THE ANATOMY
OF TERRORISM

THE ANATOMY OF TERRORISM

David E. Long

THE FREE PRESS
A Division of Macmillan, Inc.
NEW YORK

Collier Macmillan Canada
TORONTO

Maxwell Macmillan International
NEW YORK   OXFORD   SINGAPORE   SYDNEY

The Free Press
A Division of Macmillan, Inc.
866 Third Avenue, New York, N.Y. 10022

Collier Macmillan Canada, Inc.

Printed in the United States of America

printing number

1 2 3 4 5 6 7 8 9 10

Library of Congress Cataloging-in-Publication Data

Long, David E.
    The anatomy of terrorism / David E. Long.
        p.   cm.
    Includes bibliographical references.
    ISBN 0–02–919345–1
    1. Terrorism.   I. Title.
    HV6431.L66   1990
303.6'25—dc20   90–33634
                                                    CIP

To Mom
I hope I am going as strong at 82

Contents

Preface and Acknowledgments

One of the aims of terrorists is to intimidate people by making them aware of their personal vulnerability. To a degree, they have been successful. The general public is highly aware of the threat of international terrorism. People who do not follow the intricacies of strategic arms negotiations or fully comprehend how an international trade imbalance can affect them personally know that terrorists often attack the innocent and that they could be among the victims. Anyone who regularly reads the newspaper or watches television news shows has seen the results of terrorist attacks in gruesome detail. Anyone who has ever passed through a modern airport has come into direct contact with measures designed to stop terrorism.

Despite a high public awareness of the threat, there is no wide consensus of what terrorism actually is. The scholarly literature is surprisingly extensive for a subject so recently in the public eye, but no one has succeeded in establishing a general theory of terrorism. There is virtually no unanimity in defining terrorism, either among scholars or among those operationally involved with terrorist threats—politicians, diplomats, criminal investigators, prosecutors, intelligence officers, public security officers, industrial security experts, military special forces, and journalists. Each has a different professional point of view that might or might not be compatible with other equally valid viewpoints.

For the professional, scholar, and citizen alike, the most fundamental issue is one of policy: What mix of cooperative and confrontational measures is most likely to persuade terrorists and their supporters to renounce their activities. To address this issue properly, we need to explore why groups and individuals turn to terrorism in the first place, particularly when its ability to force political concessions is historically so low.

Without a general theory or even a general consensus of what terrorism is, the task of organizing government and even private resources to combat it is intimidating. Yet the grim realities of a worldwide terrorist threat that seems to increase even as Cold War tensions decrease require that all countries seek means to defend themselves as effectively and comprehensively as possible.

This book confronts the component elements of terrorism—those the author dealt with daily for three years, from 1985 through 1987, as director of regional policy formulation and coordination in the U.S. State Department's Office of Counter Terrorism, and with which his successors are continuing to wrestle. These elements group themselves into six basic questions: (1) What is terrorism? (2) Why do people commit terrorist acts? (3) What groups are engaged in terrorism? (4) What are their sources of support? (5) How do terrorists plan and execute their acts? And finally, (6) How can governments organize to combat terrorism?

No study of this scope would be possible without the help and encouragement of many people. In this case, there are so many that I wish to thank them all collectively for fear of inadvertently leaving someone out. Particular thanks go to my colleagues in the State Department: Jerry Bremmer, who arranged for me to spend time as a Diplomat in Residence at Georgetown University; Joe Reap, Al Adams, and Tom Miller in the Office of Counter Terrorism, and Ann Marie Adamo in the Office of Terrorism and Narcotics of the Bureau of Intelligence and Research, all of whom read the manuscript in whole or in part; and Georgia Rogers in the Bureau of Consular Affairs, who provided invaluable assistance. I am grateful to Dean Peter Krough and Assistant Dean Andrew Steigman of the Georgetown University School of Foreign Service for providing a place and a congenial atmosphere in which to do the research, and to colleagues in academia and the private sector, including Martha Crenshaw of Wesleyan University; Gabriella Tarazona-Sevillano of Davidson College; Jerrold Post of George Washington University; K. S. Dhillon of the State Academy of Administration, Bhopal, India; Paul Wallace of the University of Missouri; Rick McCauley of Bryn Mawr College, Ariel Merari and Anat Kurz of the Jaffee

Center of Tel Aviv University; Bill Farrell of the Naval War College; and Dick Ward and Paul Beecham of the University of Illinois at Chicago. I would also like to thank Karen Colvard of the Harry Frank Guggenheim Foundation, in whose terrorism study group I participated and gained many valuable insights, and Dr. Cynthia Hartz of Pittsburgh, whose insights on the psychology of terrorism were of great help. I also wish to express thanks to my colleagues at the U.S. Coast Guard Academy for their encouragement during the last stages of preparation of the study for publication, particularly Irv King, Al DeFilippis and Gerry Massad, and to Joyce Seltzer and Lincoln Payne of the Free Press. Most of all, I must express my appreciation to my long-suffering wife, Barbara, who put up with me during the writing of this book.

With all the generous help and encouragement I received, however, the views expressed herein are entirely my own and do not represent the views of any person or institution, public or private.

DAVID E. LONG
Old Lyme, Connecticut
January 1990

1

The Nature of Terrorism Today

For all the fervid attention terrorism has demanded and received from policy-makers, governmental security agencies, the media, and the general public, as yet no global profile or taxonomy of terrorism itself—no comprehensive classification of its aims and rationale, its adherents and supporters, its methods and its victims—has emerged. This book is an attempt to fill that gap. Without tracing the interrelationships of all the many complex and often seemingly incompatible elements of terrorism, it is impossible to understand fully the phenomenon of terrorism itself.

For the general public, there is a special urgency to the need for understanding. Unlike other threats to the peaceful and orderly conduct of domestic and international relations, terrorism directly affects the personal lives of millions of people, not only through victimization but through fear. Thousands of travelers avoid certain carriers or airports for fear of hijacking or sabotage; senior business and government officials regularly undergo training in how to avoid becoming terrorist victims; and when there is a major terrorist attack, the media bring it right into the living rooms of millions of families around the world.

In point of fact, the impact of terrorism on the general public is more psychological than physical. In the absence of accepted criteria for what constitutes a terrorist act, there can be no definitive statistics of terrorist casualties, but by even the broadest interpretation, annual worldwide terrorist casualties number only in the hundreds. By comparison, auto accident fatalities, to use just one example, number in the tens of thousands in the United States alone. Moreover, as a political tactic,

1

terrorism is not very successful. Although terrorists have played a part in successful campaigns for political goals—such as the Irgun and the Stern Gang in the Israeli war of independence and the insurgent groups in the coming to power of the Sandinistas in Nicaragua—no political goals sought by terrorists have ever been achieved by terrorist tactics alone. Nevertheless, the psychological impact of terrorism, with its unpredictability and its violation of civilized norms, on the general public and through it on government leaders has been so strong as to cry for a comprehensive policy approach to ending it.

Many people think terrorism is a new phenomenon, the product of the present age of high technology. They believe it is dependent on exotic explosive devices that can be set to detonate months after they are in place, such as the Provisional Irish Republican Army bomb in the Grand Hotel in Brighton in October, 1984, or are designed to detonate by atmospheric pressure, such as the bombs placed in TWA flight 840 in April 1986 and on Pan Am flight 103 in December 1988, and on such weapons as plastic pistols that cannot be picked up by airport metal detectors. In reality, although the weapons may change, the use of political violence is as old as recorded history. Before there were plastique bombs and microchip detonators, there were black powder bombs, and before bombs there were daggers and poisons. From the eleventh to the thirteenth century, the Assassins, a tribe that ranged from Persia to Syria, gained such notoriety for their exercise of violence that their name has stood for political murder ever since. The word "assassin," derived from the Arabic "Hashashin," was given to the tribesmen because they went about their violent business while high on hashish. Terrorism and drugs were linked long before the twentieth century.

Even ancient societies experienced what we now call political terrorism as a form of nonsanctioned violence in response to perceived injustice—that is, violence not condoned by the rules of war or required for the maintenance of public order. Over the centuries philosophers, theologians, and politicians have struggled with the issue of when and under what circumstances political violence may be justified.[1] The international community today accepts some forms of violent lethal action as legally and morally sanctioned in certain specific circumstances and conditions. Thus, conventional warfare is not considered in itself an illegal act in international law, although chemical and biological warfare is. No similar delineation yet exists for terrorist activities. There is still no consensus on whether terrorism is *a priori* unjustified no matter what the cause or grievance, whether there are circumstances that can justify such behavior, or whether moral judgment should focus on the terrorist act or the actor.

Understanding terrorism is particularly difficult because the term has come to mean many things to many people. The first step in the process, therefore, is to seek a common ground for discussion. Practitioners and academics alike have devoted a great deal of time to defining terrorism. One author listed 109 definitions for terrorism formulated between 1936 and 1981, and doubtless more have been created since.[2] Yet we do not appear to be any closer to an acceptable generic definition now than we were fifty years ago, and there is not likely to be one in the foreseeable future.

The principal obstacle is national self-interest. States (and individuals) are loath to base their responses to political violence on definitional criteria alone, because all too often such responses could conflict with more pressing foreign or domestic policy interests. The diversity of national perspectives on any single group or event makes the task of creating the international consensus necessary for concerted international action against terrorism exceedingly difficult.

Even though no international consensus exists on what terrorism is, many countries have attempted to define it. One U.S. government definition states:

> Terrorism is the threat or use of violence for political purposes by individuals or groups, whether acting for or in opposition to established governmental authority, when such actions are intended to shock, stun, or intimidate a target group wider than the immediate victims. Terrorism has involved groups seeking to overthrow specific regimes, to rectify perceived national or group grievances, or to undermine international political order as an end in itself.[3]

This is not a bad formulation, including, as it does, many of the elements associated with terrorism. But on closer scrutiny it turns out to be more of a description than a definition, and it is so broad as to be applicable to political violence in almost any form. Because of its breadth, it is unlikely ever to gain international acceptance as the basis for taking state action against specific acts of terrorism.

In addition to the political constraints in defining terrorism, there are semantic problems as well. The word "terrorism," while it has uniformly negative connotations, is so imprecise and emotionally evocative that it can be, and often is, used as a label for a wide variety of often unrelated and incompatible types of activity.

There is no question that distinctions can be and are made between terrorism and such other forms of political violence as conventional, nuclear, chemical, biological, and guerrilla warfare, as well as insurgencies, revolutions, and rebellions. There is also a distinction between terrorism and such nonpolitical criminal acts as murder, hijacking, and kidnapping.[4]

However, there is no consensus on just what those distinctions are or should be. For example, guerrilla groups and uniformed armed forces employ terrorist tactics from time to time, even when terrorism is neither their primary objective nor their preferred mode of action. Conversely, many terrorist organizations resort to criminal but nonterrorist activities, like trafficking in arms and drugs, to raise money for their terrorist operations. Drug traffickers in Peru and Colombia have become allied with terrorist organizations for mutual benefit. This relationship, commonly referred to as narco-terrorism, combines illicit commercial and political aims in a new and intimidating form of violent activity. Casualties due to narco-terrorism in Peru alone have reached nearly 15,000 since 1980.

Adding to the confusion is the question of state terrorism and state-supported terrorism. A considerable difference of opinion exists over whether one should place domestic political repression by a totalitarian regime in the same category as the activities of an opposition terrorist organization attempting to subvert the government in power. Similarly, the line between state support for "national liberation" movements and state support for terrorism is often very difficult to determine.

Most definitions of terrorism strive to be tight constructs of mutually exclusive and jointly exhaustive characteristics, all presumably adding up to a generic definition. A more fruitful approach might be to abandon the search for a definition altogether and to seek instead to identify the most common characteristics associated with terrorism, regardless of whether any particular one or combination of them is present in any given case. These characteristics can be grouped into four general categories: goals, strategies, operations, and organization.

The ultimate goals of terrorism are political. Whatever the group psychology or personal motives of organizations and individuals carrying out terrorist acts, the presence of underlying political goals is a basic consistent characteristic. The social psychologist or the law enforcement officer may see little intrinsic difference between a hostage situation involving a cornered criminal or an estranged spouse and one involving a known international terrorist. From the point of view of an expert combating the modern terrorist threat, however, the distinction is plain. Political goals are an essential element in the terrorist phenomenon and set terrorist acts apart from violent criminal acts or those of the emotionally disturbed.

Politically motivated terrorism invariably involves a deeply held sense of grievance over some form of injustice. The injustice may be social or economic, but it is nevertheless blamed on a political authority. Because terrorists believe that the injustice cannot be assuaged through any other means, terrorism has often been called the tactic of last resort.[5] Fanatically seeking vindication, they engage in terrorism despite the great probability that it will not achieve their political aims.

Related to the characteristic presence of political goals in terrorism is the transformation of political ends into moral imperatives that are used to justify whatever means are deemed necessary to attain those goals. Modern terrorist organizations justify their actions not merely with the stated political aims of the group but by appeals to some higher "universal truth." For the member of Hizballah, it is "jihad," a holy crusade against evil. For the Red Army Faction, it is to provoke a cataclysmic world revolution. For member organizations of the Palestinian Liberation Organization, it is to fulfill their national destiny and regain their homeland.

It is important to note, however, that terrorist ideologies usually reveal more about the terrorists themselves than about the ideological or theological doctrine to which they claim allegiance. The doctrine rarely mandates terrorist violence, even though individual extremists interpret it as a justification for their activities. For example, claims that Shi'a Islam espouses political suicide, given vogue by Shi'a terrorist suicide bombings in Lebanon, simply have no basis in fact. On the contrary, Islam clearly proscribes suicide. Indeed, no major religion espouses or justifies the practice of terrorism.

Another set of terrorist characteristics involves strategic and tactical objectives. The immediate objective of the terrorist group is to create terror—not destruction—and then to use the unreasonable fear and the resulting political disaffection it has generated among the public to intimidate governments into making political concessions in line with its political goals. Viewed in this context, terrorism is basically a psychological tactic, with fear and publicity two of its most important elements.

The transformation of reasonable fear into a kind of irrational hysteria as a terrorist tactic was graphically demonstrated in the summers of 1985 and 1986, when American tourists stayed away from Europe in droves in response to a spate of terrorist incidents beginning with the hijacking of TWA flight 847 from Athens in June 1985.

In order for terrorists to instill fear, they must publicize their activities. Important as secrecy is in terrorist planning and operations, maximum public exposure after the fact is still more crucial. Victims, location, and timing of terrorist acts are all chosen with public exposure in mind. Because publicity is so important, the advent of mass and instant worldwide communications has influenced modern terrorism possibly even more than advances in modern weapons technology. Live coverage of terrorists and their demands is now possible from virtually anywhere on the globe. In recent years the more successful terrorist organizations have become adept at manipulating the mass media to obtain maximum exposure. The extraordinary media coverage of the "Munich Massacre" on September 5, 1972, which resulted in the deaths of ten Israelis attending the Munich Olympics at the hands of Palestinian terrorists, played an enormous role in creating public awareness of contemporary political terrorism. Besides arousing revulsion, it confronted the viewer with the ability of a small group to hold the entire international community at bay. In the case of the TWA hijacking, the terrorists invited the international media to interview the hostages in Beirut just before their final release, and thereby received maximum worldwide media exposure both for their political cause and for their ability to breach civil airline security.

The most important operational characteristic of terrorism is the premeditated use of threat of violence. Indeed, were the element of violence not present, heinous as the act might be it would not be terrorism. Illicit trafficking in drugs, arms, travel documents, currencies, or the like to finance terrorist activities is not itself a terrorist act without the element of premeditated violence. Taking a hostage for ransom in order to finance terrorist activity, on the other hand, is a terrorist act because it involves violence. The presence of violence as a fundamental characteristic of terrorism requires that a distinction be made between terrorist acts and terrorist organizations or groups. Not all acts of terrorist organizations are themselves terrorism, and not all terroristic acts are performed by terrorist organizations, a distinction that is important to discussions of both terrorist organizations and antiterrorist policies.

Not only are terrorist acts violent, they are also criminal. Whatever their alleged political or moral justification, virtually all forms of terrorist activity involve criminal acts—murder, assault, hijacking, kidnapping, arson, sabotage, and other acts deemed abhorrent and punishable by society. The criminality of terrorist operations distinguishes them from guerrilla and insurgent operations, which, while not fully sanctioned as conventional warfare, are still considered appropriate military behavior. Terrorist acts cannot be so justified.

In recent years the United States and other countries have sought to expand both domestic and international legal sanctions against terrorist acts as criminal violations. In the absence of an internationally acceptable legal definition, terrorism *per se* cannot be considered a criminal offense, so law enforcement agencies must focus on the specific criminal acts committed by the terrorists as a part of their operations.

Another important characteristic of terrorist operations is their covert nature. Because of the violent and criminal nature of terrorism, terrorists must work undercover to avoid detection. That may sound like a truism, but it is important to note, for it establishes the need for covert antiterrorist intelligence operations in order to learn who the terrorists are and when and where they are likely to strike. The highly developed skills of many terrorist organizations in avoiding detection have made the task of carrying out criminal investigations of terrorist acts particularly difficult.

Violent, criminal, and covert, terrorism is also noncombatant in nature. That distinguishes it from low-intensity conflict and other forms of irregular warfare involving the deployment of uniformed services. Terrorism has no purely military mission, does not distinguish between military and civilian targets, and generally involves noncombatant victims.

The distinction between combatant and noncombatant action is far from precise. Noncombatants can be the targets of guerrilla forces and even uniformed services; and terrorist organizations may target combatants for terrorist attacks. Nevertheless, terrorists by and large do not have military goals, whereas regular and irregular forces do. Terrorist victims are arbitrarily chosen precisely in order to propagate fear more widely.

Another characteristic of terrorist operations is their relatively low cost. Although some operations are very elaborate, employ high-technology equipment, and are correspondingly expensive, terrorism is quite inexpensive when compared to the cost of training and equipping modern conventional forces. A "part-time" terrorist can carry out as a random bomb attack for only a few dollars. Even the most sophisticated bomb attacks, such as the sabotage of Pan Am flight 103 over Lockerbee, Scotland, in 1988, seldom cost more than about $250,000. The low cost factor greatly expands the availability of terrorism as an option to organizations with limited financial resources or to states that see the use of such organizations as a cheap way to further their own policies.

The most important organizational characteristic of terrorism is that it is nearly always carried out in groups. Cases in which individuals unaffiliated with any group have carried out major acts of terrorism are rare. Terrorist groups impose powerful constraints and bestow strong rewards on their members. For many terrorists, membership in a group is a source of self-esteem. Indeed, membership in a terrorist group can come to outweigh the group's political goals as the individual's primary motivation for carrying out terrorist acts.

Terrorist groups are almost always small, or are small operating units of larger organizations.[6] The larger an operational group becomes, the less able it is to maintain internal discipline and the more easily it can be penetrated and its members apprehended. Another organizational characteristic of terrorist groups is that they are usually subnational in scope, that is, not organized according to nation-state loyalties. They are small groups within larger population groups that seek to achieve their aims through violent, covert, and criminal means independent of any nation-state, even one that is a major sponsor.

Some people argue that totalitarian states employ similar forms of violence to induce submission from their citizens and should therefore also be called terroristic. Certainly, when one considers the records of Stalin and Hitler in this century, and the barbaric practices of the Mongols and others in earlier times, state terrorism has wrought a great deal more human suffering than what Walter Laqueur calls "terrorism from below."[7] Nevertheless, state terrorism is so different in institutional and political make-up and in social psychology that it is better studied separately.

Despite the fact that terrorist groups are not characteristically organized and directed by states, and have emerged from "below," they need external support. Terrorist organizations cannot continue to operate in a totally hostile political environment. They need to secure bases of operations, freedom of movement, safe havens, financing, and an available manpower pool from which to recruit new members. In most cases, those needs are met with the help of a segment of the general population, both at home and abroad, that either sympathizes with the organization's leadership or its political aims, identifies with its stated grievances, or is opposed to the governing authority against which the terrorist organization's efforts are aimed. Whether direct or indirect, such support is essential for the terrorist group.

Support, often crucial to their survival, is also provided to terrorist groups by states sharing their political goals. The United States State Department keeps a list of the most egregious state supporters of terrorism. As of 1988, the list included Cuba, Iran, Libya, North Korea, Syria, and South Yemen.

A number of countries that officially oppose terrorism have provided passive or tacit support to terrorist groups, either because they share their political goals or because they fear that more punitive policies will invite retaliation by terrorist groups. Several Scandinavian and East European countries allow or at least do not observe too closely the entry or transit of suspected members of terrorist organizations provided the organizations conduct no operations within their borders. The existence of such policies greatly complicate the task of determining which states are or are not supporting terrorism.

Unfortunately, the characteristics sketched here do not constitute a self-contained typology or a generic definition of terrorism. Virtually no characteristic of terrorism's goals, strategies, operations, or organization is present in equal strength in every case. Nor is there a consensus on how many of these characteristics must be present and in what degree for an action to be considered terroristic, a fact that becomes evident in certain gray areas. One is narco-terrorism, in which the ultimate motivation is as much commercial as it is political. Many terrorist groups today deal in drugs as a means of raising revenue. In South America, the symbiotic relationship between terrorist groups and drug traffickers has grown to such a degree as to constitute virtually a separate problem. The drug connection not only compounds the difficulties of creating a terrorist taxonomy but confounds efforts to wage wars on either terrorism or narcotics.

Another gray area is the distinction between domestic and international terrorism. Perhaps at one time a clear distinction could have been made, based on whether the scope of operations of a given terrorist organization was limited to a single country or crossed international boundaries. Today, however, many terrorist organizations have expanded their operations beyond the borders of the country in which they seek political change; and more and more countries perceive terrorism not only as a domestic threat but as an international threat that can victimize their nationals anywhere in the world. Domestic measures alone are no longer deemed adequate to cope with what has become an international threat.

Further complicating the ability to understand terrorism is the multiplicity of perspectives from which terrorism is viewed. In general, there are three distinct viewpoints: those of the general public, the terrorists themselves, and the people who study and seek to combat it.

The general public's perception of terrorism is all too often influenced by emotional responses to the responsible terrorist organizations: moral condemnation of groups whose acts are directed against friendly groups or countries, and political support of groups whose avowed political aims are considered worthy. The tendency to respond to terrorist acts according to personal, political, and ideological affinities has given rise to the cliché: "One man's terrorist is another man's freedom fighter." Unable always to separate the violent means from the political end, the general public and its leaders alike are often erratic in their response to terrorism.

The terrorists' perspective of terrorism is both personal—that of the individual member—and collective—that of the entire group. Individual perspectives are as varied as the members themselves, reflecting their individual circumstances and personal psychology. Terrorist attitudes are also heavily influenced by group psychology, and groups appear to develop their own "personality." One expert on terrorism, Brian Jenkins, has observed:

> Each terrorist group has its own repertoire, its own style of operations, its own *modus operandi*. The Irish Republican Army does not engage in the hijacking of airlines or kidnapping. The Italian Red Brigades kidnap and shoot journalists and others in the legs. West German terrorists seem to be thorough planners. . . . [8]

Terrorist group psychology reflects the aims and evolution of individual organizations, the backgrounds of their members, and the political and social environment in which they operate. In order fully to understand the terrorist outlook and behavior, one must analyze the history, politics, economics, and cultural anthropology of specific groups as well as the social psychology, tactics, strategies, and available technologies of terrorism in general.

Professional observers are no less immune to personal prejudices and political biases than the general public; they carry all the baggage of their professional points of view as well. Unless care is taken, professional perspectives—academic, criminal justice, diplomatic, military, and so on—can create an overly narrow understanding of the overall problem of terrorism.

Academic perspectives of terrorism differ widely. They are influenced to a great extent by disciplinary interests: cultural anthropology, religion, social psychology, history, political science (including international relations, conflict resolution, and peace science), geography, demography, weapons technology, communications, electronics, and forensics.

The perspectives of those who are operationally or professionally involved in combating terrorism also differ widely. Politicians, government spokesmen, diplomats, public security officers, intelligence officers, prosecutors, law enforcement officers, and military officers all approach the problem of terrorism from different, and occasionally incompatible, professional points of view.

Terrorism first and foremost is a political problem. Regardless of whether the solution is obtained through legal, military, or clandestine means, the primary objectives are the alleviation of the underlying political problems giving rise to terrorism, and the creation of sufficient international pressure on terrorist organizations and their supporting states to compel them to cease their activities.

Politicians, diplomats, and the intelligence community all share a predominantly political perspective of terrorism. They tend to focus more on terrorist organizations and the states supporting them than on individual terrorists and terrorist acts, because the states and groups have far more political impact than single individuals on the national interests of a given country. The politician must take into account the impact of any response to terrorist acts on other competing, and often conflicting, interests, and (a factor often ignored) whether available policy options can actually achieve sufficiently positive results to justify the political, economic, and social costs to be incurred. If the political aims of a group serve a country's national interests, the country's response to that group's terrorist activities is almost certain to be tempered; if the group's political aims are a threat to the national interest, the country's response to its terrorist activities is certain to be amplified.

A public servant's highest aim is to promote his country's aggregate national welfare, of which moral interests are a part. For the politician and the diplomat, therefore, terrorism must be defined normatively, dependent in large part on the degree to which it threatens (or supports) the national interest. In this context, the cliché about terrorists and freedom fighters is not so much a moral conundrum as it is a statement of political reality. For the single-issue advocate, however, whether an elected representative or a pressure group, no competing political, moral, economic, or other interest can justify tempering a policy of total support for or opposition to a group guilty of committing terrorist acts.

Those who are involved in criminal justice take a very different view of terrorism. For them, the primary focus is on the act, and upon the individual and organization or group responsible for it. The domestic and international political consequences of prosecuting those suspected of terrorist acts, which are of primary importance to politicians and diplomats, are of secondary importance here. To the law enforcement officer, it does not really matter so much whether the individual is a member of a terrorist organization or an organization fighting for freedom so long as he has committed a criminal act.

The problem, however is that the search for a legal definition of terrorism as a criminal act has been going on for as long as the search for a general definition, and with no more success. The reason is largely the same. Political considerations invariably take precedence over legal interpretations, and political problems are seldom solved by legal solutions. Because of the inability to arrive at a generic definition of terrorism, the trend in the area of criminal justice has been to concentrate on and to expand jurisdiction over specific criminal acts implicitly considered "terrorist" rather than to attempt to define terrorism in legal terms.[9]

Military and public security personnel generally see terrorism as a form of low-intensity conflict, at the opposite end of the spectrum of armed conflict from nuclear war. As one military analyst has noted, terrorism "has increasingly become either a manifestation of the changing nature of armed conflict or indeed a new form of warfare that is the result of a technological revolution and accompanying changes in the international political arena."[10] In considering terrorism as a form of warfare, military professionals focus on states and groups from a strategic point of view, and on individuals and acts from a tactical point of view. The idea of terrorism as a new kind of warfare seems to be borne out in recent conflicts, including the Vietnam War, the Afghan insurgency, the Tamil insurgency in Sri Lanka, and the bloody fighting between government troops and guerrillas in El Salvador. With little children hurling bombs and civilian targets chosen to break the enemy's will to fight, the distinctions between combatants and noncombatants and between military and nonmilitary targets are breaking down.

There is no set pattern in the way countries respond to terrorism as low-intensity conflict. In nondemocratic countries, military as well as public security forces may have a domestic antiterrorism (or indeed a state-terrorism) mission as well as an international antiterrorism mission. In general, however, and particularly in democratic countries, both domestic public security and law enforcement functions are generally in the hands of civilian police, whereas foreign operations are the province of the armed forces and clandestine intelligence services.[11]

Constructing a taxonomy to accommodate the many elements that make up terrorism has many obstacles indeed. But by sorting out the diverse perspectives and the many faces terrorism assumes, we can succeed in better understanding the phenomenon and fashioning a characterization that will enable us to combat it. It is not likely that a generic definition of terrorism will ever gain international recognition or that a government, even a free democratic one, will allow policy decisions in response to political violence to be based entirely, or even primarily, on definitional criteria. A country's estimate of its own interests will continue to be the basic determinant of what is and is not terrorism. On the other hand, this determination need not be purely a matter of political expediency. The identification of some of the recognizable characteristics generally associated with terrorism, which we have begun here, can form the basis of that determination.

In order fully to understand terrorist behavior, however, we must look beyond general characteristics to the social psychology of terrorist groups and the psychology of their members, as well as to the social, political, economic, and operational environment of particular terrorist groups. In order to judge the appropriateness of national and international responses to terrorism, we must consider each of the different aspects of terrorism, as political activity, as criminal activity, and as low-intensity conflict.

2

Understanding Terrorist Behavior

There are probably as many reasons for committing terrorist acts as there are terrorists. The most obvious reason is to achieve the political agenda of the group; the agenda almost inevitably involves righting perceived (and often very real) wrongs, which are cited to justify otherwise reprehensible acts. Just saying that terrorists harbor grievances and seek to right wrongs, however, does not go far toward explaining what motivates individuals and groups to risk and in some instances virtually assure the loss of their lives with often very little hope of achieving their stated aims. After all, most people who harbor grievances and seek to right wrongs do not become terrorists. For those who do, becoming a terrorist is usually a gradual process, originating in some milder form of political protest. A crucial question about terrorism, therefore, is what draws people and groups to that type of activity.

One of the chief obstacles to understanding terrorist behavior is the prevalence of popular misconceptions about what kind of people terrorists are. Among the more common misconceptions is that they are deranged. At a dinner for members of a terrorism study group, the guests were asked whether or not they thought terrorists were criminally insane. One group, made up mostly of journalists, expressed the popular view that, by and large, they were. The other, a mixture of academics and government officials dealing more directly with terrorism, maintained that they were not. The divergence between the popular view and the expert view was striking. Insanity is a simple and emotionally satisfying explanation for terrorist motivation, but it has very little basis in fact. According to one leading authority, "the outstanding common characteristic of terrorists is their normality."[1]

Another simple and perhaps even more satisfying misconception is that terrorists are morally depraved. As long ago as 1910, one writer concluded, "The ignorant mass looks upon the man who makes a violent protest . . . as upon a wild beast, a cruel heartless monster, whose joy it is to destroy life and bathe in blood; or at best, as upon an irresponsible lunatic."[2]

A cursory review of public statements by responsible authorities— the U.S. Congress, the British Parliament, the Israeli Knesset, or even the Soviet Politburo—shows that neither the "terrorist-as-evil monster" image nor the "terrorist-as-lunatic" image is restricted to the uninformed. Both of these perspectives are examples of the tendency to dehumanize and stereotype one's adversaries to cope psychologically with one's violent reactions against them. Dehumanizing the adversary helps to avoid having to deal with the very real grievances often cited to justify terrorist acts. So long as Palestinian terrorists are viewed as morally depraved, for example, one need not face the issue of their right to self-determination.

A more sympathetic explanation of terrorist behavior postulates that individuals are forced into terrorism because the intolerable conditions under which they live has left them no choice. This variation of the "innocent victim of society" model is often used to absolve terrorists and terrorist organizations of any liability for their actions. Supporters of the Palestinian cause argue, for example, that Palestinian terrorism is the fault not of the Palestinian Liberation Organization or its members but of the denial of self-determination. The fallacy of this argument is that the great majority of those who live under such conditions never resort to terrorism, and no matter how compelling their grievances, they are still legally and morally accountable for their acts.

These explanations of terrorist behavior, no matter how emotionally satisfying, are flawed. Explaining terrorist behavior as antisocial or psychopathic or as the embodiment of evil focuses on individual psychology and totally ignores the political, economic, and social environment; explaining it in terms of environmental determinism ignores individual psychology altogether. Single-factor explanations overlook the fact that terrorist behavior is an interaction between individual psychology and external environment, not the result of one or the other.[3]

The study of what motivates a terrorist—terrorist psychology—is in its infancy, and conclusions drawn from it are at best tentative. Research suffers from a paucity of reliable data that can meet even the barest standards of social science. Terrorism being a covert activity, there are few terrorists willing or available to be interviewed; most terrorists are either under cover or dead. Extensive interviews of a few captured terrorists have nevertheless been obtained, some terrorists leaders have given occasional interviews, and a few leaders have written autobiographies, including Boris Savinkov of the Combat Organization of the Socialist-Revolutionary Party in prerevolutionary Russia,[4] Saadi Yacef of the Algerian FLN,[5] and Menachem Begin of the Irgun Zvai Leumi.[6] However, in interviews and memoirs particularly, it is difficult to distinguish between genuine motivation and rationalization. The following discussion is based primarily on research on contemporary terrorists. Tentative and inconclusive though it may be, it can still be helpful in understanding terrorist motivation.

Even the principle that terrorist motivation arises from an interaction between the individual terrorist and his environment must be qualified. One cannot rule out the possibility of a psychological predisposition toward terrorism. For years, specialists in the field have been fascinated with the question of whether or not a terrorist personality or mindset exists. Coming to grips with the concept of a terrorist personality is difficult. As late as 1979 Brian Jenkins described the terrorist mindset and terrorist decision-making as "two areas of ignorance."[7]

Some have tried to create a descriptive terrorist profile. Charles Russell and Bowman Miller, basing their profile on information about captured or known terrorists, describe the "typical" terrorist as, "male (although there are many notable exceptions) in his early twenties, single, from a middle or upper class family, well educated, with some university training, although he may be a university dropout, who often joined or was recruited into the group while at a university."[8]

At the very least, this description challenges common stereotypes that portray terrorists as coming from the dregs of society. Nevertheless, while such generalizations may be an accurate reflection of the available data, they are obviously of somewhat limited explanatory value. Because they are descriptive rather than psychological profiles, they cannot really get to the heart of the problem of terrorist motivation. They fail to provide an adequate explanation for why, out of the many individuals with the same psychological traits in the same environment, only a few become terrorists.

More sophisticated studies have not come up with much better results. No comparative work on terrorist psychology has ever succeeded in revealing a particular psychological type or a uniform terrorist mindset.[9] On the contrary, terrorism seems to attract a wide variety of personalities. One could conclude, therefore, that a generic terrorist personality type does not exist.

At the same time, the absence of a terrorist personality type does not preclude the disproportionate presence of certain personality traits among such a heterogeneous group as terrorists, which might help to explain terrorist behavior. Much of the research on terrorist psychology is in pursuit of just such common traits.

Two traits that appear to be disproportionately prevalent among terrorists are low self-esteem and a predilection for risk-taking. Those with a low self-esteem tend to place unrealistically high demands on themselves and, when confronted with failure, to raise rather than lower their aspirations. Bitter at failure, they tend to be drawn to groups espousing equally unrealistic aspirations.

A common psychological characteristic among those with low self-esteem is to feel out of control of their own lives and to be convinced that their lives are controlled by external sources. This phenomenon, called "externalization," accounts in part for the accumulated wrath they direct toward outside forces believed to be the source of all their problems. They also tend to externalize the weaknesses and self-denigration they feel in themselves and transfer them to an outside enemy. Often the single-minded zeal with which terrorists oppose established authority is a projection of their own self-hatred onto an external object that reaps all their negative feelings.

Another form of displacement common to terrorists has been identified as "splitting."[10] It occurs in individuals who have incurred psychological damage in childhood and have never fully integrated the good and the bad aspects of the self. These aspects are "split," the good being identified with a idealized self and the bad projected onto external enemies. This psychological tendency appears to be more common among terrorist leaders than followers, for it provides a grandiose self-image that projects confidence and purpose and attracts others to its glow. Terrorist leaders have often been characterized as more extroverted, narcissistic, and hostile than the average follower.[11]

Many followers are likely to be drawn to a terrorist organization by the charisma of the leader and the feeling of identity provided by the group as a means of compensating for their own feelings of inadequacy.

"Terrorism," Martha Crenshaw observes, "involves reflective, not impulsive, violence and requires the ability to delay gratification through long and tedious planning stages."[12] Since impulsivity is a measurable psychological trait associated with psychological borderline cases, the reflective nature of terrorism tends to underscore the "normality" of terrorist behavior, both individually and in terms of group dynamics.

A second personality trait prevalent among terrorists is a propensity to take risks. A high proportion of terrorists appear to be stimulus hunters who are attracted to situations involving stress and who quickly become bored with inactivity.[13] Many people who externalize their feelings of inadequacy tend to be inconsiderate, self-centered, and unemotional. It is possible that the dangers of risk-taking serve as a stimulus for those who are otherwise lacking in personal feeling. Martha Crenshaw, a leading specialist on terrorist behavior, further distinguishes between individualistic risk-takers and collectivistic risk-takers. The former are exemplified by the terrorist leader who seeks danger to the point of narcissism as a form of self-affirmation, and the latter are exemplified by the follower who identifies more with the group than with its activities.[14]

Curiously enough, a predilection to violence does not appear to be a dominant aspect of terrorist personalities.[15] Among terrorists who have been interviewed for personality traits, some indeed appeared to be violence prone—that is, they had no remorse, guilt, or moral qualms about resorting to violence. Most, however, were very ambivalent toward the use of violence and human suffering. Ulrike Meinhof, the Red Army Faction leader, was apparently terrified of guns,[16] and the Palestinian terrorist Layla Khalid was able to deal with the presence of child passengers on hijacked airliner only by blotting the possible consequences out of her mind.[17] These feelings scarcely suggest the behavior of blood-thirsty, psychopathic killers. Some even went to great lengths to avoid direct responsibility for violent death. It is possible that taking hostages is a preferred tactic at least in part because of the terrorists' ability to shift the blame for any ensuing violence to the target government if it refuses to satisfy the terrorists' demands.

A conceptual framework for absorbing and organizing what is known about terrorist behavior that links the psychology of individual terrorist behavior to the environment in which the individual lives is particularly important. Erik Erikson's concept of identity might provide such a framework.[18] To Erikson, the development of personal identity is basic to the integrity and continuity of the personality. Identity is something developed not in a vacuum but in the collective experience of one's ethnic, familial, communal, and national past.

The cornerstone of a positive identity is a sense of trust, beginning in infancy. Deprived of trust, the individual will have difficulty establishing autonomy and creating a positive identity as he nears adulthood. He needs something to believe in, to have faith in something outside himself. If instead of developing a sense of trust he finds ambiguity, fragmentation, contradiction, and relativism, he is likely to have a crisis of identity and become susceptible to absolutist ideologies, which provide a false sense of certainty.

Such groups and ideologies provide not only a sense of identity but an explanation for the frustrations the individual is encountering, as well as a program for overcoming those problems. Psychoanalytic studies of West German, Italian, Basque, Armenian, and Croatian terrorists all appear to bear out the utility of using Erikson's concept of personal identity to help explain terrorist motivation.[19]

While the concept of identity is an excellent tool for comparing and understanding a broad range of personality types among terrorists, it, too, must be used with care. Espousing an extremist ideology and actively pursuing it by joining a group does not always result in violent behavior, nor does it always indicate a perverted sense of identity. The same "negative" identity traits that could lead one to join a terrorist organization, for example, could also lead one to join a religious cult or simply to adopt nonviolent means to assert identity, such as distinctive speech or dress.

Even those who espouse ideologies associated with terrorism do not necessarily support the use of violence. For example, of the many people who are drawn to religious fundamentalism in order to provide a sense of identity and certainty—Christian (Roman Catholic and Protestant), Muslim (Shi'a and Sunni), Jewish, Hindu, and Sikh, to name a few whose doctrines have been used to justify terrorism—only a minute proportion have ever become terrorists. The same can be said for those who espouse political, ethnic, or national causes with fanatical intensity.

Whatever combination of psychological and environmental factors cause an individual to be attracted to terrorism, it is basically a group activity. Individuals appear to be attracted more to the group than toward the acts of terrorism *per se.*[20] Those motivated by a strong desire to change their social and political environment can rarely hope to accomplish their goals alone and are dependent on a group in seeking to fulfill their aspirations. For others, the group identity becomes the individual's identity, and belonging to the group becomes a priority in itself. Indeed, the available evidence suggests that a dominant motive of most terrorists, particularly followers, is simply to become and remain a member of the organization.[21]

With this emphasis on group behavior, the social psychology of terrorist groups is an important element in determining terrorist motivation. Three areas of particular interest are the recruitment, cohesion, and extremism of members within the groups, especially the way they contribute to the motivation and sustenance of terrorists.

Terrorist groups and religious cults share a number of striking similarities in the relationship of the individual to the group.[22] One encounters the same difficulties distinguishing a terrorist group from a guerrilla organization that one does in distinguishing a cult from a more mainstream religious group. Both terrorist groups and cults tend to become countercultures with their own codes of behavior into which each new recruit is indoctrinated. The activities of both tend to be on or beyond the fringes of socially acceptable behavior. It has long been established in the study of cults that any deviant group will attract individuals who have a grievance or a feeling of deprivation, provided the group offers some explanation and remedy. We have seen that the same is true of terrorist groups. Populations with similar or shared grievances or feelings of deprivation constitute a pool of possible converts.

In the case of cults, it was further found that social networks—similar ethnic, social, educational, or other relationships existing before the recruitment takes place—are highly influential in determining who among the many in the pool are most likely to be among the few who are recruited. Despite the greater heterogeneity of personality types among terrorists in general, there appears to be a remarkable homogeneity in terms of social networks within specific groups.

In the case of the Lebanese Shi'a fundamentalist group, Hizballah, which has characteristics of both a cult and a terrorist group, not only are all members from the same Shi'a Islamic confessional community, but the subgroups within Hizballah are often linked through close blood ties as well. A principal reason why Hizballah took American and other foreign hostages in the mid-1980s was to trade them for Lebanese terrorists in jail in Kuwait, notably the brother-in-law of Imad Mughniya, one of Hizballah's main terrorist leaders. Similarly, the Hammadi family kidnapped two West Germans to use as leverage in the West German trial of Muhammad Ali Hammadi, who killed an American serviceman on TWA flight 847, hijacked to Beirut in 1985. Kinship is also a prominent factor in the composition of the Islamic Amal, a faction of Hizballah led by Husayn al-Musawi. Many of its members are from the Musawi clan.

Examples of the influence of close social networks on the recruitment and composition of membership can also be found within other terrorist groups. Among Palestinian terrorists, interpersonal relationships nurtured in the same village, camp, school, or religious community are important. Two of the most important Marxist Palestinian terrorists are Greek Orthodox Christians—George Habbash and Naif Hawatamah—as are many of their followers. Their Marxist ideology can be explained, at least in part, in terms of a crisis of Christian identity in a largely Muslim Arab culture. Studies of members of the Basque terrorist group ETA show a much higher percentage are of mixed Basque-Spanish parentage (over 40 percent) than the general population of the Basque region (only 8 percent), suggesting that the "half-breeds" are trying to out-Basque the Basques through terrorism to demonstrate their authenticity.[23]

Whereas recruitment into a terrorist group is largely based on individual personality needs and social networks, the cohesion of the group derives from individual commitment to the group and pressures exerted by the group on individual members to conform. Some of the motivational factors for individual commitment to the group have already been discussed. Individuals who seek a family substitute may become so dependent on the group that they abdicate independent choice in participating in terrorist activities. The same can also be said of those who seek to enhance their self-image through the sense of mission, sacrifice, and self-justification they gain by their association with the group.

Membership in a terrorist group or organization can also enhance one's social standing in a broader community—family, ethnic, confessional, or national. The admiration of relatives and peers is apparently a significant factor in consolidating membership in the ETA, the Provisional IRA, and Hizballah.[24] One also cannot rule out material well-being as a contributing factor in cementing individual loyalty to a group. Although many terrorist organizations are habitually strapped for funds, the cash flow of terrorist groups can be significant, and when one turns the corner from political terrorism to narco-terrorism, material gain becomes a primary motivating factor.

Despite all these unifying factors, most terrorist groups are characterized by constant and pervasive conflict, which group cohesion must overcome. Conflict with the outside world, "the enemy," is obvious. Just as important, however, is inter- and intragroup conflict. Conflict among members of the same group can be particularly threatening, since the maintenance of secrecy and security depends on cooperation. Thus the group itself establishes and develops strong norms to maintain cohesiveness and to oppose any form of rebellion or challenge to authority.

One way of maintaining cohesion is to exclude from the group anyone who challenges the group's internal power structure. But withdrawal or defections from the group are extremely destabilizing to those who remain, and in some groups withdrawal is so threatening that it is almost impossible except by death. The way these groups cope with doubts concerning the legitimacy of their goals and activities is to get rid of the doubters. It is a paradox of terrorist groups, which are so intensely opposed to established authority, that they so often maintain group cohesion by authoritarian insistence on conformity and unquestioning obedience.[25]

The absolutist ideologies espoused by terrorist groups reinforce the pressure to believe totally in the group and to suspend all critical judgement. The ideology becomes holy writ and dictates what is morally acceptable group behavior. To the extent that members of a terrorist group submerge their individual identities into the group identity, the group ideology becomes the determinant of individual morality. This explains how individuals who have been taught to abhor acts of violence can be induced to commit terrorist acts, which are seen as not only politically justifiable and tactically desirable, but morally imperative as well.

A shared sense of common danger also enhances group cohesion. In the face of a common enemy, individual conflicts tend to become submerged, and the solidarity imposed by a group on its members is intensified by the threat of external danger. According to members of West Germany's Red Army Faction, "The group was born under the pressure of pursuit," and group cohesion was "compelled exclusively by the illegal situation, fashioned into a common destiny." That pressure, according to one member, was "the sole link holding the group together."[26]

Another important element in the social psychology of terrorism is the creation of a norm of extreme and violent behavior. One of the imponderables of terrorism is whether terrorist acts are the result of rational choice or psychological compulsion.

At one level, terrorism is the result of rational choice. The terrorist, or more accurately the terrorist organization, chooses violent tactics as the most appropriate under oppressive circumstances to further the organization's political goals. Usually the circumstances involve a militarily and politically weak terrorist or guerrilla organization opposing the vastly superior central authority and power of a state. In light of such odds, conventional strategies would be futile.

The strategic political goal of the group is generally to redress some perceived political grievance, and terrorism is seen as an ultimate, if not the only, means of focusing as much attention as possible upon that grievance. The target of terrorism is much broader than the immediate victims of the terrorist attack. The horror that befalls the victim is merely used as a statement to shock the opponent into recognizing the existence of the group and its political goals when other means have no chance of succeeding.

The escalation of violence can also be in part a reaction to government counterterrorist measures. As the authorities crack down, the terrorists will respond with an even higher level of activity, creating what has often been described as "a cycle of violence."[27]

Groups generally resort to violent acts gradually over time. They do not spring up overnight as fully developed terrorist organizations but rather adopt increasingly violent tactics as the group itself develops cohesion. Many members of the Baader-Meinhoff gang (the RAF) started off as peace movement activists.

Moreover, even within a terrorist organization, there are many non-violent activities that a new recruit can undertake without actually committing an act of violence: administrative and logistical support tasks such as serving as an accountant, a courier, or any number of similarly mundane functions. Many members engage in the more violent aspects of terrorism only after a significant period of time within the group.

The shift from less extreme to more extreme group behavior has at least as much to do with a psychological compulsion to commit acts of terrorism as it does with the rational choice to escalate the level of violence. The dynamics of the shift have been linked to the psychological climate of the group more than to the external reality facing the group, leading to the conclusion that group psychology is a primary determinant of increasingly extreme and risky decision-making.

One explanation for this phenomenon concerns the nature of social communication within the terrorist group. As discussions of various courses of action take place within a group, there is a tendency to seek a reduction in differences of opinion. If differences remain, the strongest-held will prevail. In terrorist groups, the most extreme views are generally the strongest-held and thus tend to be adopted. Once a consensus is reached, those who continue to hold strongly to the contrary view tend either to withdraw or to be expelled from the group, thus reinforcing even more the shift toward the extreme.

Beneath the strategic political goals of the group is an often more immediate though less articulated goal relating to the survival of the group itself. Indeed, this may be the most important goal for those whose membership in the group provides them with a sense of identity and purpose. Continuing and accelerating acts of violence in this light helps to justify and rationalize the existence of the group.

This dynamic suggests that terrorist groups experience "group-think" in a somewhat extreme form. According to one scholar, the characteristics of terrorist group-think are the illusion of invulnerability and its attendant excessive optimism and risk-taking; a presumption of moral superiority by the group; a one-dimensional perception of the enemy as evil; and intolerance of any challenge to key beliefs from within the group.[28]

One can take the group psychology of terrorism a step farther. If a primary motivation of many members of terrorist groups is to perpetuate the existence of their group, then the success of the group in achieving its political agenda could be a major threat, for once the goal is attained there would be no further justification for the group's continued existence. In other words, groups must be successful enough to maintain a constituency, recruit members, and perpetuate themselves, but not so successful as to put themselves out of business. This could contribute to the absolute nature of terrorist demands. No matter how accommodating the central authority is to the legitimate demands of the group, only total capitulation will suffice, something no central authority is likely to do.

The implications of this powerful dynamic of group psychology among terrorist organizations for those responsible for combating them could be highly unpalatable. Some have argued that to prevent terrorists from continuing their activities once a reasonable accommodation of their grievances is reached, it would be better to ensure the continued existence of the groups as legitimate political parties or similar entities so that the members do not lose their sense of identity and well-being. In support of this view, one can point to former members of Israeli terrorist groups who successfully made the transition in 1948 to legitimate political party members, including Prime Ministers Begin and Shamir. However, duplicating that experience in the case of the Palestinian Liberation Organization, the Provisional Irish Republican Army, or Sendero Luminoso (Shining Path) of Peru, assuming that an acceptable political accommodation with them could be worked out, would be an extremely formidable task.

Beyond the psychological and social-psychology aspects of terrorist motivation, there are the individual and group and the social, cultural, political, and economic environment in which they operate. Analyzing terrorist environment is largely a deductive process. Beginning with the fact of terrorism, it is not too difficult to work back to the environmental factors that contributed to it. The religious confessional confrontations in Northern Ireland, Lebanon, and India; the ethno-nationalist aspirations of the Basques in Spain, the Tamils in Sri Lanka, and of the Palestinians in the Middle East; and the underlying sociopolitical disaffection in France, Germany, and Italy in the case of the New Left groups in those countries are all fairly obvious environmental factors in the rise of terrorism in those areas.

Inductive analysis, on the other hand, seeking to determine the probability of terrorism based on environmental factors, is virtually impossible, because the causes of terrorism are a mixture of interacting psychological and environmental factors, not just the latter alone. Terrorism is only one of several behavioral responses to disaffection with political, social, or economic conditions. Many responses to such conditions are nonviolent, such as participating in legitimate political parties, joining a pacifist organization or a religious cult, or simply emigrating to another country. The difficulties of prediction should not undermine the importance of environmental analysis, however. Terrorists are real people, operating in the real world. Without understanding the broader environmental causes of the political and social disaffection that leads to terrorism, one is virtually powerless to deal effectively with the threat.

Much has been written since World War II about the inability of governments to meet rising social, economic, and political expectations as a leading cause of political unrest. No one has yet been able adequately to explain why the expectations of peoples around the world rise or why some countries appear more successful in dealing with the rising expectations than others despite similar circumstances and resources. At any rate, frustration over unmet expectations does appear to be an important cause of political disaffection and, by extension, of terrorism.

No one really knows the dynamism that creates political disaffection and then transforms it into dissidence. It has to do basically with the ability of a country's political, economic, and social institutions in the aggregate to meet rising expectations.

In the case of terrorism, it is generally not whole populations in a country but segments sharing a common sense of grievance that constitute the recruiting grounds for terrorist organizations. As with more broadly based national political disaffection, however, terrorist grievances are based on a combination of social, political, or economic conditions that are viewed as oppressive and intolerable. Analysis of those environmental conditions as they relate to specific groups and organizations is thus necessary in understanding terrorist behavior.

The foregoing discussion has highlighted the difficulty in understanding terrorist motivation and the rudimentary state of research into terrorist behavior. However, even though there does not appear to be a generic terrorist personality or mindset, there do appear to be some factors more often found among terrorist groups than in the general population. It also appears that groups are drawn toward terrorism gradually and that the psychology of the group is at least as important as the psychology of the individual in determining the shift to extremism.

Probably a greater obstacle to understanding terrorist behavior than the rudimentary state of research, however, is the prevalence of public attitudes that render terrorists either insane or morally depraved on the one hand, or that absolve them as victims of circumstances on the other. If we are to combat terrorism successfully, it is absolutely vital that we understand terrorists as a cross-section of the population at large, who, through a combination of psychological, sociological, political, and economic reasons, have been drawn into terrorist activity, and who must be held accountable for their actions.

Thus far, we have been discussing terrorism in general terms. Terror ists are real people, however, operating in real groups that do untold real atrocities. Because they are active in all parts of the world, in every kind of political and social setting, and because factual information about them is sketchy at best, it is extremely difficult to put a real face on terrorists. The next two chapters, however, are an attempt to describe as accurately as possible the people and groups that are most involved in committing terrorism in today's world.

3

Terrorism in the Struggle for National Identity

Any attempt to label groups and organizations involved in terrorist activities according to qualitative or moral standards evokes strong if not acrimonious differences of opinion. It has already been noted that in a very real sense, terrorists and freedom fighters often differ only in the eye of the beholder. In a semantic sense, however, the two terms differ entirely. Freedom fighting refers to a political goal, whereas terrorism refers to a tactic used to attain that goal; terrorist tactics can be and often are adopted by organizations and groups fighting in the name of freedom. It is important to remember that participants in terrorist activities are overwhelmingly convinced that terrorism is but a means to an end, not the end itself, and virtually all of those engaged in terrorism consider themselves freedom fighters.

In discussing terrorist groups, therefore, the use of nonqualitative classifications is imperative. For this study, we shall distinguish between nationalist or ethnic organizations, which seek to achieve or maintain independence or autonomy for a specific ethnic or national group, and doctrinal organizations, which use political ideologies or religious dogmas to justify terrorist acts intended to redress perceived social, economic, or political grievances.

Use of these classifications has limitations, however. Given their diversity, no attempt to sort terrorist groups into categories can be entirely successful. Hizballah is predominantly a doctrinal group (Shi'a Islam), but it is also ethnic in composition, rooted in the Shi'a confessional community of Lebanon. Sikh terrorists in India are predominantly nationalist–ethnic, but their ethnic identity is based on the Sikh religion. Conversely, the nationalist–ethnic Popular Front for the Liberation of Palestine (PFLP) also espouses a Marxist doctrine. Since the two categories are not wholly exclusive, placement of some groups or movements is perforce a matter of subjective judgment.

Nationalist–ethnic groups and doctrinal groups differ in that the former tend to speak for larger constituencies and to use a broader range of tactics. Small groups with little ability or desire to seek broad ethnic or national support do exist, such as the Armenian Secret Army for the Liberation of Armenia (ASALA) and the Gush Emunim's now defunct Terrorism Against Terror (TNT) in Israel, but they are relatively rare and seldom politically significant.

By contrast, many doctrinal groups are small themselves and have small constituencies. That is particularly true of such utopian New Left groups as the Red Army Faction and the Red Brigades. Other doctrinal groups, however, particularly Marxist groups in Latin America, have substantial constituencies among the disaffected worker and peasant classes.

Terrorist labels become even more difficult to apply in the cases of guerrilla insurgency groups and predominantly political organizations. Although both kinds of groups are often involved in terrorist activities, there is, in the author's view, a basic taxonomical difference between them and groups involved principally or exclusively in terrorist activities. Inclusion of predominantly guerrilla or political groups in this study, therefore, will depend on the extent to which they engage in terrorist activities. Two guerrilla insurgency groups, the Nicaraguan Contras and the Afghan Mujahidin, which in the past engaged in terrorist acts but are not doing so now, will be omitted from discussion.

Another insurgency is being conducted by Palestinians in the Arab territories occupied by Israel. Called the "Uprising," or the *Intifada*, it employs mainly civil unrest and has not yet reached a high level of violence. Were it to do so, however, it is virtually certain that both the Palestinian insurgents and the Israeli authorities would commit acts that their opponents would label terrorist.

Another difficulty for those who study terrorism is that the groups engaging in it are forever splitting, disbanding, and reforming, and in doing so appear to follow no discernible pattern. Some changes may be the result of the loss of a charismatic leader such as Wadi Haddad, whose Palestinian group, PFLP-Special Operations Group, subsequently split up. Other groups, such as the Basque ETA, have experienced multiple internal schisms. In other cases the underlying political, economic, or social conditions sustaining a group's existence change, and the group either disbands or is reconstituted into a more traditional political organization.

Bearing in mind the difficulties of categorizing groups involved in terrorism and the fact that such groups number in the hundreds, the task of highlighting just a few of the more active and successful ones is necessarily a highly selective undertaking. What follows, therefore, is an overview of some of the more prominent nationalist–ethnic groups involved in terrorist activities. The next chapter will discuss some of the more prominent ideological groups.[1]

Among the currently active nationalist–ethnic groups to have employed terrorist tactics on a regular basis are the organizations that constitute the Palestinian resistance movement, the Roman Catholic and Protestant organizations in Northern Ireland, the Basque ETA (*Euzkadi ta Askatasuna*) in Spain, the Tamil insurgents in Sri Lanka, and the Sikh organizations in India.

They will be discussed roughly in order of outside, particularly American, recognition and interest, but no particular political or geopolitical significance should be attached to the order. In all cases, the political grievances have roots in ethnic conflicts that go back many years; all of the groups have at least tacit support outside their home areas, principally from those who share ethnic ties; and nearly all have employed a variety of tactics to achieve their goals, of which terrorism is only one.

Subject of myth and misinformation alike, the Palestinian resistance movement is one of the world's least understood political movements. To its supporters, the movement is the political manifestation of a high moral cause: to remedy the injustice of the denial of Palestinian self-determination caused by the creation of the State of Israel. So compelling is this moral cause that it justifies the use of terrorism if no more peaceful means can be found to achieve its political ends, the creation of a Palestinian state. For the opponents of the Palestinian resistance movement, it is the embodiment of moral depravity, ruthlessly attacking innocent victims and ultimately seeking the destruction of a sovereign state—Israel—if not its people, depriving them of their moral right to live in peace.

Neither Palestine nor Palestinianism even existed before the end of World War I. Prior to that time, the land that now comprises Israel, the West Bank, and Gaza belonged to the Ottoman Empire. The Ottoman Sultan was also Caliph of Islam and as such commanded the allegiance of Sunni Muslims everywhere. Under Ottoman rule the population was organized primarily by religious community—Muslims, Christians, and Jews. The concept of national consciousness, basically a Western idea, was very weak until the latter part of the nineteenth century.

Although the Muslims were in the majority and constituted the politically dominant community, the Ottomans recognized the Christian and Jewish communities as "Peoples of the Book" and allowed them to worship freely and to maintain their own independent communal legal systems. There was even a Grand Rabbi in Constantinople.

World War I changed that. The British, who needed Arab support against the Ottoman Turks, persuaded Sharif Hussein of Mecca to revolt against Ottoman rule in return for promises to support Arab national aspirations. The promises came in the form of letters between the British High Commissioner of Egypt, Sir Henry McMahon, and Sharif Hussein, which are collectively known as the McMahon Correspondence.[2]

It is difficult for a non-Muslim fully to appreciate the magnitude of Hussein's decision. It meant not only revolting against the virtually defunct political power of the Ottoman Empire but, far more significantly, withholding allegiance from the Islamic Caliphate, the most unifying institution in the orthodox (Sunni) Islamic world of that time.[3]

After the war, Arab national aspirations were dashed as the British and French subdivided much of the Middle East into mandates, which served simply to substitute British and French imperial power for that of the Ottomans. The British created a mandate out of the Holy Land, to which they gave the ancient name Palestine. The Muslims and Christians inhabiting this new mandate not only experienced a reawakening of their Arab identity but began to create a Palestinian identity as well. In both cases, their national consciousness took on a decidedly negative, anti-British coloration.

At the same time that the British promised to support Arab national aspirations, they also promised to support Jewish national aspirations in the Holy Land. In what has become known as the Balfour Declaration, the British Foreign Secretary, Lord Balfour, asserted in November 1917: "His Majesty's Government view with favor the establishment in Palestine of a national home for the Jewish people." The Balfour Declaration and the McMahon Correspondence were basically irreconcilable.[4] In effect, the British gave away to two groups of people a country that was not yet in existence to be created from lands the British did not own.

It is interesting to speculate how the problem might have been resolved had not Hitler come to power in Germany. With the dramatic increase in Jewish immigration to Palestine in the 1930s, many settlers fleeing from Nazi Germany, and the huge expansion of Jewish land acquisition, the problem became unmanageable. Jewish immigration rose from 5,000 in 1930 to 62,000 in 1935, and by 1936 Jews made up 28 percent of the population.[5]

Violence and acts of terrorism broke out on both sides. Between 1936 and 1939 a series of Arab uprisings and strikes called the Arab Revolt was suppressed by the British. By 1939 the British belatedly recognized the problems being created by the shift in the demographics of Palestine and issued a White Paper, which, among other things, called for a reduction of Jewish immigration and land acquisition. It was rejected by both sides, however, and soon British attention turned to Europe as the whole world was again engulfed in global war.

Following World War II, the British, realizing the impossibility of reconciling the two sides and neither willing nor able to maintain the mandate by force, turned Palestine over to the newly created United Nations. The United Nations voted to partition Palestine into Arab and Jewish areas, a resolution rejected by the Arabs. The British withdrew from Palestine on May 14, 1948, and on the following day the Jews proclaimed the State of Israel. The United States was first to give the new state *de facto* recognition, and the Soviet Union the first to give it *de jure* recognition.

The Arab states unanimously rejected the new state and mobilized their armed forces to reunite an Arab Palestine. In the ensuing Arab-Israeli war, Israel greatly expanded its territory beyond the U.N. partition lines. Approximately 650,000 Arabs fled from their homes in the zone of the fighting.[6] The Israelis refused to allow them to return or to compensate them for the loss of their property. The Arab states, on the other hand, refused to assimilate the refugees. They maintained that it was Israel's responsibility either to allow the refugees to return or to compensate them, whichever the Palestinians preferred. Out of this impasse the Arab refugee problem was born, and the bitterness engendered by it has been a major impetus for Palestinian terrorism.

What was left of Arab Palestine became known as the West Bank and the Gaza Strip. The West Bank was annexed by Transjordan's Amir (later King) Abdallah to create Jordan, an act for which he was subsequently murdered by a Palestinian nationalist. Gaza was administered, but never annexed, by Egypt.

Following the 1948 war, the Palestinian national movement was in shambles. For the next two decades, the Palestinian problem became a pan-Arab cause, taken over by the Arab states, and the Palestinians had almost no voice in how the cause was pursued. It was during this period that Palestinian nationalists took the first steps in creating an organized resistance movement.

The best-known Palestinian resistance organization and the organization most widely associated with terrorism in the public mind is the Palestinian Liberation Organization (*Munathamat Tahrir Filistin*, or PLO). Despite its notoriety, it is probably one of the least understood nationalist groups in the world today. The PLO was created by the Arab states at the first Arab summit meeting, held in Cairo in January 1964, to counter the growing importance of indigenous Palestinian resistance organizations. At the time, the Arab states, far more interested in establishing their individual primacy in the pan-Arab cause against Israel than in the fortunes of the Palestinian resistance movement itself, sought through the PLO to keep a tight rein on its activities. To the Arab states, Palestinian "armed struggle" meant creating and maintaining conventional Palestinian military units to be attached to and closely controlled by their own military establishments. Thus was the ill-trained, ill-equipped group called the Palestinian Liberation Army formed, only to be totally discredited along with the PLO leadership under Ahmad Shukairy in the humiliating Arab defeat in the 1967 war.

The 1967 war heralded a new phase for the Palestinian resistance movement. West Bankers and Gazans came under Israeli occupation and had to look to themselves for their own national survival. As a result of the military defeat, all Palestinians, whether in the occupied territories or in the Palestinian diaspora, lost faith in the ability of the Arab states to create an independent homeland for them.

Another event, a year later, also had a great psychological impact on the Palestinian resistance movement. In March 1968 Palestinian commandos from Yasser Arafat's al-Fatah organization successfully resisted an Israeli retaliatory raid at al-Karamah, Jordan. The "Karamah victory" (*karamah* means "dignity" in Arabic) seized the imagination of Arabs everywhere, who had been mortified by the defeat of the previous year. More important, it became the catalyst for a resurgence of Palestinian national consciousness.

Palestinian nationalism organized itself in two steps. First the Palestinian resistance movement coalesced into a number of full-fledged resistance organizations, and second, under the leadership of Arafat, it took over the PLO and transformed it into an umbrella organization for those organizations.

In February 1969 Arafat was elected Chairman of the PLO Executive Committee at the fourth meeting of the Palestinian National Council, a position he has held ever since. (The Palestinian National Council is made up of the heads of the various PLO member organizations, which include the Arab Liberation Front, al-Fatah, the Democratic Front for the Liberation of Palestine, the Palestine Liberation Front, the Palestine Popular Struggle Front, the Popular Front for the Liberation of Palestine, the Popular Front for the Liberation of Palestine-General Command, and al-Sa'iqa; ten Palestinian unions and syndicates for workers, intellectuals and professionals are also represented.)

While the PLO became radicalized as it came under the control of the resistance organizations, its members' commitment to armed struggle (that is, guerrilla and terrorist tactics) was tempered by political imperatives imposed by the PLO. The PLO, in fact, became two separate entities: the symbolic political voice of the Palestinian people and the organizational framework for accommodating a number of disparate, undisciplined, and often warring member organizations.

The former of those roles was legitimized by the United Nations in 1974 when it recognized the PLO as the representative of the Palestinian people and invited it to participate in the U.N. debate on Palestine. On November 13, 1974, just a year after al-Fatah's terrorist wing, the Black September Organization, killed two American diplomats in Khartoum, Arafat addressed the U.N. General Assembly.[7] Fourteen years later, at the Palestinian National Council meeting in Algiers in November 1988, the PLO constituted itself as a government-in-exile. The following month, having been denied a visa by the United States to address the United Nations (the United Nations moved the venue to Geneva to accommodate him), Arafat finally conceded the right of Israel to exist and renounced terrorism, conditions that the United States had insisted upon before engaging in direct U.S.–PLO talks, which began on December 16, 1988, in Tunis.

The Arab-Israeli peace process and the role of the PLO in it are beyond the scope of this study. In the narrower context of terrorism, the PLO must be viewed as an umbrella organization for the autonomous Palestinian resistance groups. As chairman, Arafat has virtually no power over the member groups other than the power of consensus. (Even in his own al-Fatah, there is relatively little organizational discipline.)

The power of consensus should not be underestimated. Decision-making by consensus (*ijma‘*) is an ancient Arab institution, derived from consultation (*shura*) with all those whose views bear on the decision—in this case the leaders of the member organizations. Because of its political persona and the desire of its members not to undermine the unity of the cause, the PLO has probably been more of a constraint upon Palestinian terrorism than a catalyst for it. The Palestinian resistance groups most dedicated to armed struggle have, on balance, been loath to break with the consensus of the PLO even when it has taken positions contrary to armed struggle, such as the 1974 moratorium on terrorism outside Israel and the Occupied Territories, the Arafat–King Hussein agreement of February 1985 to seek a negotiated Arab-Israeli peace, and most recently Arafat's December 1988 renunciation of terrorism.

The locus of decision-making on terrorist operations is at the member organization level, not the PLO as a whole. The largest, oldest, and most influential Palestinian resistance organization is al-Fatah. The word Fatah, which means "conquest" in Arabic, is also a reverse acronym (FTH) for its Arabic name, *Harakat al-Tahrir al-Filistini*, the Palestinian Liberation Movement. It was founded in Kuwait in 1957 by Yasser Arafat (his *nom de guerre* is Abu Ammar). Other principal founders were Salah Khalif (Abu Iyad), Khalil al-Wazir (Abu Jihad), and Faruq al-Qaddumi (Abu Lutf).[8]

Al-Fatah is committed exclusively to Palestinian nationalism and does not espouse any particular religious or political ideology. Its members represent every shade of political opinion from far left to far right. On balance, however, it is the most conservative, religiously and politically, of all the Palestinian resistance organizations. Many of its leadership are devout Muslims and consider the Marxism espoused by a number of the Palestinian resistance groups to be anathema.

Yasser Arafat, who has come to personify the Palestinian struggle for self-determination, hardly looks the part. Short, balding, with a receding chin and his famous scraggly beard, he looks more like a taxi driver than the sophisticated and highly charismatic leader who through sheer force of personality has kept the Palestinian resistance movement from splintering into a score of warring groups. Such strange bed-fellows as the Israeli Ariel Sharon, the Syrian Hafiz al-Asad, and the Palestinians Abu Nidal and Abu Musa have all tried without success to put an end to his career. As one Western observer put it, "If the Palestinians did not have Arafat to be the leader of their cause, they would have to invent him."

Arafat came from a devout Muslim middle-class family. He studied engineering in Cairo in the early 1950s and while there formed lasting contacts with the Muslim Brotherhood, a militant Muslim fundamentalist organization founded in 1928 by Hassan al-Banna.[9] Those Islamic ties have greatly enhanced the willingness of conservative Arab states such as Saudi Arabia to provide financial support to al-Fatah and the PLO.

Arafat became committed to armed struggle early in his career. Like all Palestinian nationalists of the time, he was greatly influenced by the Algerian revolution and inspired by its successful war of independence against France. To conduct commando operations, he created a paramilitary wing, *al-'Asifah* (The Storm) in 1965. Largely because of Khalil al-Wazir's Algerian contacts, its organization and doctrine were patterned on that of Algeria's FLN, and most of its early members were trained in Algeria.[10]

On the other hand, Arafat has always been basically a politician, pragmatic and opportunistic, and has never ruled out a negotiated settlement in order to achieve a Palestinian homeland. In this he has differed markedly from some of the more radical PLO leaders.

Exploiting the psychological impact of the Karamah "victory," Arafat maneuvered al-Fatah into the position of the premier resistance organization with himself as its undisputed leader. (Prior to that, leadership had been more collegial.) With Arafat as the head of both the PLO and al-Fatah, the dichotomy of moderation and extremism has been even more pronounced within al-Fatah than within the other groups. Much of the PLO's political, diplomatic, and social welfare activities are carried out by al-Fatah. Faruq al-Qaddumi, for example, has long acted as *de facto* Palestinian foreign minister in his diplomatic dealings with outside states.

At the same time, until the present moratorium al-Fatah had never totally renounced terrorism as a tactic. In September 1970 al-Fatah and the PLO leadership were driven from Jordan to Lebanon after having challenged King Hussein and having been soundly defeated by the Jordan Arab Army. The defeat and relocation in Lebanon had vast repercussions on PLO, Lebanese, Arab, and Israeli politics. Until its leadership was forced to leave Lebanon in the face of the Israeli invasion of 1982, the PLO was virtually a state within a state, a situation that contributed to the Lebanese civil war. From Lebanon, the PLO leadership moved to Tunis, where it is still situated. Concurrently with the Israeli attempt to crush the PLO in 1982, Syria also tried forcibly to remove Arafat as the head of al-Fatah and replace him with Sa'd Musa (Abu Musa). Syria's attempt failed, and Abu Musa's rival al-Fatah faction is now simply another Syrian surrogate.

The 1970 expulsion also caused al-Fatah to embrace terrorism. Salah Khalif organized the Black September Organization (the name commemorating the defeat by Jordan), which in the early 1970s went on a rampage of terrorist activity eclipsing all other Palestinian groups. Black September operations included the murder of eleven Israeli athletes at the 1972 Munich Olympics and of two American diplomats, Ambassador Clio Noel and his deputy chief of mission, Curtis Moore, in Khartoum in March 1973.

Al-Fatah's current terrorist wing is called Force 17, led by Muhammad Ahmad Natur (Abu Tayib). Although most of its attacks have been inside Israel and the occupied Arab territories, it engaged in outside activities despite the 1974 moratorium, including the murder of three Israelis on a yacht in Cyprus in September 1985. In addition, Abd al-Hamid Labib, alias Colonel Hawari, has apparently also received terrorist assignments from al-Fatah. It may have been under his direction that a bomb was placed on TWA flight 840 en route from Rome to Athens in April 1986.

When at Arafat's insistence the PLO declared a moratorium on terrorism in 1974, it so angered one of his chief lieutenants in al-Fatah, Sabri al-Banna, that he broke with al-Fatah and the PLO and created a rogue organization formally named al-Fatah–Revolutionary Council. Al-Banna's *nom de guerre,* Abu Nidal ("father of the struggle"), has become one of the most feared names in terrorism, and his group is now generally known as the Abu Nidal Organization (ANO).[11] Bitterness between Arafat and Abu Nidal was so great that each swore to kill the other; indeed, the ANO has killed nearly a dozen senior PLO officials over the years.

No two people could be as opposite in personality. Whereas Arafat courts publicity and is an expert in exploiting it for the Palestinian cause, Abu Nidal is so secretive there was speculation in the mid-1980s over whether or not he was deceased. He is known to have heart trouble and may have had open heart surgery, but most observers believe that he is still alive. Algerian news reports in late 1989 claimed that he was in a Libyan military hospital with terminal cancer.

Sabri al-Banna's early life is fairly well known. He was born in 1937 into one of the wealthiest Arab families in Palestine. Almost everything was confiscated by the Israelis after the 1948 war, and the family, after a period in a refugee camp, moved to Nablus, in the West Bank. Sabri studied engineering in Cairo but never got a degree. He also worked as a skilled laborer in Saudi Arabia in the 1960s. In his humiliatingly reduced state, he reportedly developed a hatred for wealthy Arabs and their Western trading partners to go along with his hatred of Israel. He is married and has several children, who, he claims, do not know of his identity as a terrorist.

Abu Nidal rose quickly in al-Fatah, known by his former colleagues as a taciturn but intensely stubborn person. His organizational skills and eye for detail were quickly appreciated, and he was sent to North Korea and China for guerrilla training in 1972. One of the few known photographs of him dates from that time.

The ANO first moved to Iraq, and after it was expelled in 1984, to Syria. In 1987 Syria's President Asad ordered ANO offices closed, and it is thought to have moved to Libya, although operatives are still located in Lebanon. The exact whereabouts of Abu Nidal are unknown, and his movements are shrouded in mystery. Nevertheless, he has created one of the most lethal and effective terrorist organizations in the world today. Whether working with Iraq, Syria, or Libya, ANO ultimately works for itself, being totally committed to pushing the Palestinian cause through armed struggle.

The ANO is estimated to have 900 to 1,000 members, about half of them trained terrorists. It goes under many names in addition to its official one, al-Fatah–Revolutionary Council. It is believed to be responsible for almost 1,000 deaths in twenty countries since 1974. Its attacks include the attempted assassination of Israeli Ambassador Argov in London in June 1982, which gave General Ariel Sharon a pretext to invade Lebanon in his effort to destroy the PLO; the September 1985 hijacking of an Egyptian Airliner to Malta; the bloody attacks at the Rome and Vienna airports in December 1985 (supported by Libya); the hijacking of Pan American flight 73 in Karachi, Pakistan; the September 1987 bombing of a synagogue in Istanbul, Turkey; and armed attacks in Khartoum in May 1988 that resulted in the deaths of five British and the wounding of five Americans.

The organization is among the richest of all terrorist groups, with a net worth estimated at $200 million controlled personally by Abu Nidal. Its income comes from the arms trade, forging travel and other documents, drug trafficking, and blackmail of individuals and Arab governments. Abu Nidal's SAS Foreign Trade and Investment Company, which dealt primarily in arms and money laundering, operated openly in Warsaw until the Poles were pressured to close it down in 1987. Another company, Zibado Foreign Trade Consultants, operated out of East Berlin.

There were news reports in November 1989 that Abu Nidal was in semi–house arrest in Libya after ruthlessly purging his organization of many of its top leaders. Some 150 of them, including twenty of Abu Nidal's top lieutenants, had reportedly been murdered in the previous eighteen months, embarrassing Colonel Qadhafi, who is attempting to refurbish his public image in the Arab world and the West. Libya has been under pressure from Egypt and the PLO to muzzle Abu Nidal, whose terrorism runs counter to the current Palestinian strategy to seek a political settlement to the Arab-Israeli problem. If the report of Abu Nidal's arrest is true, the result could be the disorganization if not disintegration of one of the most deadly international terrorist organizations of the last fifteen years.

Other Palestinian resistance groups fall generally into two categories: groups that are descended from or are closely related to the Movement of Arab Nationalists (ANM),[12] and those sponsored by and more or less surrogates of Arab states, particularly Iraq and Syria.

The ANM was begun as a kind of political debating society by radical Arab students at the American University of Beirut in the late 1940s under the aegis of a Greek Orthodox Palestinian medical student, George Habbash (who subsequently became a physician). Ideologically, it espouses pan-Arabism and Marxist class struggle.[13] Although the ANM itself has never amounted to much organizationally, it members have spread throughout the Arab world. Kuwaiti members include Dr. Ahmad al-Khatib, a noted radical politician; the Dhufar rebels in Oman in the 1960s and 1970s adopted ANM ideology; and their sponsors, the South Yemen regime, have their ideological origins in the ANM. It is no coincidence that a close relationship between Habbash and the South Yemenis continues to this day.

The Palestinian ANM members generally believed that a Palestinian homeland could be achieved only in the context of broader Arab unity, a world socialist order, and armed struggle. They steadfastly rejected any political solution with Israel. That orientation remains a distinguishing factor of the Palestinian groups descended from the ANM and explains in part why they are generally the most terroristic groups in the PLO.

In December 1967, in the wake of the disastrous war with Israel the previous June, ANM-related and -associated groups merged to form the Popular Front for the Liberation of Palestine (PFLP) under George Habbash.[14] Habbash favored well-publicized terrorist attacks on civilian targets, and in the 1970s PFLP was one of the world's most notorious terrorist organizations. It was responsible for the Air France hijacking at Entebbe, Uganda, in June 1976, which prompted the daring Israeli rescue raid in which all the hijackers and four civilians were killed. In recent years PFLP has concentrated its energies mainly on targets in Israel, using more conventional guerrilla tactics.

Almost immediately after PFLP was created, it began to splinter. In September 1968 Ahmad Jabril, a non-ANM Palestinian but with similar political leanings who had joined PFLP, broke off to create the PFLP–General Command. A former Syrian army officer, Jabril has always complemented terrorist tactics with more conventional guerrilla tactics. PFLP-GC was responsible for the first major Middle Eastern airline hijacking, an El Al flight from Rome to Tel Aviv in July 1968, and for the shootout at Quiriat Shemona, Israel, in April 1974, during which eighteen civilians and two Israeli soldiers were killed and sixteen wounded. In May 1985 PFLP-GC traded three Israeli soldiers kidnapped in Beirut in 1982 for 1,500 Palestinian political prisoners held by Israel. At the time of this writing, PFLP-GC is also the leading suspect for the bombing of Pan American flight 103 over Lockerbie, Scotland, though the evidence is not conclusive.

PFLP-GC further split in 1977 with the creation of the Palestinian Liberation Front (PLF)[15] under Muhammad Abu al-Abbas. At the end of 1983 Abu al-Abbas split with his own group and allied his PLF faction with al-Fatah. It was this faction that hijacked the Italian cruise ship *Achille Lauro* in 1985 and killed a wheelchair-bound American citizen, Leon Klinghoffer.

In February 1969 Nayif Hawatamah split off from PFLP to form the Democratic Front for the Liberation of Palestine (DFLP).[16] Hawatamah, who represented a younger generation of ANM members (he joined in 1954), was more Marxist ideologically and today is probably the closest of all PLO leaders to the Soviets. More important than his ideology has been his unwillingness to take orders from Habbash.

DFLP was responsible for a 1974 attack on a schoolhouse in Ma'alot, Israel, which resulted in the deaths of a number of schoolchildren before the terrorists themselves were killed.

Wadi Haddad bolted from PFLP in 1974, when Habbash accepted a PLO moratorium on terrorism outside Israel and the Territories, and formed PFLP–Special Operations Group. After his death from leukemia in 1978, PFLP-SOG fell apart, and its remaining members formed the PFLP–Special Command, the 15 May Organization, and the Lebanese Armed Revolutionary Faction (LARF).

PFLP–Special Command is led by Salim Abu Salim, and the 15 May Organization (named for the day Israel declared independence) is led by Husayn al-Amri (Abu Ibrahim), a bomb expert who either built the bomb set off in TWA flight 840 in 1986 or else helped the person who did. The bomb was designed to be activated by barometric pressure and explode at high altitude between Rome and Athens, leaving no remains. It did not work properly, however, and exploded at low altitude, doing only minor damage and enabling investigators to identify its "signature," that is, the type of bomb and the likely builder.

LARF was founded by George Ibrahim Abdallah. Although it is an offshoot of the Palestinian resistance movement, it is more Lebanese than Palestinian. Its members are mostly Christians from Qubayyat and Andaqat, two villages in northern Lebanon.

In 1980 LARF moved its operations to France, where it apparently came in close contact with the New Left group Action Directe and attained notoriety in attacks on several U.S. and Israeli diplomats.[17] They included a November 1981 murder attempt of the U.S. chargé d'affaires, Christian Chapman, and the January 1982 murder of the U.S. military attaché, Lieutenant Colonel Charles Ray. In 1984 French and Italian police arrested key LARF leaders, including Abdallah, who was sentenced to life imprisonment by the French in 1987. Since then, LARF has retreated back to Lebanon.

As the Palestinian resistance movement gained momentum following the 1967 war, both Syria and Iraq sought to maintain as much influence as possible over the movement by establishing surrogate Palestinian organizations. Sa'iqa (Thunderbolt) was formed under the aegis of the ruling Syrian Ba'th Party in October 1969, its members mainly drawn from Palestinians living in Syria. It is currently headed by Issam al-Qadi and Sami al-Attari. Sa'iqa has undertaken sporadic operations, including attacks against Syria's Arab opponents, but it generally eschews terrorism. Second in size only to al-Fatah, it is still considered a Syrian entity, and its role in the Palestinian resistance movement is minimal.

Much the same can be said for the Arab Liberation Front (ALF), the Iraqui equivalent to Sa'iqa, founded in January 1969. It is universally considered little more than a tool of Iraqi foreign policy. Both Iraq and, more recently, Libya have also given support to remnants of the old Palestine Liberation Army (the military wing of the pre-1967 PLO) that formed the Palestine Popular Struggle Front (PPSF).

In the 1970s the PPSF, PFLP, PFLP-GC, and PLF created the Rejection Front in opposition to the PLO's decision to accept creation of a state on part of Palestine (the West Bank and Gaza) as an interim step toward total liberation. The Rejection Front members considered this a capitulation to Zionism.

In sum, Palestinian terrorism is basically the work of the component members of the PLO, not of the PLO itself, which, in the context of terrorism, is little more than an umbrella organization. The acceptance by the PLO of the possibility of a political settlement, particularly since 1973, and the commitment to armed struggle including terrorism by its members, particularly those with ANM antecedents, have created major inconsistencies in word and deed between the use of terrorism and its disavowal. As of this writing, Arafat's 1988 moratorium on terrorism is apparently holding. Nevertheless, the underlying struggle between extremism and moderation within the PLO and within its constituents is not likely to disappear unless there is a breakthrough for the Palestinian cause of self-determination.

Terrorism has been associated with the Jewish side of the Arab-Israeli problem as well as the Palestinian side. Following the 1948 war, the Jewish terrorist groups disbanded or were absorbed into the political mainstream. In the late 1970s, however, there was a brief resurgence of Israeli terrorist activity by a covert group affiliated with the right wing, the fundamentalist Gush Emunim. Known as the Gush Emunim Underground, Terror Against Terror, or TNT, it was a small, illegal organization that plotted terrorist acts against Palestinians. Its members were rounded up by the Israeli police in the early 1980s, and it is now defunct.[18] Its main significance today is in having demonstrated the presence of an ideological framework (a mixture of messianic Zionism and fundamentalist Judaism) around which Israelis could respond to Palestinian violence with nonsanctioned violence of their own, should the Intifada become more violent.

Terrorism in Northern Ireland evolved out of the centuries-old issue of British political and economic domination of Ireland. Whatever "civilizing mission" the British may have felt they had throughout the rest of the empire, their record in Ireland was on balance brutal and mean-spirited.

Irish resentment of British political domination was further reinforced by the ethnic division between the Anglo-Saxon English and the Gaelic Irish, the religious division between Protestant England and Roman Catholic Ireland, and the socio-economic discrimination against the Catholic Irish by the Protestant Irish ruling class, generally of English and Scottish ancestry.

The "Irish Question," as it was called, was the cause of centuries of intermittent violence, which ultimately led to the creation of the Irish Free State in 1922. However, six counties in the northeast, historically known as Ulster,[19] had large Protestant majorities and resisted being swallowed up in an overwhelmingly Roman Catholic Ireland.

The roots of Northern Irish separatism go back to 1609 and the "plantations," when King James I of England attempted to colonize the six counties with Protestants. Similar attempts were made elsewhere in Ireland, but in Northern Ireland the plantations were designed to displace not only the native aristocracy but the tenants as well.

Animosity between the two communities was not absolute. Many of the Protestants in Northern Ireland were Scottish Presbyterians. Because Presbyterianism was looked down upon only slightly less than Catholicism by the Anglicans dominating the Irish parliament instituted by William of Orange (King William III) in 1691, a degree of affinity developed between Ulster Presbyterians and Catholics in the eighteenth century.

In the nineteenth century, however, Northern Ireland began to industrialize. From the south it drew Protestant capital as well as thousands of Irish Catholic laborers. Not only did sectarian tensions increase, but Northern Ireland was drawn farther from the Irish mainstream by its growing economic and commercial ties to Britain.

In 1800 Parliament passed the Act of Union, dissolving the Irish parliament and placing Ireland directly under British rule. Throughout the rest of the century, Irish patriots resorted to armed struggle to regain home rule. Such groups as the Young Irelanders of the 1840s and the Fenian Brotherhood of 1850s were precursors of the Irish Republican Army (IRA).

In response to the violent acts of predominantly Catholic proponents of home rule, Northern Irish Protestants organized the Orange Order (commemorating Protestant political ascendancy in Ireland under William of Orange), the lineal ancestor of Ulster Protestant terrorist groups. Its fanatical opposition to home rule further radicalized the Catholic activists, who repudiated home rule for republicanism and, in the case of the IRA, turned ultimately to Marxism.

In 1914 the British finally voted to restore home rule to Ireland, but because of Protestant agitation in Ulster and preoccupation with World War I, its implementation was delayed. In 1912 Protestants in Ulster had already organized the Ulster Volunteer Force to fight home rule in the streets if need be. It was largely in response to the UVF that the Irish Volunteers, later known as the IRA, evolved.

The IRA can be said to have officially been born on April 24, 1916, the day Irish dissidents proclaimed a republic and began a short-lived armed insurrection known as the "Easter Rebellion." The insurgents were known as the Army of the Republic of Ireland and later the Irish Republican Army.[20] Although the Easter Rebellion was short-lived, it began a process that culminated in the creation of an independent Ireland six years later.

The political arm of the IRA, *Sinn Fein* ("We Ourselves" in Gaelic), was founded by Arthur Griffith around 1905.[21] Neither a revolutionary nor a republican, Griffith advocated a dual English-Irish monarchy along the lines of the Austro-Hungarian Empire, to be achieved through passive resistance, not armed struggle.

Over time, however, Sinn Fein became both republican and revolutionary. Following the Easter Rebellion, it and the IRA captured the imagination of the people. In 1918 it controlled the Irish delegation elected to Westminster, which met instead in Dublin as the first Irish Dail, or parliament. The Sinn Fein leader, Eamon de Valera, who later served as Prime Minister and President of Ireland, was elected head of the Dail.

In 1920 the British Government of Ireland Act created two separate entities, Ireland and Northern Ireland, giving dominion status and a separate parliament to both. The south initially rejected that action, and fighting broke out between the IRA and the British. Britain and the Dail agreed to a treaty in 1921, however, and the following year the Irish Free State was created as a dominion under Great Britain. All ties with Britain were severed in 1949 with the declaration of the Republic of Ireland.

Diehard republicans in the IRA did not accept the 1921 treaty because it did not create an independent republic or include Northern Ireland. De Valera did accept it as a stepping stone toward full independence. In 1923 he left Sinn Fein to create a new party, *Fianna Fail* ("Soldiers of Destiny"). Although the Irish Free State outlawed the IRA, it still retained great popularity both there and in Northern Ireland, and Sinn Fein became its political arm. The IRA's principal aim became to reunite the six counties of Northern Ireland with the Irish Republic. Its subsequent uprisings and terrorist attacks met with little success, however, as much a consequence of Catholic apathy as of the efficiency of the security forces. By the late 1950s the IRA had abandoned armed struggle altogether, and the 1960s gave every indication of heralding a reconciliation between Ulster Catholics and Protestants.

It was not to be. The rising political and economic expectations of the Catholics and the total rejection of reconciliation by the Protestant right wing reversed the trend. After growing civil unrest and violence, the British army moved into Northern Ireland in August 1969 to keep order; thus began the "Troubles," which have continued to the present day.

The immediate cause of the Troubles was the civil rights demonstrations by the Catholics in 1967–68, influenced by the civil rights movement in the United States. A hard core of militants, less interested in civil rights than in a united Ireland, continued acts of violence even after Westminster expressed sympathy with many of the demands.

In response to Catholic violence, Protestant hard-liners, inflamed by the rhetoric and demagoguery of such leaders as the Reverend Ian Paisley, took to the streets. With the Orange Order politicized and either unable or unwilling to lead an armed struggle, other groups sprang up. Various gangs, many of them criminals, coalesced into the Ulster Volunteer Force (revived by Gusty Spence in the mid-1960s using the name of Edward Carson's anti–home rule paramilitary organization of 1912) and began to commit acts of violence and random terror against Catholics.[22] The group officially renounced terrorism in 1976, but, with no centralized control, it has continued to be involved in criminal violence.

The Ulster Defense Association (UDA) is the largest Protestant group. Formed from street gangs in September 1971, it quickly grew to almost 50,000, although the numbers have declined since then. Among its principal leaders were Charles Smith and Andrew Tyrie, who became head of the Inner Council, its highest executive body.

The UDA is basically a citizens' vigilante group, more reactive than proactive, and has managed to stay just inside the law. In many respects, it has come to replace the role of the Ulster Special Constabulary with its "B-Special" units, a citizens' militia that was disbanded in 1970.[23] With its tremendous size, the UDA would be difficult to disband. On the other hand, it is quite easy to penetrate, and its activities are generally well known to the security forces.

Two organizations more dedicated to violence and terrorism, the Red Hand Commando and the Ulster Freedom Fighters (UFF), were created in 1972–73. Both also evolved from street gangs and comprise a mixture of blue-collar toughs and criminal elements. Some sources suspect ties between the UFF and the UDA, the former carrying out terrorist acts that the latter would not wish to be associated with. Not surprisingly, this has been denied by the UDA.[24]

As the Troubles began, the Catholics turned to the IRA for protection, only to find that it, like the Orange Order, was no longer equipped for armed violence. Internal conflict in the IRA over its mission led to a split in 1969. Technically, the issue was whether Sinn Fein representatives should take their seats in Northern Ireland's parliament. (The question became moot in 1972; with violence there running out of control after the assassination of the British Ambassador to Dublin, the Ulster Parliament was dissolved.) But in fact, many members were increasingly at odds with the organization's emphasis on political action over armed struggle and its increasingly doctrinaire Marxist cast.

The schismatics called for a continued parliamentary boycott and armed struggle for a united Ireland. They withdrew and created the Provisional IRA (known as PIRA or Provos); the original organization became know as the Official IRA. In January 1970 Sinn Fein also split, making the creation of two rival organizations complete. PIRA has been far more active than the Official IRA and has become the primary instigator of nationalist terrorism in Northern Ireland.

The PIRA has a hard core of 300–400 members. Most of the rank and file are conservative Catholics, republicans, and Irish nationalists dedicated to armed struggle. The leadership consists of a younger generation mainly from the north and appears to be more Marxist than its followers. Leaders include Gerry Adams, Martin McGuinness, Sean MacStiofain (formerly John Stevenson), Seamus Twomey, Dave O'Connell, Ivor Bell, and Myles Shevlin.[25]

The PIRA is convinced that only through armed struggle can it publicize its cause, obtain outside support, and ultimately drive the British out of Northern Ireland and unite it with the south. The PIRA has not, however, ignored more legitimate political activity through the Provisional Sinn Fein, adopting the slogan, "Armilite [a British-made rifle] and the ballot box."

Realizing that a quick victory is virtually out of the question, the PIRA has adopted a long-term strategy of attrition. Its main targets have been British army personnel, local law enforcement and judicial officers, and hard-line Protestant politicians. Operationally, it seeks the maximum number of casualties and has been responsible for more than a thousand deaths. Tactics have included shootings and mortar attacks, but the preferred tactic is bombings. Kidnappings and hijackings are seldom if ever used. Most of the attacks occur in Northern Ireland, but there have been operations in the Irish Republic, Great Britain, and Western Europe, particularly against British army personnel.

Among PIRA attacks have been the assassination of Queen Elizabeth's cousin and World War II hero Lord Mountbatten and three others with a remotely detonated bomb placed on his sailboat in August 1979; the October 1984 bombing at Brighton, England, which killed a Cabinet minister and narrowly missed Prime Minister Thatcher; the November 1987 bombing at a veterans memorial service at Enniskillen, Northern Ireland, which killed eleven and injured sixty-five; the May 1988 gunning down of RAF servicemen in Roermond, the Netherlands, killing one and wounding two; and the July 1988 bombing of a British army barracks in Duisburg, West Germany, wounding nine.

PIRA terrorists are well armed, having a variety of handguns, rifles, grenade launchers, and, of course, explosives. In recent years Libya has apparently become a major supplier of arms—two shipments were interdicted by the authorities in the Irish Republic—and financial support. The PIRA also raises money from criminal activities and private donations, including a sizable amount from the United States. The PIRA has also had close ties with the Basque ETA, dating back to the early 1970s.

Originally the PIRA maintained the same organizational structure as the old IRA: geographically organized sections, companies, battalions, and brigades. The chief executive body was know as the (Provisional) Army Council. In 1977, owing to penetration by British and Northern Irish security services, it was reorganized into a cell structure, with each cell, called an Active Service Unit or ASU, so compartmentalized that members know only fellow ASU members and the individual giving orders from above. The cells are responsible to local brigades and ultimately to the "Northern Command," the main executive authority.

Despite the new cell structure, the British and Northern Irish authorities have been moderately successful at penetrating the PIRA and using informers, called "supergrasses." Nevertheless, it is still very potent, and its operations are likely to continue.

One other group that has been responsible for much terrorism in Northern Ireland is the Irish National Liberations Army (INLA), the terrorist wing of the Marxist Irish Republican Socialist Party (IRSP), headquartered in Dublin. Party founder Seamus Costello broke away from the Official IRA in 1975. Considered more Marxist than the Official IRA and the Provisional IRA, he feuded with both groups and was killed in 1977. Since then a degree of tactical cooperation between the INLA and the PIRA has existed.

The INLA uses tactics similar to those of the PIRA. Because of its Marxist ideology, it has proclaimed solidarity with such other left-wing groups as the French Action Directe and the West German Revolutionary Cells. In the 1980s many leading INLA members were arrested on the basis of supergrass testimony, forcing operations to be greatly curtailed. In 1987 internal struggle further decimated the leadership. Still, the INLA has the potential to continue a particularly brutal strain of terrorism.

Basque national consciousness did not exist until the late nineteenth century. Before that the distinguishing characteristic of the Basque homeland—four north central Spanish provinces[26] and the neighboring area in southeast France—was linguistic. Basque, or *Euskera*, is not Indo-European or, indeed, like any other language. Its uniqueness helped foster an ethnic myth and oral tradition of Basques as an ancient people, descending from Tubal, son of Japheth and grandson of Noah, whose descendants had practiced pure democracy.[27]

For centuries the Basques lived in semi-isolation in the mountains and foothills of the Pyrenees and along the southeastern shores of the Bay of Biscay, a conservative, self-contained, and self-sufficient race of herders and fishermen. By the 1890s, however, the area had begun to industrialize, attracting thousands of ethnic Spanish workers. Tensions between the secular proletarian Spanish and the conservative, devoutly Roman Catholic Basques quickly appeared, and from those tensions Basque nationalism began to grow.

It was helped along, indeed to a great extent invented, by Sabino Arana. Arana coined a name for the Basque fatherland, *Euskadi*, designed a flag, and created a national history from the region's ethnic lore to justify independence from Spain. In 1895 Arana founded the Partido Nacionalista Vasco (Nationalist Vizcaya [Basque] Party—PNV). From the beginning the PNV emphasized Basque language and culture as unifying forces and looked on the ethnic Spaniards as interlopers.

The PNV's call for regional autonomy was finally granted by the Spanish republic in 1936, but after the republican defeat in the Spanish Civil War General Franco subjected the entire region to repression and brutality and outlawed the use of the term Euskadi. The Basque government under President Jose Antonio Aguirre went into exile in Paris. (Ironically, the conservative PNV shared hardly any common ground politically with the leftist republican government that had granted Basque autonomy.)

In the 1940s and early 1950s the Spanish government felt that agitation by the working classes in the Basque region was a greater threat than Basque nationalism. With the postwar industrial boom in the region, the threat of labor unrest continued to grow and to bear an increasingly leftist coloration. In time many of the younger Basque nationalists also embraced socialism.

On July 31, 1959, a group of left-wing members of the youth wing of PNV, believing the party had lost its relevance since the Spanish Civil War, split off and created the ETA (Euskadi ta Askatasuna—Basque Fatherland and Freedom). Although calling for armed struggle, the ETA in the early days did little more than distribute pamphlets, write on walls, and argue political theory. Though the leaders were Marxists, they were mainly of middle-class origins, and their principal support came from conservative Basque nationalists who did not really understand their professed ideology.

Since its founding the ETA has been plagued with personality conflicts as well as intense differences over ideology and organization. It originally sought to create a national front with other parties in hopes both of beginning a war of national liberation and of building a Marxist workers' movement in support of world revolution. Those members for whom national liberation was the first priority looked to Vietnam, Algeria, and Cuba for inspiration. More doctrinaire Marxists, claiming that national liberation wars were for the Third World and inappropriate for their highly industrialized region, called for the working class, Spanish and Basque alike, to rise up against the Franco regime. Neither group seemed to recognize the basic incompatibility between Marxist internationalism and Basque nationalist particularism. They spent countless hours debating whether or not ethnic Spanish workers should be accepted in "Euskadi."

Another topic of intense internal debate was the appropriate balance between political activity and armed struggle. Some wished to pursue their aims almost entirely through violence, while others favored a mix of violence and more traditional nonviolent political activity.

Those two issues—national liberation versus international revolution and armed struggle versus political activity—have been the cause of numerous splits and shifts in emphasis in the organization's history. The first split occurred in early 1967, when a Marxist group broke off to form ETA Berri (New ETA), which ultimately merged with the MCE (Movimiento Communista de España). The remaining ETA then began to engage in widespread terrorism for the first time.

In 1970 the ETA split again, the more Marxist group being known as ETA VI (for the sixth party assembly) and the more nationalistic group as ETA V. ETA VI was more successful at first, mainly because of publicity surrounding the public trial of six of its terrorist members in Burgos in 1970, which elevated them to the status of Basque national heros. Ultimately, however, ETA VI turned from terrorism to political activity, as ETA Berri had done previously, and lost its popularity. ETA V continued to be dedicated to armed struggle. The most spectacular terrorist act of ETA V during this period was the assassination of Prime Minister Carrero Blanco in December 1973.

Although nationalist and populist, ETA V was still Marxist. Its justification of its terrorist acts, however, was based more on Maoist national liberation concepts than on traditional Marxism. Its ultimate nationalist origin probably contributed to its survival at the end of the Franco period, when other Spanish Maoist groups were disintegrating.[28]

ETA V had inherited four fronts created by the ETA in the 1960s to carry out the its diverse aims and missions: political, cultural, workers, and military. Only the workers' front and the military front became important to the future of ETA V. The workers' front contended that armed struggle, to be effective, must be linked to a mass workers' movement. In May 1974, having not been informed about the intention of the military front to assassinate Carrero Blanco, it withdrew and took the name LAIA (Langile Abertzale Iraultzaileen Alderdia, the Revolutionary Patriotic Worker's Party).

In October of the same year the military front also broke away, becoming known as ETA-Militar (ETA-M). It has remained the Basque group most single-mindedly devoted to armed struggle. The members left behind called themselves ETA-Politico-Militar (ETA-PM) and argued that both political action and armed struggle were necessary. For a while ETA-PM continued to be engaged in terrorism but gradually gave it up at the end of the Franco period and has ceased to exist as a significant terrorist group.

Thus ETA-M has inherited the mantle of the ETA terrorist organization. Even it has seen the need for some political organization, however, and maintains connections with Herri Batasuna, a Basque socialist political party. Nevertheless, it continues to believe that only armed struggle will win Basque independence.

Over the years the ETA-M has evolved a highly sophisticated organizational structure centering on three- or four-member commando cells. Many commandos are able to lead normal outside lives unknown to the police. The organization has extensive international ties, including the PIRA, European Marxist terrorist groups, radical Palestinian groups, and such states as Nicaragua and Cuba.

The end of the Franco regime and the advent of democracy, along with a measure of autonomy, have undermined some of the Basque sense of grievance upon which ETA-M depends. In the late 1980s ETA-M even agreed to enter into discussions with the Spanish government on a political solution, possibly a sign that it fears an erosion of its political sympathizers. So far, however, the talks have accomplished little.

Also in the past few years, Spanish and French police actions have taken a heavy toll of its leadership. In 1986 the French exiled one of ETA-M's main leaders, Iturbe Abasolo, to Gabon; in the fall of 1987 a series of joint police arrests netted Santiago Sarasolo (Santi Potros), another important leader; and in January 1989 the French arrested ETA's top leader, José Antonio Urruticoechea-Bengoechea (alias Josu Ternera). Nevertheless, the broad-based nationalist sentiment still extant in the Basque region has enabled the ETA to regroup and continue operations. Despite its leftist ideology and the essentially conservative Basque population, it is likely to survive as a nationalist organization dedicated to armed struggle and terrorism for some time to come.

At the heart of the insurgency in Sri Lanka is the ethnic division between the majority Sinhalese (about 74 percent of the population) and the minority Tamils (about 12.5 percent are Sri Lankan Tamils, and 5.5 percent are Indian Tamil emigrés; 7.6 percent are Muslims who are mainly Tamil speakers).

Although the Sinhalese claim that they were the island's original inhabitants, no one really knows when either group first came from the Indian mainland. Over the course of time, both communities have developed distinct identities, making the history of Sri Lanka one of ethnic rivalry and coexistence. The Sinhalese claim descent from fair-skinned north Indians and point out that the Sinhala language is Indo-European. They are predominantly Buddhists, and much of Sinhalese ethnic fanaticism is fanned by the Buddhist clergy, who still blame the Tamils for the thirteenth-century collapse of a Sinhala kingdom in the area of northern Sri Lanka now inhabited by Tamils, and the resulting military intervention by Tamils from the subcontinent. Today the Sinhalese mainly inhabit the southwestern coastal plain and central highlands, where rainfall is plentiful.

The Tamils speak a Dravidian language and descend from darker-skinned peoples of south India. They are predominantly Hindus, although most of Sri Lanka's Muslim community are Tamil speakers. There is also a substantial community of descendants of Indian Tamils brought over by the British in the nineteenth century to work on the tea plantations in the highlands. The Tamils still inhabit mainly the northern and eastern portions of the island, where rainfall is sparse and agriculture, the main occupation, is far less productive than in the south and west. The ethnic ties between the Sri Lankan Tamils and the south Indian Tamils have created additional resentment among the Sinhalese as well as fears of Indian–Tamil domination.

By the thirteenth century three kingdoms had emerged in Sri Lanka, two Sinhalese states in the southwest and the central highlands, and a Tamil kingdom in the north with its capital at Jafna. The Portuguese and Dutch, when they occupied Sri Lanka in the sixteenth and seventeenth centuries, left the local administration largely intact, but the British who succeeded them created a unitary administration.

Under the British, a sizable English-educated Tamil middle class developed, which became disproportionately represented in local gov-

ernment. Tamil minority rights were also maintained by ethnic representation in the legislative council. Many Sinhalese began to look on
the Tamils as a privileged community; they insisted that it was Sinhalese rights, not Tamil rights, that needed protecting, and thus concentrated on making postindependence Sri Lanka a Sinhalese state.[29]

Prior to independence in 1948, ethnic strains were somewhat muted
by the mutual desire to be rid of colonial rule. Following independence, however, Tamil minority rights were slowly eroded by a Sin-
halese-dominated government. In the new constitution the communal
representation instituted by the British was abolished, depriving the
Tamil minority of a legislative means of defending its interests. In 1949
most of the Indian–Tamil community was denied citizenship and lost
the right to vote.[30] In 1956 Sinhala became the sole official language of
government, even in the Tamil areas where few understood the language.[31]

Those and other Sinhalese measures resulted in Tamil protests, civil
disobedience, and, ultimately, communal violence. Various governments, realizing that at least some of the Tamil grievances were justified, tried from time to time to redress them, but Sinhalese hard-liners
prevented them from doing so.

In 1957 Prime Minister S. W. R. D. Bandaranaike and S. J. V.
Chelvanaykam, leader of the Federalist Party, which called for a Tamil
state in a federal union and represented the majority of the Tamil
people in parliament, negotiated a pact giving official status to the
Tamil language in the north and east without challenging the primacy of
Sinhala as the national language. The pact was not implemented, and in
the spring of 1958 communal riots broke out. By the mid-1960s a
compromise giving Tamil some status was arrived at. Nevertheless, the
language issue of the 1950s and 1960s further divided the two communities.

In the 1970s many younger Tamils despaired of coexisting with the
Sinhalese in a federal system and began turning to separatism as the
ultimate goal, calling for "Tamil Eelam"—an independent Tamil state.
Rising militancy was reinforced in part by the new constitution of 1972,
which not only reaffirmed Sinhala as the only official language but
conferred special status to Buddhism and abolished the clause in the
previous constitution proscribing any legislation that would give "un-
due advantage to a race, religion, or community."[32]

In 1972 the major Tamil political parties plus the Ceylon Workers
Congress, which represented Indian Tamils, created a common politi-

cal front. The following year the militants forced through a resolution in the front's action committee making a separate state of Tamil Eelam its ultimate goal. In 1976 the Tamil United Liberation Front (TULF), as it had been renamed, reaffirmed Tamil Eelam. (The Ceylon Workers Congress, however, continued to support a Tamil state in a federal system.) In the parliamentary elections of 1977 TULF swept the Tamil areas, giving a clear signal to the Sinhalese majority that Tamil Eelam had broad popular support.

The rise of militant Tamil separatism, including the call by some Tamils for south Indian Tamil support, confirmed every fear the Sinhalese had of ultimate Tamil irredentist intent and set the stage for the renewal of large-scale communal violence. Communal riots broke out in September 1977 and again in 1983. By 1984 the conflict had spread to most of the Tamil areas.

During the 1970s more than twenty Tamil insurgent groups were established espousing armed struggle to attain Tamil Eelam,[33] By 1986 they are estimated to have had more than 10,000 members. The Tamil insurgent groups were generally all called "Tigers" by the Sinhalese after the oldest and largest group, the Liberation Tigers of Tamil Eelam (LTTE). The Tiger organization was founded by Veluppillai Prabakaran 1972, but it did not turn to the use of violence until 1975, when it claimed credit for the killing of Jafna's Mayor Alfred Durayappah. Its terrorist activities began in earnest in 1977 with bank robberies, raids on police and security forces, and assassinations of civil officials and civilians. Following the communal riots of 1983, it expanded its operations into full-scale guerrilla warfare, virtually controlling large areas in the north and east, including most of the Jafna Peninsula, the organization's main base of support.

LTTE terrorist acts have included the suspected bombing of an Air Lanka Tristar in 1986; bombing the Colombo central bus station in April 1987, killing 106 and wounding 295; a rampage of killing of more than 200 in October 1987 in the wake of the suicide of twelve captured LTTE members; and planting two land mines in Trincomalee in May 1988, which killed seven Indian soldiers who were part of a peace-keeping force.

Only four other organizations have attained prominence. In 1980 the Chairman of the LTTE Executive Committee, Uma Maheswaran, broke with Prabakaran and founded the People's Liberation Organization of Tamil Eelam (PLOTE). Drawing on support from the north and the east (including predominantly Muslim areas in the latter), it has engaged in similar terrorist activities but has eschewed killing Sinhalese civilians.

Another rival group, the Tamil Eelam Liberation Organization (TELO), was formed in 1983 by a man named Thangathurai, who was killed while participating in the Welikade Prison riots of 1983. The Eelam Revolutionary Organization of Students (EROS) was founded in 1975 in London and directed by a Mr. Rajanayagam there and V. Balakumar in Madras. It specializes more in sabotage than in killings and robberies.

One other group that became significant in the 1980s is the Eelam People's Revolutionary Liberation Front (EPRLF), led by K. Padmanabha. It claimed credit for the rescue of Tamil prisoners from Batticaloa Prison in 1983 and the kidnapping of an official of the U.S. Agency for International Development and his wife in 1984. (The couple was released after pleas from the Sri Lankan government.) Both EROS and EPRLF drew much support from plantation workers in the hill country.

In 1985 the violence spread to the Sinhalese areas, finally causing the government to call for a ceasefire and for talks to work out a political settlement. The government and Tamil politicians (TULF) were joined by representatives of the five main insurgent groups—LTTE, PLOTE, TELO, EROS, and EPRLF—who formed the Eelam National Liberation Front (ENLF) for the purpose. Although the talks failed, the fact that the militant Tamil groups were willing to enter into a dialogue with the government showed some flexibility on their part.

Both sides took advantage of the ceasefire to rearm, and in 1986 fighting again broke out. The government launched a major military offensive and was fairly successful in the east. The militants failed to unite; in addition to fighting the Sri Lankan army and security forces, they attacked one another in a battle for preeminence that LTTE ultimately won. During this power struggle, LTTE killed TELO leader Sri Sabaratnam and most of his lieutenants in April 1986, and more than ninety EPRLF members the following December.

The Indian government had become involved in the dispute following large-scale communal riots in 1983 and had pushed for a negotiated settlement. Its efforts were resented by Sinhalese hard-liners, however, who alleged that India was providing covert support for the Tamil insurgents. As civilian casualties mounted in 1986, the Indians increased their peacemaking efforts, and a political settlement was concluded on July 29, 1987. It gave a modicum of autonomy to the Tamils and provided for an Indian peacekeeping force of some 70,000 to be stationed in Tamil areas.

The settlement did not bring a respite from the killing, however. By the end of 1988 more than 4,000 civilians and combatants had died since the settlement went into effect.[34] In the north, where the LTTE refused to surrender its weapons, the Indians undertook a major campaign to suppress it by force. They were joined in their efforts by LTTE's rival, EPRLF.

In the south the Sri Lankan armed and security forces have also had to confront a serious Sinhalese terrorist threat in the nominally Marxist Janatha Vimukthi Peremuna, or People's Liberation Front (JVP). It was founded in 1965 by Rohan Wijerwee, a student at Patrice Lumumba University in Moscow, and was proscribed after a bloody insurrection against the government in 1971. Its leaders were jailed but were released in 1977 after promising to renounce force, and it became a rather insignificant trade union organization. Following the 1987 settlement it reemerged to wage a terrorist war against low-ranking government officials and civilians in opposition to the settlement, concessions to the Tamils, and the presence of Indian troops in Sri Lanka.

Wijerwee and six of his leading lieutenants were reportedly killed in November 1989 under somewhat mysterious circumstances (the bodies were said to have been immediately cremated), and Sri Lankan security forces claim that the group was finished. It remains to be seen whether or not new leaders will rise to take their places; even if the JVP disbands, Sinhalese Marxist terrorism is virtually certain to continue. Despite partial success in isolating the Tamil and Sinhalese extremists and increasing Tamil participation in the political process, particularly the elections of early 1989, the cycle of violence has not been entirely broken in Sri Lanka. The unyielding fanaticism of both ethnic groups will make ending terrorism and restoring peace and order to Sri Lanka a long-term task at best.

Sikh terrorists seek an independent state of Khalistan in the Indian portions of the Punjab, a region now split between India and Pakistan. The region straddles the frontier of two states created out of Hindu—Muslim rivalries that still sorely strain the relations between the two countries, but Sikh terrorism has almost nothing to do with Hindu—Muslim communal strife. The confessional animosities of Sikh terrorism are focused on Hindus.

The origins of Sikh terrorism are both old and new. The Sikh religion was founded some five hundred years ago in the Punjab by a Hindu guru named Nanak (1469–1539). Nanak attempted to reform Hinduism and to synthesize it with Islam in reaction to what he saw as the inequities of the Hindu caste system. His followers were called disciples, or "Sikhs."

Nanak was succeeded by nine gurus, hereditary after the fourth, until the death of the tenth and last, Gobind Singh in 1708. According to Sikh tradition, the ten gurus are regarded not as a succession but as manifestations of the same guiding spirit.[35] The fourth guru, Ram Das, founded the holy city of Amritsar. His successor, Guru Arjan, built a Sikh temple (gurdwara) there, which he called the Harimandir. The temple complex, which also includes the Akal Takht ("throne of the timeless one"), is now known as the Golden Temple and is the principal Sikh shrine. Arjan also compiled the *Guru Granth Sahib*, the Sikh sacred book, at Amritsar in 1604–5.

According to Sikh tradition, Gobind Singh declared that there would be no more gurus to succeed him and that religious authority would be embodied in the writings of the *Guru Granth Sahib*. In 1699 he also established a religious order, the Khalsa, which was ultimately to incorporate Sikh identity. All men who joined the Khalsa were to add the name Singh (lion) to their given name; women were to add Kaur (maiden or princess).

Not all Sikhs were inducted into the order, and many continued to perceive Sikhism as a reformed branch of Hinduism. All the gurus were of the Khatri caste (a mercantile class), and many of the converts were of the Jat caste (an agrarian class) of Hinduism. It was common for a family to have some members belonging to the Khalsa and others not,[36] and even some Khalsa Sikhs considered themselves Hindus.

Nevertheless, it was through the Khalsa that the idea of a separate confessional identity took root. The Khalsa also became the institution through which Sikhism was transformed from a pacifist religion to a militant one, and also through which Sikhs become known for their military prowess and bravery. By the eighteenth century Sikh military bands called *misls* were established. The army, the Dal Khalsa, became more unified in the early nineteenth century, when most of Punjab was governed by a Sikh ruler, Maharajah Ranjit Singh. The name Dal Khalsa was later adopted by one of the current Sikh terrorist groups.

Ranjit Singh's kingdom was a powerful force in the development of Sikh national identity. Upon his death in 1839, the kingdom began to fall apart, but it took two Anglo-Sikh wars before the British were able to annex it in 1849. Following annexation, Sikh ethnic consciousness began to diminish, but in the 1880s it was again gathering momentum. The British contributed to the process by recruiting large numbers of Sikhs into the army. They prized the Sikhs not only for their bravery but for their loyalty—the Sikhs by and large remained loyal in the Indian mutiny of 1857, for example. Another impetus to ethnic awareness was the threat of Western Christian missionaries (Christianity had been introduced long before), who first came to the Punjab in 1835 and actively converted outcasts as well as prominent members of the Sikh aristocracy.

By the 1920s Sikh agitation was on the rise. A prominent issue was the administration of the gurdwaras, which had come to be virtually hereditary. Agitation resulted in the Sikh Gurdwara Act of 1925, which placed administration of the shrines and temples in the hands of the Shiromani Gurdwara Prabhandak Committee (SGPC). Control of funds accruing to the Sikh holy places has made the SGPC a very powerful religious institution. Its political counterpart, the Akali Dal, has become the main Sikh political party in India and the Punjab today.

After the partition of Punjab by India and Pakistan in 1947, Sikhs from Pakistan moved to India or emigrated abroad, principally to Britain, Canada, and the United States, where older Sikh communities already existed. Indo-Pakistani tensions have been a complicating factor in dealing with the Sikh problem. Although there is no evidence of official Pakistani support for Sikh terrorism (nor any indication that the Sikhs would consider joining Pakistan), it is difficult for many Pakistanis, including some in prominent positions, not to empathize with a movement opposed to "Hindu domination." It is equally difficult for Indians not to suspect Pakistan of covertly aiding the terrorists. The Indo-Pakistani dimension and expansion of Sikh communities abroad has given Sikh separatists an international base from which to conduct terrorist activities.

Following independence, the Akali Dal continued to agitate for more concessions to the Sikh community, including more local autonomy in Punjab, declaring Amritsar a holy city, and incorporating various Punjabi language areas into the Punjab. By 1979 a number of Sikh extremists were calling for a completely independent Sikh state to be called Khalistan. One such extremist, Dr. Jagjit Singh Chauhan, broadcast a call for a "Republic of Khalistan" from Pakistan in 1971 and created the National Council of Khalistan, which he runs from self-exile in London, canvassing support in Great Britain, West Germany, Canada, and the United States.[37]

The most charismatic Sikh extremist, however, was a young fundamentalist priest, Sant Jarnail Singh Bhindranwale, who turned to terrorism as one tactic for obtaining an independent Khalistan. Bhindranwale preached orthodoxy and militancy, and gathered a group of extremists around him who began to engage in terrorism. It has been alleged that the ruling Congress-I Party of India covertly backed Bhindranwale early in his career as a means of challenging the political power of Akali Dal in the Punjab.

In 1978 some of Bhindranwale's followers clashed violently with a group of Nirankari Sikhs, a small splinter group viewed as heretics because they venerated a live guru. In 1980 the head of the Nirankari sect was murdered in Delhi, and in 1981 a prominent Hindu editor critical of Sikh fundamentalism was also murdered. Bhindranwale was arrested for the murders but released for lack of evidence. He and his entourage moved into a building in the Golden Temple complex, and other gurdwaras were also used as secure bases for extremists.

Public order continued to deteriorate. In June 1984 the Indian army was finally called out to crush the extremists in an operation code-named "Blue Star." A principal target was the Golden Temple in Amritsar. When the defenders refused to surrender, the army stormed the temple. Bhindranwale and other top leaders were killed.

The violence continued, however. In August 1984 Sikh terrorists hijacked an Air India plane to Lahore. They demanded to be flown to the United States but after negotiations gave up in Dubai. In October Prime Minister Indira Gandhi was murdered by her Sikh bodyguards as a reprisal for Blue Star. The resulting communal violence left thousands of Sikhs dead and wounded in Delhi and elsewhere. (Again, there were allegations of Congress-I party connivance in the riots to discredit Sikh political power.)

In May 1985 a plot was uncovered to assassinate Prime Minister Rajiv Gandhi during a visit to the United States. Another plot was uncovered to kill an Indian parliamentarian in New Orleans. On June 23, 1985, an Air India flight from Canada to London blew up over the Atlantic. That is thought to have been the work of Sikh terrorists (two Sikh groups and an obscure Kashmiri group claimed responsibility). The same day, a bomb planted in baggage being transferred to an Air India flight in Japan blew up, no doubt prematurely; it, too, has been credited to Sikh terrorists.

In 1987 the Punjab was put under "President's Rule," placing all state law enforcement under the central government in New Delhi. In May 1988 the Indian government launched another operation, "Black Thunder," which uncovered further evidence in the Golden Temple of continuing torture and murder. Although it was tactically more successful than Operation Blue Star, it also failed to reduce the incidence of terrorism. In 1989 Indian newspapers reported casualties of Sikh terrorism almost daily. International Sikh terrorism has tapered off in recent years. Most Sikh activities abroad—principally in Britain, Canada, and the United States—are aimed at fundraising for operations back home.

Actual terrorist operations are carried out by a number of covert groups about which very little is known other than that they probably first turned to terrorism after the Sikh independence movement turned violent under Bhindranwale in 1981. An effort was made to coordinate their activities through the creation of the Panthic Committee, but it failed to unite them, and they continue to operate more or less independently.

One of the earliest Sikh terrorist groups, Dal Khalsa, was created in 1978 by Jagjit Singh Chauhan, allegedly with support from Congress-I party politicians who wished to cause a split in the Akali Dal and remove it from power in the Punjab (the party did indeed split in 1981). In September 1981 five Dal Khalsa members hijacked an Indian airliner and diverted it to Lahore, where they were captured by Pakistani commandos. The group also claimed responsibility for the 1986 murder of General A. S. Vaidya, who was Army Chief of Staff during Operation Blue Star.

At present there are many Sikh terrorist groups and factions. Among the more prominent is the Dashmesh "Tenth" Regiment, founded around 1982 probably under the aegis of Bhindranwale. It is named for the tenth guru and founder of the Sikh military tradition, Gobind Singh. Many believe that it was founded and trained by Major General Shahbeg Singh, a Sikh who trained Bangladeshi guerrilla forces and who was cashiered from the Indian army shortly before his scheduled retirement. Shahbeg Singh was killed along with Bhindranwale in the attack on the Golden Temple in 1984. The Dashmesh Regiment has been responsible for a number of assassinations, arson, and bombings and claimed responsibility for the two Air India attacks in 1985.

The All-India Sikh Students' Federation, which replaced the Communist Party student wing as the dominant student group in the

Punjab, has allegedly been involved in some terrorism but seems to have been more important as a recruiting ground for terrorists and is primarily a political front organization. It is split into rival factions.

Other key groups include the Khalistan Commando Force, probably the largest of all the Sikh terrorist groups, which has staged many major incidents. It suffered substantially in Operation Black Thunder in May 1988, and even further when its leader, General Labh Singh, was killed in a shootout with security forces in June of that year. The Khalistan Liberation Force was organized by a shadowy figure called "Brahma," who was also killed by the police in Rajasthan near the Pakistan border the following month. The Bhindranwale Tiger Force of Khalistan is believed to be led by Gurbachan Singh Monochahal, one of the most wanted men in India. He is also a prominent member of the Panthic Committee. Babbar Khalsa is a highly organized group known for its religious fervor. It spends much time on religious indoctrination, particularly the cult of saint-soldier (sant-sipahi), based on the life of Gobind Singh. Its operations are generally very carefully planned.

There is evidence that many common criminals have adopted the Khalistan cause as a cover for extortion and murder, a factor that makes it even more difficult to assess the nature and extent of political Sikh terrorism. One source estimates that over 60 percent of the terrorist killings in the villages are not politically motivated but criminal acts performed under the umbrella of the Khalistan cause.[38] There is also a nexus between Punjabi smugglers and the terrorists; the smugglers buy protection from the terrorists by smuggling arms for them from Pakistan.

In addition to those relatively high-visibility groups, there are many smaller nationalist−ethnic groups throughout the world. For example, a number of Corsican groups were organized in France in the late 1970s and early 1980s, notably the National Front for the Liberation of Corsica (FLNC). Others include the Kanak insurgents in New Caledonia and the Renamo guerrillas of Mozambique, who seem to have no political platform beyond the overthrow of the government.

The *Umkhonto We Sizwe* (MK, or Spear of the Nation) is the paramilitary or operational wing of the African National Congress (ANC) in South Africa. In 1960 racial tensions culminated in riots at a black township, Sharpeville, during which white police fired on and killed a number of black demonstrators. The ANC was outlawed, and its leader, Nelson Mandela, was jailed. Convinced that the government would not moderate its repressive white supremacist policies without violence, the ANC created the MK in 1961. At first it engaged in sporadic attacks on transportation facilities. In 1980 it intensified its operations, targeting strategic installations, and in 1983 it began indiscriminate attacks involving civilian, including black, casualties. The MK operates primarily out of Botswana, Zimbabwe, and especially Zambia.

Two of the more visible of the smaller nationalist–ethnic groups are Armenian terrorist organizations. A resurgence of Armenian national consciousness followed the murder of two Turkish diplomats in Los Angeles in 1973 by Kirkan Yanikian, an eighty-four-year-old survivor of the pre–World War I Turkish genocide of Armenians. In 1975 the Secret Army for the Liberation of Armenia (ASALA) was founded by a Lebanese Armenian, Hagop Hagopian. It espouses a Marxist ideology, and its goals are to reestablish an independent Armenian state in eastern Turkey, northern Iran, and the Armenian Soviet Socialist Republic of the USSR. It also wished to raise world consciousness about the Turkish genocide of Armenians in 1915–17.

ASALA's main targets have been Turkish representatives and institutions worldwide, and NATO and Israeli targets as well. In 1983 ASALA split into the Militant group under Hagopian (who was killed in Athens in March 1988) and the Revolutionary Movement group under Monte Melkonian. ASALA-RM argued that indiscriminate terrorism was hurting the cause and wanted to limit attacks to Turkish targets. ASALA-M favors unrestricted attacks against Turkish and "imperialist" targets.

Terrorist activities have been reduced since the split; ASALA was nevertheless reportedly a participant in a series of terrorist attacks in Paris in September 1986, along with LARF and a French New Left group, Action Directe. ASALA hoped to force the release from jail of one of its leaders, Varoujan Garabedjian, while LARF sought the release of its founder and leader, George Ibrahim Abdallah. ASALA gunmen also attacked the French Embassy in East Beirut in October 1987 with the same purpose in mind.[39]

Another Armenian group, the Justice Commandos of the Armenian Genocide (JCAG), is a non-Marxist socialist rival that seeks an independent Armenia excluding the Armenian Soviet Socialist Republic. Sensitive to Western public opinion, it has avoided indiscriminate terrorist attacks and limited its targets to Turkish officials and Turkish facilities. Beginning around 1983, terrorist acts of the kind known to be JCAG acts have been claimed by the Armenian Revolutionary Army (ARA), possibly a cover name for JCAG.

When looking over the nationalist–ethnic groups involved in terrorism, one is struck by the lack of common characteristics among them. Some, such as the Sikh terrorist organizations, are part of larger political movements; others, such as the PLO, are large groups in their own right; and still others, such as Force 17, are small operational units or cells of larger organizations. Some groups, such as the PLO, are primarily political organizations; some have separate political wings (like the PIRA's Sinn Fein); and others, such the Abu Nidal Organization, are almost totally dedicated to terrorism and engage only minimally in political action. Some groups have accompanying political ideologies—the Marxist ETA and LARF are examples—and a case could be made for including them among doctrinal groups. Others, such as al-Fatah, espouse no single political ideology.

The single factor that all these groups have in common is the primacy of national or ethnic identity. This identity is invariably the most important element in creating a sense of grievance and in articulating the political resolution of such a grievance.

4

Doctrinal Terrorism

Doctrinal terrorism is generally based on a universalist political ideology or religious dogma, in contrast to nationalist–ethnic terrorism, based on a particularist national or ethnic identity. Although the two categories are logically incompatible, many terrorist groups attempt to appeal to both universal "truth" and a particularist sense of common cause. We have seen that a number of nationalist–ethnic groups, including the Basque ETA and the Irish Republican Army, have adopted Marxism, a universalist ideology. Similarly, many doctrinal groups are national or ethnic in appeal and scope, despite claims of doctrinal universalism. Peru's Sendero Luminoso (Shining Path), for example, while Marxist–Maoist in ideology, is uniquely Peruvian, and the backbone of its support is the Indian population in the high country.

Two principal motivating factors underlie most doctrinal terrorism: either disaffection with the prevailing political system or a fear that a favored political system be overturned because the government security forces are incapable of sustaining it. These characteristics are not unique to terrorist groups; they apply to most left-wing or right-wing political organizations. Terrorist groups can be seen as occupying the most extreme positions on the left and right of the political spectrum. They are generally so extreme, in fact, that it is sometimes difficult to tell the two poles apart.

Since World War II leftist doctrines have been the primary vehicles for expression of political protest. For left-wing extremists, including terrorists, Communist doctrines of armed struggle and of wars of national liberation have provided a doctrinal justification for acts of violence. In the last two decades, however, right-wing doctrines, particularly religious fundamentalism, have become increasingly popular among the politically disaffected. Right-wing extremism has also increased dramatically in support of the status quo, particularly among those who feel that their privileged political, economic, or social positions are threatened by even the most moderate, equitable reforms. Such groups generally reject democratic ideals and justify their actions on the basis of "anti-Communism."

Among left-wing terrorist groups there are probably more differences than similarities. The common denominator, socialist ideology, is less a motivating force than a justification, and it is often interpreted in a cavalier fashion, tailored to the circumstances and needs of the individual groups. Broadly speaking, there are two categories of left-wing terrorist groups: utopian groups and national revolutionary groups.

Utopian groups tend to espouse abstract or remote causes, such as "world revolution of the working class." Because they are among the most thoroughly interviewed and studied of all terrorist groups, their profile tends to set the popular stereotype of terrorists as young, single, mostly male, from middle-class backgrounds, and with good, if incomplete, educations.[1]

Most contemporary utopian groups grew out of the New Left student protests of Western Europe and Japan in the late 1960s, which paralleled the student antiwar movement in the United States but took on a more violent form. Many utopians began as pacifists, protesters against nuclear proliferation and the Vietnam War, and advocates for various groups, including the Palestinians, whom they considered victims of the evil "capitalist system." Over time, a small number of protesters adopted increasingly violent tactics to draw public attention to their political agendas and finally coalesced into terrorist groups. Having arrived at a violent stage, utopian groups seldom consider nonviolent tactics suited to their aims. It is not unreasonable to conclude that terrorism for them becomes as much an end in itself as it is a means to an end.

Of the many utopian groups in existence, eight stand out as the most representative of the species: the Red Army Faction (RAF) and Revolutionary Cells (RZ) of West Germany, the Red Brigades of Italy, Action Directe of France, the 17 November Revolutionary Organization and the Revolutionary Popular Struggle (ELA), both based in Greece, and two Japanese New Left organizations, Chukaku-Ha and the Japanese Red Army. There are, of course, many other smaller groups, including Belgium's Combatant Communist Cells under Pierre Carette, the First of October Anti-Fascist Resistance Group (GRAPO) in Spain, and the Popular Forces of 25 April (FP-25) in Portugal. Most of them appear to have ties with other New Left groups.

The Red Army Faction, also known in its early years as the Baader-Meinhof Gang, was formed in the wake of the student demonstrations that swept much of Western Europe in 1968.[2] Among the founding members were Andreas Baader, Ulrike Meinhof, Gudrun Ensslin, Holger Meins, and Horst Mahler. All were from prosperous families and were well educated. Baader was the son of a historian, Meinhof the daughter of an art historian and a graduate in philosophy, Ensslin the daughter of a clergyman and a graduate in philosophy, and Mahler was a lawyer. It could hardly be said, as they claimed, that they were victims of social or economic injustice. There was, though, a conscious effort by RAF's basically affluent members to identify with the poor and exploited, particularly the Vietnamese (until the war ended in 1975) and the Palestinians, and in so doing, to make common cause with similar New Left groups abroad. In addition, the members, all of whom grew up in the immediate post–Nazi Germany period, were particularly antagonistic to all forms of authority, which they called "Fascist."[3]

The group was initially indistinguishable from other antiwar student activist groups. As it slowly drifted toward violence, its ideology evolved toward utopian Marxism with an emphasis on armed revolutionary struggle. Mahler and Meinhof produced much of the theoretical writing, the latter as a frequent contributor to the leftist journal, *Konkret*. Though shallow, this writing appealed to a number of would-be dissidents who were looking for an ideological justification for their acts.

The RAF considers armed struggle against capitalism to be a universal goal as well as a coming reality; hence it is but one "faction" of a universal revolutionary army which will come together to overthrow the capitalist system. (The name Red Army Faction was adopted by Baader in 1970 from the Japanese Red Army Faction, precursor of the Japanese Red Army, much admired by Baader and Mahler.) The founders did not regard the RAF as a political party; in the words of Ulrike Meinhof, it was instead "organizationally, practically and conceptually an essential component of a Communist Party worthy of the name."[4] The fact that the group operated outside the mainstream of Communist party politics is the primary indication of the RAF's essential utopianism.

The RAF's first terrorist act was an attempted arson at a Frankfurt department store in April 1968, for which Baader and Ensslin were arrested, convicted, and sentenced to prison. They were subsequently released, pending appeal, jumped bail, and went underground. Around 1969 a number of RAF leaders apparently went to Jordan to train with the Marxist Popular Front for the Liberation of Palestine.

Returning to Germany in 1970, Baader was rearrested but escaped with the help of Meinhof, Mahler, and others. Between 1970 and 1972 the group successfully carried out a number of spectacular terrorist attacks on German, NATO, and U.S. buildings, installations, and officials. Mahler was arrested in October 1970, and in 1972 Baader, Ensslin, Meinhof, Holger Meins, and others were also arrested, tried, and convicted. Meins died of a hunger strike in 1974, and Meinhof committed suicide in 1976. Baader and Ensslin also committed suicide in 1977 after the failure of a rescue attempt that involved the kidnapping of Dr. Hanns-Martin Schleyer and the hijacking and diversion of a Lufthansa airliner to Mogadishu, Somalia. Schleyer was murdered, but the German counter-terrorist force GSG-9 recaptured the airliner (which had actually been hijacked by the PFLP), and the RAF demands were not met.

With most of the original leadership either dead or in prison, a new generation took over the RAF, and in 1980 it merged with a closely allied utopian group, the Second of June Movement. Many of the new leaders were arrested in 1983, and their places were taken by others. Among the contemporary leaders are Barbara Mayer, Inge Viett, Wolfgang Grams, Horst Meyer, Suzanne Albrecht, Tomas Simon, Birgit Hogefeld, and Silke Maier-Witt.

The contemporary leadership appears to be more sophisticated than its predecessors. Its tactics are two-tiered: infrequent but carefully planned attacks on prominent personalities by the hard-core members (some twenty to thirty in number), and, concurrently, more frequent low-level bombing attacks of economic and commercial targets by RAF sympathizers and supporters. This latter group, which probably numbers several hundred, also provides safe haven and financial and logistical support to the hard-core membership.

Among their more prominent attacks were a 1985 bomb attack at Rhein-Main Air Base that killed two and injured seventeen (possibly in cooperation with Action Directe) and a 1986 arson attack that ignited over a thousand gallons of fuel at a U.S. military pumping station. The RAF has also carried out successful assassinations. In July 1986 Karl-

Heinz Beckurts, director of research at Siemens Electronics Company, was murdered, and in October of that year Gerold von Braunmuehl, a German diplomat, was murdered outside his home in Bonn. In November 1989 Alfred Herrhausen, head of Germany's largest commercial bank, Deutsche Bank A.G., was killed in a Frankfurt suburb by a bomb placed in his car.

Even though the pool of possible recruits has decreased as student unrest has diminished in recent years, the RAF appears to have a facility for regeneration, perhaps in large part because of the psychological needs it meets for the members.

Revolutionary Cells (or RZ, from the German *Revolutionaere Zellen*) has a utopian Marxist ideology similar to that of the RAF. Formed in 1973, it carries much less ideological baggage than the RAF and has less grandiose aims and a much simpler and less expensive organizational structure. The RZ's journal, *Revolutionaere Zorn (Revolutionary Wrath)* states that its intent is "immediately and everywhere to begin the armed struggle" to undermine public order and faith in existing governmental institutions.[5] It seeks mainly to disrupt politics by arson and bombings as well as demonstrations, riots, and civil disturbances in which bystanders are invited to join. It claims that it eschews assassinations, although one German official was killed "by accident" in 1981 and another was wounded by two RZ gunmen in 1986. The RZ also has an affiliated women's group, *Rote Zora,* which in addition to the usual Marxist goals seeks an end to oppression of women, sexism, and racism.

Unlike the tightly organized RAF, the RZ is basically a loose confederation of small cells having limited contact with one another. They conduct operations in their home areas, seeking to exacerbate local political conflicts and rivalries. The RZ generally avoids intricate terrorist acts requiring professional expertise and time-consuming planning.

The hard-core activists number less than a hundred, and most RZ members are what is known in German as *Freizeitterroristen*, "after-hours terrorists." Because of its pragmatic goals and aversion to political assassination, the RZ appears to have little trouble recruiting such members. This approach is also much cheaper than maintaining full-time terrorists in hiding. One 1984 study estimated that it cost about $50,000 a year to maintain a single RAF member, including arms and other terrorist materials, safe haven, and security, and costs have no doubt increased since then.[6]

In sharp contrast to the Revolutionary Cells' avoidance of targeting people, Italy's Red Brigades (*Brigate Rosse* or BR) has had one of the most brutal records of all groups involved in terrorism in recent years, with murder, "kneecapping," and kidnapping its favorite tactics. Like other activist utopian Marxist groups, the BR has its roots in the 1968 student riots, but it is also the product of the Italian political scene from the late 1960s to the early 1980s, when the country experienced a succession of weak governments. In some ways Italian politics during that period resembled the interwar period, when the political center was under attack by the increasingly violent extremes of left and right. The BR attempted to exacerbate the instability through terrorist attacks against leading business and professional leaders. They saw it as the first step in a proletarian revolution to overthrow the capitalist system in Italy and worldwide. In 1981 the BR also "declared war" on NATO as an intermediate objective.

The intellectual founders of the BR were Renato Curcio and his wife, Margherita Cagol, who also provided inspired leadership in the early 1970s. Cagol was killed in a shootout with the police in 1975, and Curcio, having broken out of jail with her help in 1975, was rearrested in 1976. Terrorist couples, with or without benefit of clergy, are not rare among the New Left groups. The groups tend to be self-contained subcultures that share common experiences dating back to student days, and personal relationships are closely entwined with group experiences.

The organizing mind behind the BR was Giorgio Semeria. He created its pyramidal structure, setting up semi-autonomous cells, collectively called columns, in major cities, including Milan, Rome, Turin, and Genoa. No cell contains more than five members, and only one member has contact with a member of the next higher cell. Each column operated independently of the others.

Mario Moretti was responsible for contacts with other groups and individuals in Italy and abroad. The BR has consistently been linked to some of the Marxist Palestinian groups and also has regular contacts with the RAF and with the French Action Directe. However, it has probably received more aid from former Argentinean Montaneros and Uruguayan Tupamaros who fled to Italy in the 1970s and passed their expertise and experience on to the BR. Those two South American groups were among the most active terrorists in the world until the Tupamaros were crushed by Uruguay in 1973 and the Montaneros by Argentina in 1977. Escapees from both groups fled to Europe, including Italy, from where many of their families had immigrated after World War II.

By 1975 most of the BR's original leadership was either dead or in jail, and a new leadership emerged, less steeped in ideological concepts but just as proficient and far more brutal. The most spectacular Red Brigades terrorist act of this period was the kidnapping and murder of the former Christian Democratic Prime Minister, Aldo Moro, in March 1978. The BR apparently held the Christian Democratic Party particularly responsible for "capitalist crimes." In December 1981, after declaring war on NATO, the BR kidnapped U.S. Army Brigadier General James Dozier in Verona. After forty-two days he was rescued by the Italian police.

As it turned out, weak democratic governments in Italy did not mean weak democratic institutions. Despite the large-scale terror and intimidation by the BR and other right- and left-wing groups, the Italian democratic system withstood the challenge. All the major political parties, including the Italian Communist Party, opposed terrorism. After two years of debate, the Italian parliament passed an amnesty law in May 1982. With many terrorists renouncing their groups and collaborating with authorities, hundreds of arrests were made before the law expired in January 1983.[7] So decimated were the terrorists that Front Line (*Prima Linea* or PL), another Italian utopian Marxist group—less brutal than the Red Brigades—declared itself no longer in existence in April 1983.

Though many observers thought, and certainly hoped, that the BR had been dealt a fatal blow, such was not the case. Despite a split within the organization, the BR began a comeback in 1984. The majority, calling itself the "militarists" or Fighting Communist Party (no relation to the Italian Communist Party) holds to the more traditional Leninist view that only acts of violence can prepare the way for Marxist revolution. The minority, called the "movementalists" or Union of Fighting Communists, argues that before the revolution can take place the proletariat must first be indoctrinated to support it. Both factions believe in armed struggle, however, and their terrorist tactics do not greatly differ.

In February 1984 BR, working with the Lebanese Armed Military Faction, participated in the murder of Leamon "Ray" Hunt, an American serving as director-general of the United Nations Sinai Multinational Force and Observers. In March 1987 the director-general of

Italian Space and Armaments, Air Force General Lucio Giorgieri, was murdered by two gunmen on a motorcycle.

Subsequently the Italian police, with the help of French and Spanish authorities, succeeded in arresting many BR terrorists, including the Giorgieri murderers. Since then, the BR has been relatively dormant. Nevertheless, its capabilities have not been totally destroyed, and it is likely to be heard from again.

The French New Left movement stems from the same tradition as its German and Italian counterparts, the student uprisings culminating in the disturbances of 1968. Its initial concerns centered on such student issues as living expenses and student housing. The Vietnam War subsequently became an issue, and by the 1970s the French New Left had also politicized the ecology issue.

The leading French New Left group, Action Directe (AD) was created in 1979 from elements of two other groups, the International Revolutionary Action Groups (GARI) and the Armed Nuclei for Popular Autonomy (NAPAP). The new group adopted the Maoist doctrine espoused by NAPAP and enunciated by the political writer and activist Frédéric Oriach.[8] Although Action Directe is better organized than its predecessors, it has never attained the organizational and tactical sophistication of the Red Army Faction, Revolutionary Cells, or the Red Brigades.

Action Directe adopted a cellular structure, with each cell operating independently and having minimum contact with other cells. It is divided into a domestic wing operating within France and a more violent international wing organized by Jean-Marc Rouillan and operating out of Paris and Belgium. The domestic wing prefers bombings of unoccupied sites, whereas the international wing has been responsible for a number of murders, including that of Georges Besse, the chairman of Renault, in November 1986. AD finances its activities mainly through bank robberies.

From the start AD appeared to seek ties with Belgian, Spanish, German, and Italian New Left groups as well as with the Lebanese Armed Revolutionary Force (LARF). AD and the RAF may have conducted joint operations, including the January 1985 murder of French General René Auran and the August 1985 bombing of Rhein-Main Air Base. It is also believed to have joined with the Combatant Communist Cells of Belgium and the RAF to establish the now defunct

Anti-Imperialist Armed Front, aimed primarily at the U.S. presence in Europe and at NATO.

AD may have also been involved with a LARF terrorist campaign in the early 1980s.[9] When the French police arrested Oriach in October 1982, they found evidence linking the two organizations. The French hoped that his capture would put an end to both AD's and LARF's terrorist activities, but starting in 1985 there were renewed attacks, and in September 1986 Paris was rocked by a series of bloody attacks linked to attempts to free LARF leader Georges Ibrahim Abdallah, a leader of the Armenian Secret Army for the Liberation of Armenia (ASALA); Warujian Garabedjian; and a Lebanese Shi'a, Anis Naccache. The attacks were reportedly spearheaded by the Committee for Solidarity with Arab and Middle Eastern Political Prisoners (CSPPA), a previously unknown entity apparently representing both AD and LARF. Its links with ASALA are less clear.[10]

In February 1987 the French arrested the leadership cadre of the international wing, including Rouillan, Nathalie Menigon, Joelle Aubran, and Georges Cipriani. Since then AD terrorist activities have been greatly curtailed. Nevertheless, as is the case with other utopian Marxist underground groups, Action Directe is probably capable of regenerating itself if and when a new generation of leaders emerges.

One of the least known but most lethal utopian terrorist groups is the Revolutionary Organization 17 November (*Epanastaiki Organoisi 17 Noemvri*) in Greece, which takes its name from the date of a 1973 student riot at the Athens Polytechnic Institute. The brutal suppression of the riot resulted in at least twenty killed and precipitated the downfall of the military junta then in power. The group's ideology is a nebulous mix of anti-Americanism, antimilitarism, anticapitalism, and revolutionary armed struggle. It initially concentrated on prominent Greeks and Americans. In the late 1980s it also started hitting Turkish targets. The 17 November attacks have been mainly assassinations of prominent Greeks and Americans by three-member hit teams that typically escape on a motor scooter in Athens traffic. It often uses the same pistol, either out of frugality or to leave a signature. It also has been involved in vehicle bombings, including two attacks on cars owned by the Turkish Embassy in May 1988.

The first known 17 November attack was the December 1975 murder of an American Embassy official, Richard Welch, who had been named as a U.S. agent in a scurrilous U.S. magazine, *Counterspy.* In

1983 it killed a U.S. Navy captain, George Tsantes, and in June 1988, the U.S. defense attache (Navy) Captain William Nordeen. It has also killed some prominent Greeks, including a newspaper editor and a retired industrialist.

Unlike most New Left groups, 17 November is not known to have any ties with similar groups abroad. In 1987 the Greek police believed they found links to another Greek Marxist terrorist group, the Revolutionary Popular Struggle (*Epanastikos Laikos Agonas*, or ELA).

The ELA is an equally shadowy group which appears to have evolved at the same time as the 17 November. Although it has expressed "solidarity" with Action Directe and the RAF, there is no evidence of formal ties. Most of its attacks are bombings.

Japanese terrorism is mainly an offshoot of the New Left, a radical political movement that currently includes some twenty-three factions with a combined membership of some 35,000, including sympathizers.[11] Many New Left extremists engage in terrorism against the state, but factional infighting is also endemic.

The origins of the Japanese New Left movement go back to the *Zengakuren*, the National Union of Autonomous Committees of Japanese Students, founded in 1948 when 400 delegates from 138 universities came together to demand more student grants and better living conditions. *Zengakuren* came increasingly under the influence of the Japanese Communist Party, and by 1952 many of its members advocated armed struggle. There were continuing debates over tactics, however, and in 1958 two factions split off over its support of peaceful coexistence: the Trotskyite League of Communists (*Kyosando*) and the League of Revolutionary Communists, (*Kakkyodo*). Both organized extensive demonstrations to protest the U.S. security treaty of 1960.

The real shift toward extremism that marked the birth of the Japanese New Left movement occurred in the middle to late 1960s. Around that time, Kakkyodo split further over whether developing New Left utopian Marxism or initiating mass struggle should have greater priority. The League of Revolutionary Communists–Marxist Revolutionary Group (*Kakumaru-Ha*) favored the former, and the League of Revolutionary Communists–National Committee (*Chukaku-Ha*) favored the latter. Initially Kakumaru-Ha was more prominent, but by 1983 it had been eclipsed by Chukaku-Ha, which had adopted terrorism as a preferred tactic.

Chukaku-Ha is strictly a domestic group comprising many laborers as well as students. It has shown no interest in international operations or in cooperation with any other groups. It has developed a proficiency in explosives and incendiary devices and has targeted government buildings, railroad facilities, and airports, as well as U.S. facilities. In 1987 it undertook a series of bombings at the new Tokyo International Airport site at Narita and the new Kansai airport at Osaka; in January 1988 it fired five rocket bombs at the Narita site. However, in its periodical, *Zensen* (*Advance*), it has also indicated that it might begin targeting particular individuals, a source of increasing concern to Japanese security officials. Chukaku-Ha is believed to have some 200 full-time dedicated activists, supported by a much larger number of sympathizers.

Probably the Japanese terrorist group best known in the West is the Japanese Red Army (JRA). It also has a convoluted history. In 1969 a group known as the Japanese Red Army Faction or *Sekigun-Ha*, broke off from the League of Communists (*Kyosando*). Its first important terrorist action was the hijacking a Japanese Airliner in 1970, Japan's first hijacking. Even then, some of its leaders disagreed with the use of terrorist tactics. In the same year it made contact with the Marxist Popular Front for the Liberation of Palestine (PFLP), a relationship that was to flourish.

An intense debate arose in Sekigun-ha over whether to concentrate on world revolution or to limit efforts to Japan. In 1971 Fusako Shigenobu, who favored world revolution and had been a liaison with the PFLP, moved to Lebanon with about twenty-five hard-core activists and organized the Japanese Red Army.[12] She has continued to operate out of Lebanon, probably in cooperation with the PFLP and possibly also with Libyan financial support. The JRA also still has a small group of about a hundred sympathizers in Japan.

Between 1972 and 1977 the JRA conducted a number of brutal terrorist attacks on behalf of the PFLP and on its own behalf as well. They have included bombings, murders, and hijackings. The most noteworthy was the Lod airport massacre in May 1972 in which sixteen Puerto Ricans pilgrims visiting the Holy Land were killed. Since 1977 the JRA has not claimed any attacks but is believed to be using the cover name Anti-Imperialist International Brigades. Individual acts have been linked to the JRA. In April 1988 a suspected JRA member, Yu Kikumura, a former Japanese Red Army Faction member, was arrested in New Jersey with three crude pipe bombs in his possession.

(What he planned to do with the bombs was never established.) Because of its offshore base of operations (in Lebanon), its close relationship to another Marxist group (PFLP), and its international area of operations, the JRA remains a stereotypical international terrorist group.

Left-wing national revolutionary groups are more concerned with revolutionary change within national boundaries than with the abstract cause of international Marxist revolution espoused by the utopians. Distinguishing between the two categories can be difficult, however, since many national revolutionary groups operate across international boundaries and many utopian groups operate almost exclusively within national borders.

Left-wing national revolutionary groups are also distinguishable from nationalist–ethnic groups that espouse leftist doctrines in that the former claim the same nationality as the regime they seek to overthrow, whereas the latter consider themselves nationally or ethnically different and seek independence or at least autonomy from the regime they oppose. This distinction can also become blurred, however, in cases where there are ethnic differences between the political elites and the politically (and economically) dispossessed represented by national liberation groups. For example, many of the Latin American national revolutionary groups represent Indian and Mestizo constituencies, whereas the regimes they seek to overthrow are of Spanish-European descent.

Another distinguishing characteristic of most left-wing national revolutionary groups is that they are generally more involved in guerrilla insurgencies than in pure terrorism. When they use terrorist tactics, they usually consider them the first step in starting an insurgency or else a tactic of last resort in cases where insurgencies have either failed or reached a stalemate. National revolutionary terrorism is thus primarily a Third World phenomenon and takes place in countries where democratic traditions are weak and government despotic. Though found throughout the Third World, during the 1980s national revolutionary terrorism occurred most often in Central and South America, where all the traditional elements of political unrest are abundantly present: widespread urban and rural poverty, illiteracy, and concentration of economic wealth and political power in the hands of a few, against an ethnic background of Hispanicized elites and largely Indian peasants.

National revolutionary activity in Latin America gained a prominent supporter in 1959, when Fidel Castro established a Marxist regime in Cuba. Castro lost little time turning Havana into a regional support base for insurgencies throughout the southern hemisphere, particularly Central America, resulting in an upsurge in guerrilla warfare. The strong Marxist flavor of most of the insurgencies convinced Washington that they constituted not a merely regional threat to stability but a global threat as well. In the early 1960s President Kennedy responded to the Cuban-supported insurgency threat by establishing counterinsurgency programs throughout Latin American. With both sides better armed and trained, the level of violence escalated.

The establishment of the Marxist Sandinista regime in Nicaragua in 1979 further inspired Central American left-wing insurgency groups. It also confirmed U.S. anxieties over a communist threat to the hemisphere. For its part, Nicaragua, though hard-pressed to cope with its own economic problems, supports neighboring insurgencies to the extent that it can.

Armed uprisings have been endemic in Central America since colonial days. Only Costa Rica and Panama, both with a strong middle class, have largely escaped. The two most active left-wing insurgency movements in recent years have been in the countries of El Salvador and Guatemala.

The plight of the landless Salvadoran peasants under a harsh aristocratic regime led to a communist-peasant insurrection in 1932 that contemporary Marxist insurgents look back upon as the beginning of armed struggle in El Salvador. The then leader of the Communist Party of El Salvador (PCES), Farabundo Martí, played an important part in the insurrection and has acquired legendary status. The PCES did not embrace violent revolutionary tactics, however, and it took forty more years for other left-wing groups dedicated to armed struggle to begin to appeal.

There are currently five principal Salvadoran insurgent groups, which collectively control some 7,500 fighters. The largest and most active is the Farabundo Martí Popular Liberation Forces (FPL), founded in 1974 by Salvador Cayetano Carpio, who used the *nom de guerre* Comandante Marcial. Involved in labor agitation in the early 1960s, Carpio became Secretary General of the PCES in 1964 but broke with the party in 1969 over its reluctance to sanction armed violence.

In 1983 renegade members of the FPL's San Salvador organization, the Clara Elizabeth Ramirez Front (FCER), began their own operations, specializing in assassinations. In March 1985 they killed the retired General José Alberto Medrano, founder of the quasi-official right-wing paramilitary organization ORDEN. Since then, however, government countermeasures have apparently undermined their capabilities, at least for a time.

A group of Trotskyite (those who refuse to accept any outside direction) and Maoist dissidents left the CPES in 1972 to found the People's Revolutionary Army (ERP). Its leader, Joaquín Villalobos, expounds a utopian-style doctrine of "people's revolutionary warfare." Like Carpio, Villalobos considers terrorist acts a form of "revolutionary justice." The group quickly gained a sinister reputation for kidnapping and assassination. In 1975 the ERP was riddled with dissension, and the intragroup struggle led to the murder of one of its own founders, the revolutionary poet Roque Dalton-García. Ernesto Jovel and Fernán Cienfuegos left the ERP to found the Armed Forces of National Resistance (FARN).

The PCES, which was founded in the mid-1920s, continued to eschew armed violence until 1979. In October of that year the government was overthrown by civilian–military reformers, with whom the party had initially decided to cooperate. Moderation was simply not workable, however. Right-wing hard-liners adamantly opposed reform, and left-wing extremists remained committed to armed struggle. In December the PCES bowed to the voices of extremism and, under Jorge Shafik Handal, created its own paramilitary wing, the Armed Forces of Liberation (FAL).

A fifth organization, the Revolutionary Party for Central American Workers (PRTC), was founded in the late 1970s by Trotskyites under Fabio Castillo, a former rector of the University of El Salvador living in exile.

Each of the groups controls a political party, somewhat analogous to the Irish Republican Army's Sinn Fein. The PCES has for years controlled the National Democratic Union, a legal political party; the FPL controls the Popular Revolutionary Bloc (BPR); the ERP controls the Popular Leagues of February 28 (LP-28); the FARN controls the United Popular Action Front (FAPU); and the PRTC controls the Movement of Popular Liberation (MLP). All the parties are used for public relations, as recruiting bases, and as a manpower pool for demonstrations and civil disobedience.

At a secret meeting in Havana in May 1980, Castro made the five active groups form an executive coordinating body, the Unified Revolutionary Directorate (DRU), as a prerequisite for Cuban assistance. The following October the DRU, which was made up of three representatives from each organization, created the Farabundo Marti National Liberation Front (FMLN) to serve as an umbrella organization for the insurgent groups and their political parties. The FMLN, which operates somewhat like the PLO but more collegially, receives far more publicity in the foreign media than its little-known constituent groups. It coordinates all political and military action, such as the ceasefire proposals made during peace talks with Salvadoran political officials in Mexico City in February 1989 and the major guerrilla attack on the capital, San Salvador, in late 1989.[13]

FMLN external headquarters are now located in Managua, Nicaragua, and it maintains "political-diplomatic" offices in Panama, Mexico, and Europe. The FMLN also coordinates training, usually in Nicaragua and Cuba, and the channeling of arms and supplies to its various groups.

Despite its political activities (generally conducted by its political wing, the Democratic Revolutionary Front, or FDR), the FMLN is still basically an insurgent organization. It began an all-out guerrilla war in 1980, which, despite a 1989 attack on the capital and other cities, has basically turned into a stalemate. In the absence of concrete gains in the jungle battlefields, FMLN groups continue to employ terrorist tactics as a means of making their presence felt.

Among their terrorist acts have been numerous assassinations and kidnappings, including the 1985 kidnapping of Inez Duarte Durán, daughter of then President José Napoleón Duarte. In the past few years they have sought to undermine civil authority by systematically assassinating rural mayors: Forty-two mayors resigned rather than face death.[14] FMLN's latest strategy appears to be to keep up pressure on the government through guerrilla and terrorist operations, while offering peace in return for a share of political power as a first step toward overturning the regime.

The roots of the Guatemalan insurgency movement go back to the 1940s and 1950s. In 1945 a left-of-center reformer, Juan José Arevalo, replaced a right-wing military dictatorship and attempted a variety of reforms to modernize Guatemala's feudal society and economy and bring the Indian population into the mainstream of Guatemalan life. In 1951 he was succeeded by Colonel Jacobo Arbenz Guzmán, a Marxist reformer who tried to build on Arevalo's agrarian policies to create a socialist state. Among other things, Arbenz sought to expropriate the holdings of the large landowners, including the U.S.-owned United Fruit Company, to give to the largely landless peasants.

U.S. Secretary of State Dulles saw in the Arbenz regime a threat to democracy in the Western Hemisphere, and in 1954 Arbenz was overthrown by a U.S.-supported right-wing coup. The new government restored title of the lands to their original owners, purged the armed forces of reform-minded officers, and banned the communist party (Partido Guatemalteco del Trabajo, or PGT), which had been legalized by Arbenz. The reformers were forced either to cease their activities or to go into exile.

On the night of November 13, 1960, a number of left-wing officers at Fort Matamoros in Guatemala City mutinied, killed their base commander, and fled into the jungle with arms and sympathetic troops. The insurrection was quickly put down, but the leaders escaped to Honduras. Among the officers was Marco Antonio Yon Sosa, a nationalist Marxist who, ironically, had been trained at the U.S. counterinsurgency school in Panama. He later organized an insurgency group, which came to be known as the 13 November Movement of 1960 (MR-13).[15]

In 1962 Yon Sosa and two other leaders, Luis Trejos Esquivel and Luis Turcios Lima, went to Havana to confer with Ernesto "Che" Guevara and Arbenz. Upon returning to Guatemala, they collaborated with the PGT to organize a full-fledged urban and rural insurgency organization, the Rebel Armed Forces (FAR). Its most famous terrorist attack at the time was the assassination of U.S. Ambassador John Gordon Mein in August 1968.

Yon Sosa later split off from the FAR and reconstituted the MR-13, which he led until he was killed in 1970. By then all the original rebel leaders had been killed by government forces, and the insurgency was contained. The FAR, however, has survived, and over the years it has engaged in both guerrilla and terrorist tactics. It operates mainly in the far north and in Guatemala City and is now led by Jorge Soto García (alias Pablo Monsanto).

The 1970s saw a renewal of insurgent activity. In 1975 César Montés, who had been a member of the PGT's central committee, helped create the Guerrilla Army of the Poor (EGP), which quickly became active in guerrilla operations. Its main base of operation is the northwest highlands. The EGP is currently led by Ricardo Ramírez de León (alias

Rolando Morán). Another group, established about the same time, is the Revolutionary Organization of People in Arms (ORPA), which operates mainly in the southwest and is led by Rodrigo Asturias Amado (alias Gaspar Ilom).

In 1980 Castro insisted that the leading Guatemalan insurgent groups coordinate their activities as a prerequisite for Cuban support, as he had with the Salvadoran groups. In February 1982 FAR, EGP, and ORPA formalized the creation of an umbrella organization, the Guatemalan National Revolutionary Union (URNG), with the Guatemalan Committee for Patriotic Unity (CGUP) as its political arm. The URNG has not been as effective as the FMLN, however, and government counterinsurgency efforts have kept the groups on the defensive in recent years.

South America has a long heritage of left-wing nationalist terrorism. Until they were crushed by government forces in 1973 and 1977 respectively, Uruguay's Tupamaros and Argentina's Montoneros were among the most active terrorists in the world, and they included not only pro-Soviet and pro-Castro groups but Maoists and Trotskyites as well.

Left-wing nationalist revolutionary groups involved in terrorism are still found throughout South America. In Chile, for example, there are the Manuel Rodriguez Patriotic Front (FPMR)—associated with the pro-Soviet Communist Party of Chile—which almost succeeded in assassinating President Pinochet in 1986, and the older pro-Castro Movement of the Revolutionary Left (MIR), founded in 1965. Venezuela has the indigenous Americo Silva Front, the armed wing of *Bandera Roja* (Red Flag), dedicated to armed struggle and terrorism. In Ecuador, *Alfaro Vive ¡Carajo!* (Alfaro Lives, "Expletive"!), named for a revolutionary president killed in 1912, was founded in 1983, apparently with the help of M-19 of Colombia. In scope and ferocity, however, the left-wing insurgency movements of two countries stand out: Colombia and Peru.

The Colombian insurgency movement has been one of the most brutal in South America, and with the added violence generated by narco-terrorism, the level of brutality is not likely to subside despite the May 1984 ceasefire accord between the government and most of the insurgency groups.

Until the 1960s the Communist Party of Colombia (PCC) eschewed terrorism and armed struggle, as did most pro-Soviet parties in Latin

America. The change came largely as a result of Castro's successful revolution in Cuba in 1959, which was an inspiration to young Colombian radicals and resulted in direct Cuban support for armed struggle.

In recent years Colombian insurgent groups have developed a close relationship with local drug traffickers, called narco-terrorism, which will be discussed in more detail in the following chapter. The funds provided by the drug traffic have enabled the insurgent groups to expand greatly. In 1978 the total number of insurgents was estimated at 1,700; by 1988 the number had risen to more than 7,500. In the countryside, killings increased from 303 peasants in 1982 to more than 1,300 in the first seven months of 1988.[16]

One of the oldest insurgent groups is the National Liberation Army (ELN), founded in 1964. It is a classic Cuban-style, Marxist insurgent group dedicated to dictatorship by the working classes, expropriation and nationalization of the private sector, and agrarian reform. Its estimated 1,700 members are divided into various factions and fronts, concentrated mainly in the north. It had funded its operations by extracting millions from kidnap victims, by extortion, and by robbing banks. In recent years it has concentrated on sabotaging oil installations to undermine the economy and the government's ability to maintain power. It was the only significant group to refuse to agree to the 1984 ceasefire.

The largest, best-trained, and best-equipped insurgent group is the Revolutionary Armed Forces of Colombia (FARC), which fields some 4,000 to 5,000 guerrilla fighters organized in fronts, which numbered forty-eight in early 1989. Its leader, Manuel "Dead Shot" Marulanda Velez, was a PCC central committee member who had for years led peasant uprisings against wealthy landowners. In April 1966 FARC was "adopted" by the PCC as its military and operational wing. The organization had only mixed success until 1975, when it extorted $1 million for the release of the kidnapped Dutch vice consul in Cali. Thereafter, holding wealthy Colombian ranchers, Americans, and Europeans for ransom enabled Marulanda to expand his operations.

While nominally observing the 1984 ceasefire, FARC has continued terrorist operations. It appears to be buying time during the truce in order to build up a political wing, the Patriotic Union (UP) and to increase the strength of its paramilitary forces. FARC seems to have a closer association with the Colombian drug trade than any other group and has greatly profited from narco-terrorism.

In March 1984 a FARC faction, the Ricardo Franco Front (RFF), broke away and for about two years instituted a wave of terrorism aimed particularly at Americans and American property. In December 1985 a bloody internal purge resulted in the deaths of about a hundred members, and the group has not been active since.

The Popular Liberation Army (EPL) was created in 1967 under the auspices of the small Maoist PCC-ML (Marxist-Leninist Communist Party of Colombia), and the EPL ideology has since moved further toward a Maoist style. Its founder, Jario Clavo (alias Ernesto Rodas) was killed in a shootout with police in 1987. Relatively small by Colombian standards (around 1,000), it is supported mainly by urban intellectuals. In the 1970s it engaged in kidnapping, bank robberies, assassinations, and bombings. Despite its Maoist ideology, it was not until 1987 that it finally began to develop the rural guerrilla campaign in which it is now engaged.

Probably the most notorious of the Colombian groups is the 19 April (1970) Movement, or M-19, which now numbers between 800 and 1,000. It earned international headlines in 1979 when it built a tunnel 100 yards long beneath a military arsenal and stole more than 5,000 weapons (which were quickly recovered). In February 1980 it was again in the news after seizing the Dominican Embassy in Bogotá and taking eighty hostages, including eleven ambassadors from the United States, Latin America, and the Middle East. After sixty-one days the terrorists were allowed to fly to Havana but without the $10 million ransom they demanded.

M-19's seizure of Bogotá's Palace of Justice in November 1985 also became international news. Nearly 500 people, including justices of the Supreme Court and members of the Council of State, were held hostage. Security forces stormed the building, rescuing most of the hostages, but fifty hostages (including eleven justices), all the terrorists, and eleven security police were killed.

M-19 was founded by Carlos Toledo Plata and Jaime Batemán Cayón. Batemán was a longtime extremist who had earlier been associated with the FARC. Toledo, who was captured in 1981, was a physician and member of Congress for the National Popular Alliance (ANAPO), a populist party founded in 1961 by a former president, General Gustavo Rojas Pinilla. The party was defeated in elections on April 19, 1970, the date that gave M-19 its name, and Toledo and Bateman turned to armed struggle. M-19's first known act was symbolic rather than violent, however. In January 1974 it stole the sword and spurs of Simón Bolívar on exhibit at his villa.

M-19 is organized into columns in the major cities, broken down into independent cells. It apparently received early training and organizational advice from the now defunct Tupamaros and Montoneros, as well as from Cuba and possibly Libya. It has raised money from bank robberies and kidnapping, and may also extort money from drug traffickers. M-19 has also established ties with other South American groups and the Basque ETA. (It apparently helped create Ecuador's Alfaro Vive ¡Carajo! organization, which in August 1983 imitated M-19 by stealing the sword of Ecuador's national hero, Eloy Alfaro.

On May 25, 1985, a number of leading national revolution groups, including M-19, ELN, EPL, and two smaller groups, the Free Fatherland Movement (MPL) and the Workers' Revolutionary Party (PRT), created the National Guerrilla Coordinator (CNG) to function as an umbrella organization to coordinate their activities. Its strategy involves a three-stage process: terrorist tactics, rural and urban insurgency, and, finally, general insurrection. In 1987 FARC, which was not included in the CNG, created a similar group under its auspices, the Simón Bolívar Guerrilla Coordinator, which apparently has cross-membership with the CNG. It has yet to become a cohesive force along the lines of the PLO or the FMLN.

Although a number of Peruvian left-wing insurgency groups appeared in the 1960s, inspired in large part by the Cuban revolution, they never amounted to much, in large part as a consequence of the remarkable land reform program instituted by the military government of General Juan Velazo in the 1969. Peru thus largely avoided the Marxist insurgencies that plagued much of Latin America throughout the 1970s. In the 1980s, however, Peru became the victim of one of the most brutal insurgencies anywhere, largely the work of a single group, *Sendero Luminoso* (SL), or "Shining Path," short for the Communist Party of Peru in the Shining Path of José Carlos Mariategui. (Mariategui was the founder of the Communist Party of Peru in 1928.)

The seeds of Sendero Luminoso's success are in many ways attributable to the success of the Peruvian government's land reform program. Not only did the peasants obtain title to land in the form of cooperatives, but they also obtained access to education and with it political awareness. Although some SL members are recruited from middle-class families of European descent, most are Quechua-speaking Indians, descendants of the Incas, or of mixed Indian-European blood (Mestizos).

Sendero Luminoso emerged in 1970 from a radical intellectual movement of students and professors at the University of San Cristóbal de Huamanga at Ayacuchu, in the Andean highlands. Its leader, a philosophy professor named Abimael Guzman, synthesized the teachings of Mao Zedong (Mao Tse-tung) and José Carlos Mariategui, who defined class struggle in Peru.[17] Guzmán's student converts became converters. Many went into the countryside as part of a national program to bring the peasants into the national mainstream, but instead indoctrinated them with Sendero's unique revolutionary ideology. In addition to Marxism, that ideology stressed violent opposition to the hated landowning classes, manipulated Indian (especially Inca) myths and symbols, and encouraged the active role of women in the movement. The result was a powerful organization with grassroots membership and a university-educated leadership. As villages were converted, they were added to the "liberated zones." In time the movement spread to the slums of the cities, where "people's schools" were establish to spread the Sendero ideology.

Sendero has operations in fifteen of Peru's twenty-four administrative departments. No one really knows how many members it has, but estimates are about 20,000 members, of which 5,000 are fighters. The group is organized along classical cellular lines: a national central committee that oversees six regional committees—north, south, east, central, metropolitan, and a primary region that includes Ayacucho. The regions are subdivided into zones, which direct the individual small hit squads.

Sendero Luminoso began its "people's war" in 1980, and since then murders, kidnappings, and sabotage have become commonplace in Peru. Murder victims are often brutally mutilated. The movement receives very little outside support; bank robberies were its main source of revenue at first, now narco-terrorism has become by far the leading source.

A tiny (200–300) rival left-wing insurgent group, the Tupac Amaru Revolutionary Movement (MRTA)[18] is also engaged in narco-terrorism in the Upper Huallaga valley but to a lesser degree than Sendero Luminoso. MRTA is a more traditional Castroite group founded by student activists in 1982. In 1986 it announced a merger with the almost defunct Movement of the Revolutionary Left (MIR). With small numbers and low overhead, MRTA can continue to function with robberies and extortion. It engages mainly in urban terrorism.

There is a world of difference between the secular and sectarian right-wing groups involved in terrorism. The former are elitist, generally aristocratic, and both distrustful and disdainful of democratic institutions. The latter are mainly religious fundamentalists. A number of secular right-wing terrorist groups have emerged since World War II, but their international political impact has not been comparable to religious fundamentalists or to Marxists. They include neo-Nazis in West Germany, neo-Fascists in Italy, and the so-called "death squads" in El Salvador and Guatemala. All have attempted to justify their activities ideologically in terms of fighting communism, but most, particularly in Central America, act mainly to preserve the economic and political privileges of their class.

Although there are also a number of sectarian groups engaged in terrorism (Sikhs in India, Tamil Hindus and Sinhalese Buddhists in Sri Lanka, and Catholics and Protestants in Northern Ireland, among others), the only significant militant right-wing religious groups that consistently place doctrine over national or ethnic identity are Muslim extremists.

There are two primary arenas of secular right-wing terrorism in the world today, Western Europe and Central America. At present the groups in Europe are relatively quiescent. It is harder to tell in Central America, where a great deal of the right-wing terrorist activity may be carried on by government-sponsored organizations.

In Western Europe most of the groups are neo-Nazis centered in West Germany and neo-Fascists in Italy. A few groups have also appeared in France from time to time but have been quickly suppressed. Most were established, or at least began to adopt terrorist tactics, in the wake of the 1968 student riots that began in Berlin and spread throughout Western Europe. Their broad aim is to create a political system in which political and economic power is concentrated in the hands of a small elite, but these groups are more noted for what they are against than what they are for. All are generally anti-Semitic, and the French groups in particular are also anti-Arab and anti-black. Italian neo-Fascists, not encumbered by the holocaust image of German Nazism, also enjoy a certain chic among the minor aristocracy and

those elements who like the melodrama of secret societies and depre-
cate the "common man."

The essentially negative nature of their ideologies appeals most to
the lower middle class, the element of society that is the least economically and politically secure, just as it did in the 1930s. The difference is
that Western Europe today is far more secure economically and politically than it was during the Depression years. Should conditions again
deteriorate precipitously, West European right-wing groups could
experience a major revival.

Although the aims of these groups differ radically from those of
Marxist underground groups, their terrorist targets are often quite
similar. In Germany, for example, they have concentrated their efforts
on the American presence (military and business) and foreign
workers.[19] Right-wing groups also, of course, target left-wing political
leaders, parties, and groups.

The right-wing groups include the German Action Groups in West
Germany and the New Order, its successor the Black Order, and the
Mussolini Action Squads in Italy. Most are far less structured organizationally than their left-wing counterparts, and the need to identify with
a particular group does not appear to be as strong. One noted right-
wing attack, the 1980 Octoberfest bombing in Munich, was done by a
lone neo-Nazi terrorist.[20] Although right-wing terrorist activity varies
inversely with the success of security forces in penetrating clandestine
organizations, the number of committed neo-Nazis and Fascists appears to be relatively stable. One source estimated in 1984 that in
Germany there were as many as a thousand hard-core disciplined Nazis
and about 20,000 sympathizers.[21]

Nearly all right-wing terrorism in Central America grew out of United
States–sponsored counterinsurgency programs of the 1960s, established in conjunction with Alliance of Progress aid programs to stem the
growth of Cuban-supported Marxist guerrilla insurgencies, particularly in Guatemala and El Salvador. The citizens' counterinsurgency
organizations set up under these programs quickly degenerated into
assassination teams, the so-called death squads, dedicated to killing
and intimidating not only communist guerrillas but trade union
leaders, missionaries, and liberal clergy—in short, anyone thought to
threaten the political and economic monopoly of the right-wing oligar-
chies that controlled the governments and economies of those countries.

It is difficult to gauge the extent of official support for these groups. Much of what is considered right-wing terrorism in Central America is actually the work of government military and security forces. Direct government counterinsurgency operations conducted by the military and security services, however, no matter how violent, are outside the scope of this study.

On the other hand, although the "death squads" are not operational government units, they have certainly had the active if not the official support of leading members of the military, security, and political establishments of their countries. The most difficult question to assess is the degree of operational control the governments have over them.

Another difficult question involves the U.S. role in the activities of these groups, given the fact that many right-wing terrorists received their initial training and arms from U.S. counterinsurgency programs. Some critics of American policies in Central America, seeing guilt by association, have contended that right-wing terrorism in Central America is an extension of U.S. policy.[22] In fact, the United States strongly condemns such behavior but has virtually no ability to force these groups to stop so long as they receive support from their own governments—governments the United States supports against communist insurgents.

The death squads are status quo underground vigilante organizations (just how underground is a moot point) in the mold of the Protestant groups in Northern Ireland and the Gush Emunim underground in Israel. Their motives are probably as mixed as any comparable group involved in terrorism—personal psychology, ethnic chauvinism (Ladino or non-Indian versus Indian), and class struggle (fear of losing vested political and economic privilege, contempt for the poor and underprivileged). To justify their activities, however, they have raised the banner of "anticommunism"—though not, it should be noted, of democracy—to the status of a universalist ideology. It is not only a convenient way to avoid having to face some of their baser motives, but fighting communists in the Western hemisphere is virtually guaranteed to find a receptive audience in the United States, one they hope will aid them in battling their "communist" adversaries.

The death squads in Guatemala go back to 1966, when paramilitary citizens' groups were established in Izqal and Zacapa provinces to counter communist guerrilla and terrorist activities. About the same time the first of a series of handbills appeared bearing the acronym MANO (Movimiento de Acción Nacionalista Organizado). Mano means "hand" in Spanish, and the group soon acquired the name Mano Blanco (White Hand). In succeeding years several other groups also appeared, including the New Anti-Communist Organization, the Anti-Communist Council of Guatemala, and Eye for an Eye. Their most active period was in the 1960s and 1970s. In 1968 White Hand kidnapped the Archbishop of Guatemala.

The death squads in El Salvador share the same origins as those in Guatemala: U.S.-assisted efforts to enhance internal security in the face of growing Cuban-supported communist insurgency movements. In the mid-1960s the Salvadoran government created a rural auxiliary civilian paramilitary group, ORDEN, short for the Democratic Nationalist Organization, but also meaning "order" in Spanish. Its members, which reached 100,000, were indoctrinated with anticommunist ideology.

As in Guatemala, a number of nonofficial right-wing groups also sprang up, financed by private members of the elite and with close ties to the military and security forces. The principal group, which emerged around 1976, was the White Fighting Union (*Unión Guerrera Blanca*, or UGB), but others appeared, including a Salvadoran White Hand and the Falange.[23]

Terrorist acts attributed to the death squads were carried out by both ORDEN and the unofficial groups, making the issue of government culpability even harder to determine. Among the victims were three American nuns and a Catholic lay worker, killed in December 1980, and the outspoken reformist Archbishop of El Salvador, Oscar Romero, assassinated in March 1980.

The UGB in particular aimed many attacks at the Catholic Church and especially the Jesuits during late 1970s and early 1980s, convinced that they were communistic. Those views were reinforced by the popularity of "liberation theology," embraced by many of the clergy, particularly, though not exclusively, among those priests in closest contact with the poor. Liberation theology is essentially a selective amalgam of Biblical scriptures that express special concern for the poor. These teachings are often (though not necessarily) communicated through the medium of Marxist semantics but do not have even a remote connection to Marxist or communist principles or ideology.

The activities of the death squads in both Guatemala and El Salvador declined in the 1980s, in part because of more stable political conditions. The squads have not disappeared, however, and are still ready and willing to defend through acts of terror the privileges of the oligarchical elites when they believe the government is not adequately protecting their interests against their leftist enemies, real or imagined.

The single exception to the anti-insurgency origin of right-wing terrorism in Central America is the Nicaraguan Contras, who are themselves insurgents against the Marxist Sandinista regime. The Contras include a wide variety of political persuasions, from right-wing supporters of former Nicaraguan President Somoza to former Sandinistas disillusioned with the antidemocratic and repressive policies of the government. Like their left-wing guerrilla counterparts in Central America, the Contras have been primarily involved in a guerrilla insurgency, and their terrorist actions are generally regarded as tactics associated with the insurgency rather than as components of a separate terrorist campaign. Unlike the left-wing insurgents, however, the Contras have not sought to transform terrorism into an ideological imperative, a right-wing equivalent of "revolutionary justice."

At the time of this writing, the Contras are not actively engaged in guerrilla operations, mostly because of the cutoff of U.S. funding. They have shown little inclination to disband, however, and for the most part remain just across the border in Honduras. If they are not able to resume the insurgency, it is not beyond the realm of possibility that at least some among their numbers might consider a terrorist campaign as a tactic of last resort.

A great deal of public attention has been focused on Islamic fundamentalism as a source of terrorism in recent years. The murder of Egypt's President Anwar Sadat in 1981 by Muslim fundamentalists; the support of terrorism by Iran to spread its Islamic revolution; and the bloody exploits of Hizballah in Lebanon, including attacks on U.S. and French installations—particularly the suicide attack on the Marine barracks in 1983—and the taking of foreign hostages, have all served to make Islamic fundamentalism almost synonymous with terrorism in the public eye.

This perception is far from accurate. Not all fundamentalism is Islamic, and not all Islamic fundamentalism is militant or even politicized. Islamic fundamentalism is part of a worldwide trend to identify with one's roots by attempting to go back to unequivocal "fundamental truths" in the face of a threatening, relativistic world. All major religions, including Christianity, Judaism, Islam, Buddhism, Sikhism, and Hinduism, have fundamentalist strains. The attraction of militant Islamic fundamentalism is not so much theological as it is political, psychological, and sociological.

One must nevertheless have a basic idea of the teachings of Islam to understand how they are used to justify terrorism. Islamic theology is very simple and straightforward and is summed up in its profession of faith: "there is no God but God and Muhammad is his messenger." It is a single-minded monotheism in which God is the ultimate causality, a concept neatly summed up in the Arabic phrase, *insha'allah*, or "God willing," for if God does not will it, it cannot happen.

There is no chosen people in Islam; all peoples are equally under God's dominion. Islam thus recognizes earlier revealed monotheistic religions: Christianity, Judaism and Zoroastrianism, called "Peoples of the Book." (The "book" refers to the holy scriptures of each religion, which Muslims accept as divinely inspired.) One of the salient characteristics of militant Islamic fundamentalists is not only refusing to recognize the political legitimacy of the other Peoples of the Book, but also refusing to recognize the legitimacy of Muslim rulers with whom they disagree.

There are five principal obligations or "pillars" of faith in Islam: profession of faith, prayer, alms, fasting, and a pilgrimage to the Islamic holy city of Mecca (if one is physically and economically able). *Jihad*, the personal and corporate struggle for good and against evil and the enemies of God, is an obligation sometimes called the "sixth pillar."[24] Because the struggle against evil includes opposing heretical political rulers, it has taken on the connotation of "holy war," a connotation emphasized by modern Islamic revolutionaries.

Islam is basically a system of divine law. According to Islamic teaching, God revealed himself to mankind through the prophets (including the Jewish prophets and Jesus), the greatest and last being the Prophet Muhammad. To Muhammad, God revealed his holy law for regulating all human behavior, called the *Sahri'a* (the word in Arabic literally means the "pathway"). It is made up of the sacred writings of the Qur'an and the divinely inspired sayings (*hadiths*) of Muhammad, collectively called the Sunna.

The central question for Islamic political theory revolves around the legitimacy of an earthly, temporal ruler in a world absolutely ruled by God and regulated by divine law. The question came to a head when Muhammad died in A.D. 632 without giving clear instructions on how a successor was to be chosen. The prevailing view was that a successor should be selected from the Muslim community at large. Abu Bakr, a close companion of the Prophet, was selected as the first in a line of successors or caliphs that continued until the caliphate was abolished in 1924. Followers of the caliphs were called Sunni Muslims.

The dissenting view held that the leader must be of the family of the Prophet. Their candidate, Ali, was Muhammad's cousin and son-in-law (Muhammad had no sons). They were called Shi'at Ali (the partisans or followers of Ali). Ali was elected the fourth Caliph but was murdered in A.D. 661. His eldest son, Hassan, succeeded him but resigned, and Shi'as believe that he was later poisoned. They consider Ali the first Imam, or leader of Islam, Hassan the second, and his younger brother, Husayn, the third.

The final schism came in A.D. 680, when Husayn was killed at the Battle of Karbala (in present-day Iraq) by troops of the Caliph Yazid. Thereafter Sunni and Shi'a political theory began to develop along different lines. As a result, one must look separately at Shi'a and Sunni fundamentalism to trace the origins of contemporary Islamic terrorism.

Sunnis, who form the majority of Muslims, came to terms with temporal authority through the institution of the caliphate and, after it was abolished, by legitimizing secular governments in Muslim states so long as they uphold Islamic law. Since the tenth century, most Sunni theologians have maintained that independent reasoning (*ijtihad*) in interpreting the holy law is no longer allowed, and that secular governments should look to one of the four Sunni schools of jurisprudence (Hanafi, Maliki, Shafi'i and Hanbali) to apply the law.

Throughout Sunni Islamic history there have been efforts to purify the religion by returning to the fundamentals of the Shari'a. One of the greatest influences on contemporary Muslim fundamentalist revivalism is Taqi al-Din Ahmad Ibn Taymiya (d. 1328),[25] a follower of the Hanbali school of jurisprudence, the most fundamentalist school in Sunni Islam. He called for reform based on the fundamental teachings of the Shari'a.

Ibn Taymiya claimed that political legitimacy could come only from the holy law. The revolutionary aspect of his teaching, however, was his claim that any ruler who did not follow the Shari'a should be removed by *jihad*. The implications of this view for contemporary Muslims seeking to justify violent opposition to secular governments of both Muslim and non-Muslim states is obvious. In their eyes, it raised the act of political violence and terrorism to a religious obligation.

Ibn Taymiya spent most of his adult life in prison for his radical views, and his works, though respected for their erudition, had little influence among Islamic scholars until the mid-eighteenth century, when Muhammad Ibn Abd al-Wahhab made it the basis of the Wahhabi revival, which still serves as the political ideology for Saudi Arabia. More recently it has become the principal doctrinal basis for Sunni Islamic revolutionaries, particularly in Egypt. Ibn Taymiya's interpretation of *jihad* has had a strong influence on the Muslim Brotherhood.[26]

To date, most of the significant militant Sunni fundamentalist organizations have originated in Egypt. The earliest was the Muslim Brotherhood (*Ikhwan al-Muslimin*), founded in 1928 by Hassan al-Banna, who was appalled by growing secularization in Egyptian society. By the time of al-Banna's murder in 1949 by an unknown assassin, the Ikhwan had spread throughout Egypt and had organizations in Syria, Jordan, Iraq, and elsewhere in the Muslim world. Al-Banna and the Ikhwan had a great influence on Yasser Arafat during his student days in Egypt.

Under al-Banna, the Ikhwan organized a "secret organ" to carry out violent acts in the name of *jihad*. The Egyptian government made a serious effort to crush the Ikhwan after its unsuccessful attempt to assassinate President Nasser in 1954, but the organization was revitalized in the 1960s under the charismatic leadership of Sayyid Qutb. Qutb had a Western education but turned to Islamic fundamentalism as the only salvation from the political, social, and economic ills plaguing Egypt and the rest of the Muslim world under the influence of Western secularism. His teachings found an audience among those who felt that Nasser's Arab socialism was an affront to Islam.

In August 1965 the government uncovered another Ikhwan plot to kill Nasser and institute an Islamic government. The authorities were astounded at the depth of grassroots support for the organization. Large-scale arrests followed, and in 1966, despite pleas for clemency from throughout the Arab and Islamic worlds, Qutb was executed.[27]

Under President Sadat the government attempted to co-opt the Ikhwan into the Egyptian political process. Sadat allowed some prominent exiled Muslim Brothers, including Said Ramadan, to return to Egypt. Although the Ikhwan was still officially banned during the parliamentary elections of 1974, the government made no effort to interfere when Ikhwan candidates ran on the New Wafd party ticket.[28]

As the Ikhwan began to lose its militancy, a number of younger members, many of whom had been drawn to the Ikhwan by the fiery personality of Qutb, dropped out to form smaller, more revolutionary Islamic organizations. The three most prominent were *al-Tahrir al-Islami* (Islamic Liberation), also known as *Shihab Muhammad*, or

Muhammad's Youth, which was responsible for the attack on the Technical Military Academy in Heliopolis in April 1974; *al-Takfir w'al Hijra*,[29] responsible for the 1977 kidnap-murder of Husayn al-Dhahabi, a noted religious scholar and former Minister of Islamic Religious Endowments and al-Azhar (the Islamic university) Affairs; and *Tanzim al-Jihad* (the Sacred Struggle Organization), which assassinated President Sadat in September 1981 and subsequently attacked a police headquarters in Upper Egypt.

The leaders of these organizations were nearly all from the educated middle class. Salih Siriya, founder of al-Tahrir al-Islami, had a PhD in science, and Takfir founder Shukri Mustafa had a BS in agriculture. Al-Jihad's leadership was a cross-section of Egyptian society—civilian, religious, and military.[30]

All three organizations rejected working within the political system, which they considered heretical. All three espoused *jihad* (which they defined as armed struggle) as the only available means for creating an Islamic state. Disillusionment with Sadat's use of Islamic symbols to legitimize his policies, combined with opposition to the Camp David accords and Sadat's treaty with Israel, increased their militancy. Though Sunnis, they were also doubtless encouraged by the success of the Shi'a Islamic revolution in Iran in 1979.

Following the murder of Sadat, the Egyptian government launched a large-scale crackdown on all Islamic fundamentalist organizations in the country, and the activities of those groups has greatly declined. The potential still exists in Egypt, however, for a charismatic leader under the right set of circumstances to channel political, economic, and social frustrations into violent Islamic fundamentalist reaction.

Elsewhere, few militant Sunni fundamentalist groups have met with the same degree of operational success. In Syria, Adnan Sa'd al-Din founded the Syrian Islamic Front in 1980 to unite and coordinate radical activities of various fragmented Sunni Islamic fundamentalist groups there. Although Sunni Muslims form the majority in Syria, a small Shi'a sect, the Alawis, has controlled Syria through its domination of the armed forces. Islamic fundamentalism was beginning to attract Sunni followers, frustrated with Alawi political domination, but efforts to organize Sunni fundamentalists collapsed after President Asad's ruthless attack on Hama in February 1982 crushed the movement.

Islamic fundamentalists have also been found in East Asia. In Indonesia a lesser-known Sunni fundamentalist group, Kommando Jihad, was founded in 1977 by members of a religious minority called *santris*. With 140 million Muslims (85 percent of its total population), Indonesia has the world's largest Muslim community. Most Muslims, called *abangan*, believe in a syncretic mixture of Shafi'i Islam and local Indo-Buddhist traditions adapted by the mystic Sufi Muslim missionaries who first converted much of the interior. (Shafi'is comprise one of four recognized Sunni schools of Islamic jurisprudence, roughly analogous to mutually recognized denominations in Protestant Christianity.) The santris live along the coast and are much more orthodox.

A santri separatist movement arose in the late 1940s, more along ethnic than religious lines, but was put down by the Indonesian government in 1952 after much fighting. In the worldwide Islamic resurgence of the 1970s, santri militants reappeared; influenced by the Iranian revolution, many younger santris called not for a separate Santri state but for a fundamentalist Islamic state of Indonesia. By 1981 Kommando Jihad, led by the charismatic Muhammad Imron Zain, had become an active terrorist organization, receiving money and support from both Iran and Libya. Indonesian authorities, who called it the Imron gang, have more or less succeeded in suppressing Kommando Jihad, at the same time making a conscious effort to invoke Islamic symbology in its official policies.[31] Nevertheless, the potential still exists for its revival.

The original Sunni–Shi'a schism arose over the political struggle for leadership of the Muslim community. The legal tenets of the two branches—Islam is more a legal system than a theological system—have not varied a great deal. However, substantial theological differences have developed over time. Unlike Sunni caliphs, Shi'a Imams were believed to have had divine guidance to interpret the holy law to succeeding generations. Moreover, according to Shi'a tradition the twelfth Imam, Muhammad al-Muntazar, miraculously disappeared in A.D. 873 74.[32] Called the Hidden Imam, he will "at the end of time" return as the Mahdi, a savior, to restore equity and justice to the world.[33]

This millenarian tradition has several implications for Shi'a political theory. First, it assumes an intercessor between God and man (the earthly Imams) not found in Sunni tradition. Second, because the twelfth Imam, though hidden, is still living, no temporal ruler can attain his stature. Thus, the legitimacy of any temporal leader can be challenged. Moreover, the Muslim community is obligated to overthrow all illegitimate rulers as an act of *jihad*.

The Ayatallah Khomeini took this line of reasoning a step farther. Beginning with the premise that the Shi'a clergy (*mujtahids*) represent the Hidden Imam until his return and retain the right to interpret the sacred law, he developed his idea of *wilayat al-faqih*, rule by Islamic jurist. In his view, the only way to protect society from corruption was for the clergy actually to rule.

In addition to millenarianism, Shi'a history has also bequeathed its followers a strong tradition of martyrdom, which is traced back to the first Imams. Ali was murdered, Hassan is believed to have been poisoned, and Husayn was martyred at the battle of Karbala. Many Persian Shi'as were subsequently martyred until the Safavid dynasty made Shi'ism the state religion of Persia in the early sixteenth century. Elsewhere, Shi'as have been routinely persecuted under Sunni rulers. As a result, martyrdom has come to be venerated by Shi'as, and to die for the religion holds a strong emotional appeal for Shi'a fanatics. In sum, the ability to challenge the legitimacy of temporal rulers plus the tradition of martyrdom have greatly enhanced Shi'a doctrine as a justification for political terrorism.

Shi'a underground organizations gained incalculable inspiration form the Iranian revolution in 1979. Terrorist activities, however, have been based not in Iran itself but in Iraq, where there is a Shi'a majority under Sunni political leadership, and in Lebanon, where the Shi'a community is the largest of all the confessional groups and has never had political power commensurate with its numbers.

Although more than half of Iraq's population is Shi'a, the country has traditionally been governed by Sunni regimes. The Shi'a community is generally conservative and devoutly religious, but historically it has not been highly politicized. By the late 1960s, however, many Iraqi Shi'as had become inspired by the fundamentalist teachings of a highly charismatic individual, Ayatallah Muhammad Baqir al-Sadr, the most respected Shi'a cleric of his day. His influence was so great in Iraq that after the Iranian revolution many of his followers saw him as the Khomeini of Iraq. He was considered so great a threat to the regime that he was arrested and executed in 1980.

Baqir al-Sadr's message was traditional Shi'a reformism: God is the sole ruler of the universe; all mankind is equal under him; the business of temporal government is to abolish inequity and injustice; and this can be done only by a return to the Shari'a.[34] His lucid writing style and strong personality further strengthened the appeal of his message. Although Baqir al-Sadr was not directly involved in politics, he was certainly the spiritual and intellectual father of Iraqi Shi'a political fundamentalism.

The oldest Shi'a political organization in Iraq is al-Da'wa al-Islamiya (Islamic Call). The party's origins are somewhat hazy, but it was probably founded in 1968 or 1969 by politicized Shi'a clergy concerned about the decline of Islam in the socialist Iraqi Ba'th party regime.

During the 1970s al-Da'wa became increasingly involved in anti-government terrorist activities. It also established links to the Shah at that time because of his opposition to the Iraqi regime, much to its embarrassment following the Iranian revolution. Nevertheless, its popularity reached its zenith in 1979 following the Iranian revolution. With Iranian support it began to escalate antigovernment activities. At the same time Baqir al-Sadr publicly endorsed the Iranian revolution and Khomeini's concept of wilayat al-fiqih, which theoretically could have been construed as denying the legitimacy of the Iraqi Ba'th regime.

In 1980 al-Da'wa attempted to assassinate a cabinet member, Tariq Aziz, because he was Christian; in December 1983 Da'wa members were involved in seven attacks in Kuwait, including the U.S. Embassy, the French Embassy, Raytheon company residential and headquarters facilities (Raytheon is a U.S. company which makes Hawk missiles purchased by Kuwait), the airport, the Ministry of Electricity, and a desalination plant. By the end of the month seventeen terrorists, including ten Da'wa members, were arrested. All were later convicted, and three were sentenced to death, but Kuwait did not carry out the death penalties.

After the execution of Baqir al-Sadr the emotional appeal of al-Da'wa declined. Many Iraqi Shi'as were horrified by the social and political excesses and economic decline in Iran under the new regime. By the mid 1980s al-Da'wa had split into a moderate group, led by Shaykh Mahdi al-Khalisi, and a militant faction, led by Hajat al-Islam Muhammad Baqir al-Hakim, which is still committed to terrorism. Al-Hakim, whose faction has the backing of the Iranian clergy, is chairman of the Iranian-based "Higher Council of the Islamic Revolution," which supposedly leads the struggle against the Iraqi regime, and heads the "Iraqi government in exile" from Teheran.[35]

Two other militant Iraqi Shi'a underground organizations were established after the Iranian revolution but have accomplished very little. The *Mujahidin* (no relationship to the quasi-Marxist Mujahidin-i-Khalq of Iran or the Afghan Mujahidin; the term means Islamic Warriors, from *jihad* in the context of armed struggle) was founded in

1979 and is led by two mujtahids who eschewed indiscriminate terrorism, Muhammad al-Shirazi and Hadi al-Mudarissi. *Munathamat al-'Amal al-Islami* (Organization for Islamic Action) was founded in 1980. It is committed to armed struggle but disdains clerical political leadership.

In Lebanon society and politics have for centuries revolved around four confessional communities: Christian, Sunni, Shi'a, and Druze. The Shi'a population is concentrated in three physically and culturally distinct areas: the Jabal Amil (Mount Amil) area of southern Lebanon, where a feudal agrarian system prevailed right up to present times, the northern Biqa' (Bekaa) valley, and the suburbs and slums of south Beirut, swollen in recent years by the migration of peasants from the countryside seeking employment. Because of their separation, the Shi'as seldom have acted as a single community.

Except for a brief period in the eleventh century, Lebanese Shi'as have been politically dominated by first the Sunnis and then the Christians. Shi'a history has generally been a tale of religious and political discrimination and persecution, which has reinforced the tradition of martyrdom and the appeal of the messianic promise of the return of the Hidden Imam to avenge the injustices to the faithful.

Confessionalism still dominates Lebanese politics. In 1920 the French broke Lebanon off from Syria and created a Christian-dominated principality, Greater Lebanon. During World War II the British supplanted the French as the dominant power in the region, and in 1943 they were instrumental in negotiating a National Pact among the Lebanese confessional groups, which became the constitutional basis for an independent Lebanon in 1945.

The Christians, led by the Maronite sect, were the largest group, based on the census of 1932, and dominated the system through the presidency and command of the army; the Sunnis received the premiership; the Shi'as, reflecting their smaller size, received the largely titular speakership of parliament; and the much smaller Druze community had to make their influence felt through appointments to cabinet and other posts. At the time few Shi'as were politicized, and the community was content to let their feudal aristocracy represent them in the political system.

In the nearly half-century since Lebanese independence, revolutionary changes have taken place. In the 1950s and 1960s huge injections of oil money flowed into Lebanon, making Beirut a regional banking center. The affluent capital became a playground for wealthy

Arabs and was known as "the Paris of the Middle East." As a result of this influx of money, however, the income gap between the rich (mainly Christians and Sunnis) and the poor (mainly Shi'as), began to widen dramatically.

The Shi'as were the poorest community, but as public education, modern communications, and transportation linked their remote villages to a wider world, their economic and social expectations grew, and thousands of Shi'as migrated to the cities for work. Many of them settled in slums in south and west Beirut, which has become a haven for terrorists today.

The Shi'as also experienced the highest population growth; in recent years they have become the largest community in Lebanon. No one knows the exact numbers, however, because the distribution of political power is based at least theoretically on population figures, and Christian-dominated Lebanese governments have refused to hold a new census to update the 1932 figures. The Maronites, though no longer the largest group, have consistently rejected sharing more political power with the Shi'as (or the Sunnis).

In September 1970 the demographic and political balance of Lebanon was further upset by the influx of hundreds of Palestinians into Beirut and southern Lebanon following the expulsion of the PLO from Jordan by King Hussein for challenging his rule. (The expulsion was known among the Palestinians as "Black September.") Operating out of Palestinian refugee camps established in Lebanon following the 1948 Arab–Israeli war, the PLO quickly became virtually a state within a state.

All these changes set the stage for a major political upheaval, the Lebanese civil war, which broke out in 1975 and continues today. At the same time there appeared a charismatic religious leader, straight out of the heroic Shi'a historical mold, to give the Shi'a community a political awareness that it had not had before, Musa al-Sadr.

Sayyid Musa al-Sadr was a descendent of the seventh Imam and a member of the distinguished Iraqi Shi'a family of al-Sadr, which had originally come from Jabal Amil, Lebanon. He was born and reared in the Iranian holy city of Qum, the son and grandson of distinguished ayatallahs. Musa al-Sadr was physically imposing (6 feet, 6 inches in height) and flamboyant in style and bearing. In 1959 he moved to Tyre, in southern Lebanon, to make his way out from under the shadow of his distinguished forebears.[36]

Through political acumen, force of personality, and patience, Musa al-Sadr forged political support within the community along traditional Shi'a reformist lines. His ultimate goal was to win for the Shi'as power within the existing confessional political system commensurate with their numbers.

In 1968 he created the Higher Shi'a Islamic Council and forced the government to deal with it as the representative of the entire Shi'a community, dealing a heavy blow to the old Shi'a political leadership. The following year he became the Council's president. In 1975 he held a huge political rally in the Biqa' Valley and established the *Harakat al-Mahrumin* (the Movement of the Deprived). The movement's paramilitary arm, *Afwaf al-Muqawama al-Lubaniya* (Battalions of the Lebanese Resistance), became known by its acronym, Amal (which also means "hope" in Arabic), and quickly became the leading Shi'a political and military organization. By 1980 it boasted some 4,000 fighters, and by 1982 the number had risen to an estimated total of 30,000.[37]

In August 1978, however, Musa al-Sadr disappeared while on a visit to Libya. He is presumed to have been murdered at the hand of the Libyan government, though for what reason is unclear. He was immediately seen as a martyr by the Lebanese Shi'a community, in line with Shi'a symbology, and he continues to be revered, even in death. Leadership of Amal ultimately went to a secular lawyer, Nabih Berri. Berri lacked Musa al-Sadr's charisma, however, and cracks quickly appeared in the Amal political structure. Those cracks would further split the Shi'a community and would pave the way for the advent of Shi'a terrorism.

The Israeli military invasion of Lebanon in 1982 was a turning point in the radicalization of the Lebanese Shi'a community. Prior to the invasion, Amal's main military enemy was the PLO, which virtually ruled much of southern Lebanon. Many Shi'a peasants initially welcomed the invading Israeli army as enemies of their enemies. Military occupation soon changed their views, however, and when they perceived that the Israelis supported Maronite hegemony, they resisted, leading to the *de facto* partition of Lebanon.

At the same time many of the more militant Shi'a clerics opposed having a layman at the head of Amal as well as Berri's policy of seeking to work within the old political system. For those clerics the Iranian revolution not was not only a great inspiration but resulted in direct Iranian support. The Iranians wished to see an Islamic republic of

Lebanon on the Iranian model, dominated by fundamentalist Shi'as and rid of all secular Western influences and institutions.

Their chance came with the Israeli invasion. Elements of the Iranian Revolutionary Guard were sent to Lebanon, ostensibly to aid in the struggle against Israel. In fact they were there to organize, train, and indoctrinate a militant Lebanese Shi'a political and terrorist organization from their headquarters, the old Shaykh Abdallah barracks near Ba'lbak in the Biqa' Valley.

The task was directed by the Iranian Ambassador to Syria, Ali Akbar Muhtashamipur (later appointed Iranian Minister of the Interior). He brought together militant young Shi'a clerics and the leaders of Lebanese Shi'a paramilitary groups, including Husayn al-Musawi's Islamic Amal (which broke away from Amal about that time), the Lebanese faction of the Da'wa party, and Imad Mughniya's gang. One of the young militants, Ibrahim al-Amin, became the official spokesman. The new organization was called *Hizballah* (the Party of God).

To coordinate Hizballah's activities, Muhtashamipur created a Council of Lebanon, which, in addition to Hizballah leaders and Shi'a clergy, included himself and the commander of the Revolutionary Guard. Later, Hizballah created its own organizational structure, and it is now governed by a consultative council, three regional councils (the Biqa', Beirut, and the south), and seven administrative committees. The consultative council is composed mainly of Shi'a clerics with close ties to Iran.[38]

Among the more prominent Shi'a clerics affiliated with Hizballah are Shaykh Subhi al-Tufayli and Shaykh Abbas al-Musawi, both from the Biqa' Valley. By far the most influential, however, is Sayyid Muhammad Husayn Fadlallah, born in Najaf, Iraq, in 1935 of a south Lebanese family. He moved to Beirut in 1966 and began quietly to build a reputation as a scholar and preacher. Following the Israeli invasion, he became an outspoken and impassioned critic of secularism and foreign involvement in Lebanon and called for the establishment of an Islamic republic.

Though widely considered to be Hizballah's spiritual guide, which in most Shi'a organizations would mean political leadership, Fadlallah outwardly distances himself from the organization, denying any official connection with it. This decision not to break entirely with the old political system, which Hizballah seeks to destroy, appears to be an indication of his pragmatism and his considerable ambition.

Shaykh Fadlallah shares the Iranian clergy's views on Islamic reform and shares Khomeini's concept of wilayat al-fiqih. If there is to be an Islamic jurist-ruler of Lebanon, he would like to be it. He is not, however, simply a creature of Iranian Islamic foreign policy, nor does he entirely subscribe to Hizballah's view that an Islamic republic can be attained through terrorism and intimidation. He also has a following in Amal, and if he believed that fundamentalist Shi'a hegemony could be attained through the existing constitutional framework, he would probably not be averse to working with Amal for an expanded Shi'a political voice within the old system.

On balance, therefore, Hizballah is in many ways a loose coalition of Shi'a fundamentalist clerics and semi-independent warlords, each with his personal followers, and none desiring to abdicate any freedom of action to Fadlallah or anyone else, including Iran. As indoctrinated Shi'a fundamentalists, however, they accept the need for Iranian guidance as well as for clerical approval of their activities, the more senior the cleric the more binding his *fatwa*, or legal opinion.[39] Thus a symbiotic relationship has developed among Fadlallah, the Hizballah warlords, and their mutual Iranian mentors.

A good example of Fadlallah's relationship with Hizballah centered on the so-called suicide missions, which Hizballah wanted Fadlallah to sanction. Suicide is strongly proscribed by Islamic law, and Fadlallah would not unequivocally condone the missions in a fatwa. Drawing on Shi'a tradition, however, he praised those who were "martyred" in the struggle to preserve the good and combat evil.[40]

All Shi'a clerics steadfastly claim that terrorism is against Islamic law, and Hizballah virtually never directly claims credit for its attacks. Most of terrorist attacks by Hizballah elements (as well as the Da'wa attacks in Kuwait) have been done under *noms de guerre,* in particular Islamic Jihad. Because of their success and notoriety, Hizballah quickly began to rival Amal for Lebanese Shi'a allegiance, and the number of fighters grew to more than four thousand.

The most spectacular terrorist attacks were the April 1983 suicide bombing of the American Embassy in West Beirut, killing forty-nine; the October 1983 suicide bombings of the U.S. Marine and French military barracks in Beirut, killing 241 Americans and fifty-six French soldiers; the suicide bombing of the American Embassy Annex in East Beirut, killing twenty-three; and the June 1985 hijacking of TWA flight 847, during which an American serviceman was killed on the ground in Beirut. The plane was hijacked out of Athens, flown to Beirut, on to

Algiers and then back to Beirut, where it remained until the hostages were finally released with Syrian and Amal intercession after almost three weeks of captivity. The release of 1,500 Israeli-held Shi'a prisoners from southern Lebanon reportedly figured in the freeing of the hostages.

In addition, Hizballah murdered Malcolm Kerr, President of the American University of Beirut in January 1984, and between 1984 and 1988 kidnapped numerous Americans, French, English and West Germans. The release of some of the kidnap victims was attributed to negotiations by the American, French, and German governments with Iran. In April 1988 Hizballah hijacked a Kuwaiti airliner, but after Syrian officials at Beirut International Airport refused landing permission, it ultimately flew to Algeria, where the hostages were released and the hijackers disappeared.

Despite the high spiritual ideals to which Hizballahis subscribe, much of their activity is rooted in practical politics and personal considerations. The individual generally held responsible for kidnapping most of the American and other foreign hostages is Imad Mughniya. Despite all the public justifications of these acts by Hizballah, the fact remains that the single consistent demand by Mughniya for releasing them throughout most of their captivity had been the release of the Da'wa prisoners in Kuwait, one of whom is his brother-in-law.

Since the middle 1980s Hizballah and Amal have continued to battle each other for primacy within the Shi'a community. Amal, though weakened by Berri's lackluster performance, has managed to avoid disintegration, and it is also supported by Syria, which sees Hizballah as more of a threat to its long-term interest in hegemony over a peaceful Lebanon. Hizballah, for its part, has been hampered in gaining broader Shi'a support by the continued lack of cohesion within the Shi'a community. Its influence is still essentially limited to strongholds in the Biqa' Valley and portions of the West and South Beirut suburbs.

In the late 1980s the confrontation between the two groups more or less reached a stalemate, with Iran and Syria pushing them to accept a truce. Iran, in particular, had to temper its support of Hizballah as its attentions were focused on internal problems—the catastrophic economic situation which caused it to withdraw from the Iran–Iraq war in the spring of 1988, and the death of Khomeini in mid-1989, which has caused the Iranian leadership to be preoccupied with the struggle over the succession.

The result of the stalemate and Iran's preoccupation with internal affairs has been to curtail possible expansion of Hizballah terrorism outside Lebanon for the present, although at the time of this writing little progress has been made in freeing the remaining foreign hostages. The struggle for political control of the Shi'a community is not likely to end, however, until one or the other is victorious or a new charismatic leader appears to capture Shi'a loyalties. In the meantime, given the chaotic state of Lebanese politics, Shi'a terrorism, particularly by Hizballah component groups, is likely to continue inside Lebanon.

In reviewing the characteristics of doctrinal groups involved in terrorism, one is struck by the heterogeneity among them, as much if not more than among national–ethnic groups. The only commonality they seem to share is their emphasis on a universalist doctrine, and even their doctrines are more often than not interpreted in cavalier fashion.

No universalist doctrine, however, has ever specifically mandated terrorist activity or spawned a terrorist organization. Terrorist organizations are created slowly over time by individuals who, for a combination of psychological and social-psychological reasons, react to social, economic, and political conditions by developing a deep sense of political injustice, which they seek to redress through violent action. It is to justify these acts that they seek the higher moral authority of a universalist doctrine—a doctrine that will enable their political ends to justify their otherwise morally reprehensible means.

5

Support for Terrorism

Like biological organisms, terrorist groups are born, mature, and die. The death of a terrorist organization can come from many causes, the most obvious being decisive action by government security forces. Less obvious but no less fatal is deprivation of outside support. No terrorist group can exist for long in total isolation. Some have become more or less financially independent, and some have even attained a measure of political independence of action, but all depend to at least some extent on outside financial, logistical, political, legal, and even moral support.

There are three basic types of support for terrorist activities: state support, other group support—including support from constituent groups, other terrorist organizations, and, more recently, drug traffickers—and, though not by intention, media support. In covering terrorist events, the media provide the terrorists with the means to communicate their political message to a much broader audience than they could reach by themselves.

It is impossible to remain actively engaged in terrorism for long in a totally hostile political environment. In one way or another, some degree of state support is crucial to the continuation of terrorism as a threat to international stability. The task of identifying states that support terrorism, however, to say nothing of the task of inducing them to stop, is exceedingly difficult. There is no objective set of criteria for determining which states are guilty of supporting terrorism, and no state openly admits to it. Even such notorious offenders as Libya and Iran piously condemn terrorism in the abstract—and are quick to label any forceful counterterrorist actions by their opponents as state-supported terrorism.

Virtually all states have at one time or another, wittingly or unwittingly, directly or indirectly, taken measures that have aided the conduct of terrorist activities. The real problem is to determine the point at which such measures constitute a policy of state support for terrorism.

Leaving aside violence carried out in the name of state security, direct operational control by a state over the operations of a terrorist organization is rare. The risks of discovery and international condemnation are usually considered too high. It is more expedient to hire a radical group willing to undertake terrorist operations, allowing the state to distance itself from the acts themselves and thereby maintain plausible denial of involvement.

The opposite extreme—passive and tacit support for terrorist groups—is far more common but equally hard to determine. One could make a case, for example, that all democratic states give constitutional support to terrorists. The very existence of democratic institutions, including constitutional guarantees of human and civil rights such as freedom of speech and due process of law, make it immeasurably easier for terrorists to avoid arrest and punishment than it is in states with authoritarian regimes.[1]

That might seem like a purely academic argument, but it becomes real enough for frustrated policy-makers in democratic countries who are tempted to suspend basic human and civil rights guaranteed by their own constitutions in order to protect themselves from the threat of terrorist attacks.

A case in point is the alleged Israeli murder of a top PLO leader, Khalil al-Wazir (Abu Jihad), in Tunis in April 1988. An assassination team infiltrated Tunisia, killed al-Wazir, and escaped. The Israelis believed him to be one of the masterminds behind Palestinian terrorism, which had so victimized their country, and to them his guilt was beyond doubt. Nevertheless, their response constituted a denial of due process of law and thus violated their own constitutional guarantees of human and civil rights.[2]

Another manifestation of passive state support is turning a blind eye to nonviolent activities of suspected terrorists transiting or residing in one's country on the assumption that such an accommodationist policy will persuade the terrorists to refrain from conducting operations inside one's own borders. A number of West European powers once held this view, only to find that ultimately there was no way to insulate one's own citizens from terrorism; it is everyone's problem. Several East European countries, as well as some smaller West European countries, still cling to the view that they have no terrorism problem. While they would never admit to being state supporters of terrorism, their policies of indifference doubtless contribute to the ability of terrorist organizations to conduct international operations.

Financial aid to groups engaged in terrorism is a more active form of support, but it too is difficult to assess, because there is no consensus about whether economic support to political opposition groups engaged in terrorism or serving as fronts for groups engaged in terrorism constitutes state support. Certainly, regular economic support to groups that are almost entirely devoted to terrorism, such as Libyan support to the Abu Nidal Organization, is easily identified. Support for multipurpose opposition or insurgency groups with both political and terrorist or paramilitary wings is more difficult to characterize.

For example, although both Libya and Saudi Arabia provide financial support to the PLO, there are substantial qualitative differences. Libya supports hard-line PLO splinter groups that have engaged almost exclusively in guerrilla and terrorist tactics against Israel and its allies. Saudi Arabia, on the other hand, strongly opposes the Marxist ideology of such groups and directs its financial support to al-Fatah and to the PLO bureaucratic infrastructure under Yasser Arafat's control. While al-Fatah has engaged in terrorism, the bulk of both al-Fatah's and the PLO's budget has always been devoted to bureaucratic and social welfare expenses, even before the 1988 moratorium on terrorism.

Virtually no country has line-item budgetary control over how its financial support is used. While groups heed their patrons' stipulations for fear of being cut off, they also know that the donors provide the aid primarily out of their own self-interest and would be loath to cut it off except in extreme circumstances. Thus the groups enjoy a degree of freedom of action, which increases as they move toward financial independence.

The PLO has never accepted budgetary control by its patrons. Because only a relatively small proportion of its current account expenditures has been budgeted for terrorism, it has been virtually impossible to trace PLO funding from the donor to the terrorist attack. Any blanket statement that PLO funding is tantamount to state support for terrorism is therefore difficult to confirm.

A related problem is regulating private donations to groups engaged in terrorism. A significant amount of funding comes from democratic states whose governments are most deeply engaged in countering international terrorism, including the United States.[3] On the other hand, some states encourage private donations to augment public funding or as a means of keeping at arms length from the organizations they wish to support when public funding is either unfeasible or undesirable. As an example, much of the Saudi financial support for the PLO comes private "donations" levied by the government from Palestinians working in the kingdom and transferred to the PLO.

A far more flagrant form of state support than financial aid—and just as difficult to pin down—involves terrorist training and arms transfers. As popularly conceived, terrorist training resembles conventional military training and takes place in a camp complete with barracks, barbed wire, and a guard at the gate. Whenever a U.S. State Department spokesman raises the subject of terrorist training, for example, the media still ask if there are any satellite pictures of the installations. In fact, terrorist training may take place almost anywhere and will seldom involve specially constructed terrorist facilities. The use of firearms and explosives, the subjects most likely to be taught at a military installation, are only one aspect of training; terrorism involves a number of other special skills: covert communications, surveillance, recruitment, falsifying and counterfeiting documents, and so on. Terrorist operations usually involve small groups of people that are strictly compartmentalized. To maintain security, training is often conducted in safe houses and at remote spots less accessible or obvious to human or technical surveillance.

Finally, some states in effect "lease" the services of terrorist groups, providing them not only with financial support but with training, logistical support, and a base of operations. After his break with the PLO in 1974, Abu Nidal entered into such a relationship in turn with Iraq, with Syria, and with Libya.

In addition to state support to terrorist groups, there is a gray area of that could be termed "guilt by association support" for insurgency and counterinsurgency groups. Most state support to such groups is for paramilitary operations, not terrorist operations *per se*. As we have seen, however, guerrilla and terrorist tactics overlap. The degree to which a state intends for its insurgency or counterinsurgency support to be used for terrorism and the degree of responsibility it should share if a group commits acts of terrorism against its wishes are extremely difficult to determine. No matter how dependent a group is on a sponsor, it has its own political agenda, its own internal dynamics, and its own irreducible priorities, which it will not or cannot change. If the survival of the group is sufficiently important to the sponsoring state, it will simply put up with the actions of its client, like it or not.

In short, determining what state support for terrorism is and deciding which states qualify is an issue more political than definitional, particularly in the absence of an internationally acceptable set of criteria for what constitutes terrorism in the first place. Virtually every state at one time or other must make such determinations, however. One of the biggest problems a state faces at such a time is maintaining a degree of consistency.

For example, the U.S. Congress has mandated that the State Department maintain a list of the most flagrant state supporters of terrorism—states that regularly and as a matter of policy provide financial aid, arms, explosives, training, and logistical support for organizations regularly engaged in terrorism. The U.S. list currently includes Libya, Iran, Syria, South Yemen, Cuba, and North Korea.

Of all those on the list, Libya has been the most catholic in its support of terrorist groups. It has not only contributed generously to such hardline Palestinian groups in the PLO as the Popular Front for the Liberation of Palestine (PFLP), PFLP-General Command, the Democratic Front for the Liberation of Palestine, and the Palestinian Popular Struggle Front, but also sponsored the Abu Nidal Organization and contributed to European groups, including the Provisional IRA, the Basque ETA, and the Red Army Faction.

There is no doubt that Colonel Qadhafi is committed to terrorism as a foreign policy tactic, but he is also a very pragmatic man and is not totally impervious to international pressure. For example, he moderated his terrorism policies following the 1986 U.S. raid on Libya. The raid was in retaliation for large-scale Libyan support for terrorism culminating in the bombing of a West Berlin disco in which an American was killed. Though many countries did not fully approve of the raid, no one strongly condemned it or came to Libya's defense. Thus, in order to reduce Libya's political isolation and to improve his image in the Arab world and in the West, Qadhafi curbed (but did not cease) his support for Palestinian and other terrorist groups, and in November 1989 he reportedly placed Abu Nidal under "house arrest" at the urging of Egypt and the PLO. Despite his current "good behavior," however, it is doubtful that Qadhafi has abandoned or ever will permanently abandon support for terrorism; he is likely to resume more active support whenever he determines that it will achieve his objectives and the costs are not prohibitive.

Iran's support of terrorism has been channeled almost totally to Shi'a fundamentalist groups as an adjunct of its revolutionary foreign policy of spreading its brand of Islamic revolution. The main recipients have been Shi'a groups in Iraq and the Gulf region and, in particular, Hizballah in Lebanon. There have also been signs that the Iranian Revolutionary Guard might be trying to develop its own terrorist capability in Europe.

Since the death of Ayatallah Khomeini in 1989, a more pragmatic leadership has come to power in Iran under former Speaker Rafsanjani. He has tried to moderate some of Iran's more extreme foreign policies in order to concentrate on its chaotic economic situation and other domestic problems. He is opposed by hard-liners like former Minister of the Interior Muhtashamipur, who continue to believe that spreading Islamic revolution should be Iran's first priority. The result of the extended power struggle is that government-sponsored terrorism may decline, but the hard-liners in and out of government are not likely to cease covert support of terrorist organizations.

Syria supports various militant Palestinian groups, particularly Sa'iqa and Abu Musa's breakaway Fatah organization, both of which it virtually controls, and PFLP-General Command. President Asad is totally pragmatic about the use of terrorism and supports it only when he believes it is an effective tactic. In 1987 he withdrew support from Abu Nidal, no doubt calculating that support of the ANO was counterproductive in his relations with Western Europe. Acts of terrorism by Syria's clients have further declined since the PLO ban on terrorism in late 1988.

Of the others on the list, South Yemen's support is largely focused on the Marxist Palestinian groups, which like its own regime trace their roots to the Movement of Arab Nationalists (ANM). Cuba is the principal outside source of military support and training for Marxist insurgencies throughout Latin America and has also attempted, with indifferent success, to play a revolutionary role in Africa. North Korea was placed on the list in 1988 after it was established that a North Korean agent tried to blow up a South Korean airliner.

A good case can be made for all these entries, but some are far more egregious than others. One might ask whether South Yemen and North Korea really deserve to be considered on a par with Libya, Iran, Syria, and Cuba, for example. Politics aside, a case as good or better might be made for countries not on the list—Nicaragua's support of communist insurgencies throughout Latin America and El Salvador's domestic right-wing organizations come to mind.

A related problem for democratic countries is how to categorize communist countries that are not directly linked to terrorist activities but do support the Marxist concepts of wars of national liberation and armed struggle. In seeking to identify states supporting terrorism, such ideological empathy alone does not make a particularly strong case, and the United States, among others, has tried to avoid blanket condemnation of communist states. Such distinctions have sometimes come as a surprise to the countries themselves, which often see the terrorist issue in East–West adversarial terms. The point is illustrated by an exchange at a symposium on terrorism a few years ago between the author and a communist diplomat from a Balkan country. The diplomat asked if his country were on the State Department list, and, looking slightly surprised when he heard the answer was no, replied, "Ah? Good."

Despite the widespread belief that the Soviet Union has organized an international network of terrorists,[4] the Soviets themselves have been very ambivalent toward terrorism, even before the thawing of the Cold War. They have always opposed specific types of terrorist acts, including airline hijacking, kidnapping, and attacks on diplomatic and other official overseas installations and personnel, and they are signatories to all the international conventions proscribing these practices.

The pragmatic reasons are fairly obvious. The Soviet Union itself has a large official presence overseas, operates an international airline, and is very much a potential victim. In the fall of 1985, for example, four Soviet diplomats were kidnapped in Lebanon. One was murdered, but with the help of the Syrians and Lebanese Druze, allegedly backed up by a brutal threat in the form of severed fingers of a relative of one of the kidnappers, the remaining three were released.[5]

The Soviet Union's opposition to terrorism as a superpower has come in direct conflict with its role as guardian of communist revolutionary doctrine, particularly in the case of groups propounding world Marxist revolution. Not only could these groups be a political embarrassment to the Soviet Union in its dealings with the West, but their internal instability makes them less than trustworthy clients. On the other hand, to the degree that these groups could undermine Western military capabilities against the Soviet Union by stirring up popular opposition to the U.S. military presence in Europe and Japan and by fostering anti-American sentiment generally, their activities have been considered, at least until recently, to be in Moscow's interest. Soviet relations with these groups, therefore, have tended to be distant and cautious but not totally negative.

Soviet support for left-wing insurgency movements and wars of national liberation has until recently been less cautious. Until the late 1980s, the Soviet Union was heavily involved, both directly and through surrogates such as Cuba and Nicaragua, in supporting Marxist insurgency movements throughout the Third World. Even so, its support was not so sweeping as is commonly believed. Though opponents of the PLO emphasize close PLO ties to the Soviet Union, the Soviets have never provided the PLO with more than token support. It has provided limited guerrilla training for some of the Marxist member groups, but, in good capitalist style, it has required them to pay for their weapons in hard currency.[6] And while the Marxist groups in the PLO do have an ideological affinity with the Soviet Union, the Muslim fundamentalists in the PLO consider Marxism anathema.

Many observers, particularly critics of Cold War politics, have been quick to point out that the political behavior of the two superpowers toward clients involved in insurgencies has been virtually identical. From an ideological point of view, however, there has been a difference. The United States espouses a democratic philosophy, which values personal freedom and places a high value on individual human life. The Soviet Union espouses a doctrine condoning the revolutionary overthrow of noncommunist systems, which justifies terrorism as an integral part of class struggle. To the degree that the Soviets will continue to aspire to being the final arbiter of Marxist orthodoxy, they are stuck with that doctrine regardless of whether it conforms to their interests as a superpower or to their national interests. It is, therefore, more as guardians of Marxist doctrine than as patrons of insurgent or terrorist groups that the Soviets support terrorism.

Just as more legitimate political parties need the broad support of a public constituency, terrorist organizations require public support groups. Such groups provide crucial financial, logistical, political, and even legal support (for terrorists facing trial). The degree of constituent support that terrorist groups can muster depends on public apathy or antipathy to their cause as well as attitudes toward the social order generally. One of the reasons that the United States has had such relatively few instances of terrorist activity within its borders, for example, is that the public generally holds terrorist tactics in revulsion, no matter what the political grievance or cause.

The underlying motivations of persons providing constituent support to terrorist groups are very similar to those of active members. Regardless of the credibility of terrorists' motives or the efficiency of their tactics, they are only extreme manifestations of the frustrations, rationalizations, and ambitions of ordinary people. Their constituents are no different. They are in no way limited to the downtrodden and dispossessed on the fringes of society and are as easily to be found in the middle-class suburbs as in slums and refugee camps.

A feeling of identity with a terrorist group can stem from national and ethnic loyalties, political or professional loyalties, class distinctions, or merely a shared sense of grievance and a common enemy. In addition, a genuinely charismatic leader usually appeals to a much broader constituency than the membership of the group he leads.

Nationalist–ethnic resistance groups and left-wing insurgency movements both require and generally command the broadest constituent support. They draw on the shared loyalties and sense of identity of members of a national–ethnic community or of a socio-economic class. The PLO, for example, commands at least the symbolic allegiance of virtually everyone claiming to be a Palestinian. In Latin America, landless peasants and urban poor, many of them of Indian descent, provide a built-in constituency for left-wing nationalist insurgencies. The depth of support among individual constituencies varies considerably. At the broadest level are the sympathizers who, while they do not support the terrorist activities of the group, share the same general political goals, or at least the same opponents. For example, substantial financial support for the IRA and Provisional IRA comes from law-abiding Irish-Americans in the United States who would never consider becoming personally involved in terrorist activities and must rationalize or ignore the brutal tactics of their clients.[7] Constituent logistical and financial support for the Red Army Faction in Germany comes largely from well-educated and relatively affluent members of the middle class.

At a minimum, a broad public constituency contributes by not impeding or informing on terrorist groups, that is, by helping to create a favorable environment for terrorist operations. At most, it also provides financial aid and broad political support of the organizations' political agenda.

Within this general constituency is a smaller group that not only supports the organizations' general goals but can also become directly involved in nonterrorist operational support activities, such as providing safe haven or surveillance and acting as couriers. In some cases these people are actual members of the organizations engaged in terrorism or of their political fronts. It is from among this group that the organizations generally recruit their hard-core members.

Constituent attitudes are vitally important to terrorist and insurgent groups that depend on their support. In some cases they may serve as a constraint on terrorist activities. While constituent supporters can favor or at least acquiesce in some types of terrorist targets, they might be repelled by others. For example, American contributions to organizations that funnel money to the IRA declined noticeably following the broad television coverage of the bloody terrorist bombing at a British war memorial service at Enniskillen in November 1987. On the other hand, even an act that elicits international condemnation might be considered a highly desirable means of advancing the group's political cause if it does not repel that group's constituency. Whatever the strategy or tactics, it is certain they will never totally jeopardize constituent support.

Another important source of terrorist support is cooperation among terrorist groups. The degree of cooperation can be exaggerated, however. There is a broadly held view in America and elsewhere, nurtured to some extent by Claire Sterling's *The Terrorist Network*, that there is an international conspiracy of terrorist groups receiving help from each other and all supported by the KGB.[8] As anyone who has ever worked in a large bureaucracy knows, however, while conspiracies abound, they rarely overcome the crippling effects of bureaucratic turf wars, organizational inertia, and sheer incompetence. Moreover, there is no compelling evidence either for an international terrorist network or for its being supported by the Soviet Union. There are too many differences in the sociology of the different groups, their political and operational environments, leadership rivalries, and ideological differences for an international network to exist. Even organizing small numbers of groups is a cumbersome process, as the Cubans learned when they tried to coordinate the activities of Marxist Salvadoran and Guatemalan groups in the early 1980s.

Though terrorist groups will never coalesce into an international network, there is evidence of tactical cooperation among certain groups. It is motivated in part by the need to acquire expertise and technical skills unavailable within one's own organization, or known to exist at a higher level in another group. The bomb planted on TWA flight 840 in 1986 resembled the work of Husayn al-Amri (Abu Ibrahim) of the Palestinian 15 May Organization, but the operation may have been carried out by Abd al-Hamid Labib (alias Colonel Harawi) working for al-Fatah.

Some cooperation may be bartered on a *quid pro quo* basis, trading technical expertise for forged travel documents, or training for arms. In other cases it may be sold to raise cash. For example, Abu Nidal for years ran a "legitimate" arms trading firm out of Poland, both to raise cash and to supply himself and other groups with weapons.

Ideology can also be a motivating factor for cooperation among groups; the closer the congruence of political goals, the closer the cooperation. The greatest cooperation exists among groups that have banded together under an umbrella organization. They include the component members of the PLO, the Salvadoran FMLN, the Guatemalan URNG, and the Colombian Simón Bolívar Guerrilla Coordinator. The first two, in particular, have reached a significant degree of cooperation.

There has also been a degree of tactical cooperation among European New Left utopian groups. For example, France's Action Direct, Belgium's Combatant Communist Cells, and West Germany's Red Army Faction are believed to have carried out joint operations, but their attempt to establish an intergroup coordinating body called the Anti-Imperialist Armed Front was short lived. The broadest cooperative efforts by a single Marxist group have been those of the Popular Front for the Liberation of Palestine under George Habbash. In addition to its ties with other hard-line groups in the PLO, the PFLP has developed ties with the RAF, the Red Brigades, Action Directe, the Basque ETA, and the Provisional IRA, and its ties with the Japanese Red Army are particularly close.

One of the most ominous developments of recent years has been the growing tie between terrorists and drug traffickers, called narco-terrorism.[9] In fact, drugs and political violence have been companions for centuries. The contemporary relationship between drugs and terrorism has less to do with drug use than with drug trafficking. The drug traffic has become the most lucrative illegal source of revenue in the world today, and it is probably inevitable that terrorist and insurgent groups would look on it as a source of funding.

Terrorist groups throughout the world have benefited from the drug trade to finance their activities.[10] However, the most extensive working relationships between terrorist groups and drug traffickers are found in South America. By the late 1980s cocaine had greatly surpassed heroin and psychedelic drugs in popularity among hard drugs in the United States. The three greatest exporters of illicit cocaine are Colombia, Peru, and Bolivia. Peru is the largest grower and Colombia the largest processor. Together they account for about 90 percent of the world's supply. Existing terrorist organizations in those countries have developed extensive relationships with drug planters and traffickers that have come to be known as narco-terrorism.

The relationships are very complex, part cooperational and part confrontational, especially the latter in Colombia. In some cases the terrorist groups offer the drug growers and traffickers protection from government security forces and U.S.-financed antidrug operations. In other cases the drug syndicates have attempted to co-opt the terrorist groups. Terrorist groups extort "protection" money from the growers or more often, from the traffickers by threatening retaliation themselves. They also extort landing fees, fees for the use of land, and other forms of "taxation." In some instances they are directly involved in the drug trade. In Colombia government agents have discovered terrorist-prepared tax tables along with instructions to growers on how and when to plant.[11]

The type and degree of involvement in narco-terrorism depends on the particular circumstances of the group and the overall political and operational environment. In 1978, for example, the Peruvian government outlawed free cultivation of coca, creating great resentment among the peasants. Not only did coca provide their livelihoods, but it had become increasingly profitable. The main area of cultivation is the Upper Huallaga Valley in the north central part of the country. The local Indians there have long grown coca, but the major growers are migrants from other parts of Peru, mainly from the highlands and the city slums. They have no cultural unity, but they share the attitudes and frustrations of the disadvantaged.

Sendero Luminoso first penetrated the area in 1980, establishing planters from Ayacucho who later began politicizing the valley. It secured the cooperation of the peasant planters by protecting them from the police and by forcing the drug traffickers to use Sendero as a middleman in negotiating with the planters. In this way Sendero built up not only an area of political control but a solid economic base. It is estimated that the Peruvian drug trade generates more than $1 billion annually. If Sendero Luminoso skimmed off just 5 percent of that, it would net $75–$100 million a year. Sendero Luminoso also values the drug trade for contributing to the undermining of society in "imperialist" America.[12]

Though Sendero Luminoso exploits the drug trade in areas it has "liberated," narco-terrorism is not considered essential to its economic survival. Prior to its involvement in narco-terrorism, it was very successful in robbing banks and holding hostages for ransom to raise money for its activities. Moreover, in seeking to win the support of the peasants, it carefully nurtures its image as a protector of the growers, not as an extortionist, and it seeks to ensure that the growers get a "fair" return from the traffickers.

Another Peruvian group, the Tupac Amaru Revolutionary Movement (MRTA), also involved in narco-terrorism, is in fact more dependent on the drug trade as a source of income than Sendero Luminoso. But, having lost out to Sendero Luminoso in dealings with the traffickers, it is more directly involved in efforts to establish ties to the growers.

In Colombia narco-terrorism runs the entire gamut from protection to extortion to direct involvement. The largest group and the most heavily involved in narco-terrorism is the Revolutionary Armed Forces of Colombia (FARC) which, largely thanks to narco-terrorist funds, has been able virtually to double in size between 1985 and 1989. Its strongholds are in the major coca growing areas, and it is estimated that over 80 percent of its revenues comes from the drug trade. FARC has become involved in every aspect of the drug trade but trafficking, and it is entirely possible that in the next few years it could either absorb some of the main traffickers into its organization or even develop a new drug cartel. On the other hand, there are those who believe that FARC itself has already been co-opted by the drug traffickers.

Other Colombian groups are involved in narco-terrorism, but to a lesser extent. The Maoist Popular Liberation Army (EPL) receives about one-third of its revenues from the drug trade. M-19, even though its stronghold in Cauca Department is not a main coca-growing area, nevertheless receives 30 to 40 percent of its revenues from narco-terrorism, principally through extortion from traffickers.[13]

Just as political terrorists have been drawn to the drug trade, drug traffickers have also been drawn to political terrorism (as distinct from the brutality associated with their criminal operations). Its main purpose is to intimidate the Colombian government into dropping legal actions and charges against the drug traffickers. An example of such activity is the blowing up of a Colombian Avianca airliner with 107 people on board in November 1989. The group responsible, called the "Extraditables," is linked to the Medellín drug cartel and takes its name from a U.S. Justice Department's list of twelve Colombian drug lords most wanted in the United States. The head of the cartel, Pablo Escobar, heads the list. Apparently the terrorist act was to dissuade the Colombian government from seeking to extradite them to America.

Another problem resulting from the unholy union of insurgent terrorist groups and drug traffickers, one that is expected to grow in magnitude, is gun running. The groups most involved in narco-terrorism are primarily insurgent groups, and a great deal of their operational expenses go into purchasing weapons. Increasingly, the drug traffickers are using their exporting and distribution networks to import illicit arms, not only for their private armies and hit men but for the insurgent groups as well.

Gun running involves a commercial as well as a political element since transactions can involve hundreds of thousands of dollars. It is possible, therefore, that the insurgent groups may soon try to cut out the middlemen (the drug traffickers) and create their own commercial arms distribution networks. Panama and Libya appear to be growing sources of black market arms to Colombia, which go directly to the insurgents.[14]

The point has been made that terrorism is essentially a psychological tactic. It is effective only if the intended target audience (the regime it opposes or the general public that forms its constituency) is intimidated, and to be intimidated, it must be made aware of each terrorist act or threat in all its gruesome details or implications. Thus, the importance of mass communications to terrorism is incalculable.

Realizing this, terrorists have become very adept tailoring their operations to draw maximum media coverage. Many terrorist acts, such as the hijacking of TWA 847 in June 1985 and the hijacking of the Italian cruise ship *Achille Lauro* the following October, are carefully planned theatrical events that virtually guarantee evocative, emotional treatment by the media. Thus, by their coverage, the media provide the terrorists with the means to publicize their political agendas to a mass audience otherwise not available to them.

The media's response to terrorists' attempts to exploit them has been mixed. Part of the problem stems from the media's image of themselves. They have always considered themselves to be recorders of human events, but in the case of terrorism, though they are reluctant to acknowledge it, they have become participants as well. The media's mission to cover the news and the terrorists' ability to "create" news have led to a symbiotic relationship between the two, one in which the media not only convey the news but help the terrorists to create it.

Part of the problem centers on the concept of what news is. The avowed aim of the media is to provide timely information to meet the public's "need to know" what is happening in the world around it. In fact, however, the media are less in the business of providing information than of surveying stories that the public will find interesting or entertaining. If there is no story of interest, there is no news; if an event has interest value, it almost automatically becomes news no matter how trivial it might be substantively.

One also cannot ignore the commercial aspects of the media. As a highly competitive industry, the privately-owned media must generate sales and profits to survive. Profitability translates largely into maintaining one's audience, and to a great extent, this is done by appealing more to the emotions than to the intellect. Coverage of terrorist events, particularly live coverage by the electronic media, is highly profitable if nothing else; lack of coverage means loss of audience share to one's competitors.

Live coverage by the electronic media is also particularly prone to exploitation. It eliminates the editorial process with which the media can at least attempt to provide balanced coverage, and by emphasizing only the most spectacular aspects of the incident, it tends to hinder the public's understanding of the true significance of the events unfolding before its eyes.

Media coverage can also be positively harmful. During the 1977 hijacking of a Lufthansa plane to Mogodishu, the terrorists discovered by listening to radio broadcasts that the captain was passing information to the ground along with routine transmissions; they subsequently killed him. There have also been cases during hostage situations in which direct communication between the media and the terrorists has hampered efforts by government authorities to bring them to a peaceful conclusion. Widespread coverage can also contribute to the "copycat" effect by encouraging other politically disaffected factions to chose violence to express their views.

This discussion is not intended to imply that all media coverage of terrorist events is negative. The public does have a need to know about such events, and in many cases media coverage has been restrained in order to deny the terrorists the full psychological impact on the audience that they seek. For example, since 1987 the media have run stories on the Lebanon hostage situation, including letters and videotapes of the hostages, but have not created major media events that the terrorists could use in trying to pressure the U.S. and other governments to meet their demands for release of the hostages.

There are those in the industry who claim that it is not the media's responsibility if their coverage is exploited by the terrorists.[15] Their responsibility is to provide the facts and let the public decide for itself the merits of a given story. That line of argument ignores the fact that the public can never obtain all the facts, but at best gets only a selection made by the media. Besides, admit it or not, it is neither the event nor the public but the media in the first instance that determine what the public needs to know.

In recent years a great deal of thought has gone into how to make the media in democratic countries more responsible in their coverage of terrorism. Most thoughtful people and the media themselves prefer self-regulation, but this has not always been effective in the past. With the possible exception of stories that could be directly linked to a threat of loss of life, there is virtually nothing that at least one representative of the media would not carry if it were considered "newsworthy," no matter how much such free publicity serves the terrorists' purposes by submitting the public to the full psychological impact of their deeds, and no matter how much it hampers antiterrorist efforts. And when one carries the story, the rest inevitably follow suit.

The real question, however, is not so much how ineffective self-regulation is as how bad the alternatives are. Some frustrated officials have called for more stringent legislative restrictions. That sentiment ignores the fact that the bulwark of a free society is freedom of speech, and limitations on the media would limit that freedom.

On the other hand, virtually all democratic societies have acquiesced in the imposition of press restrictions by government in extraordinary circumstances, as in time of war. Some countries have media restrictions—Britain's official secrets act, for example—even in peacetime. If the media in democratic countries wish to avoid a public outcry for legislative restrictions on their freedom to cover terrorism, particularly crisis events where the public deems media coverage could damage national interests and contribute to loss of life, it would behoove them to do a better job of self-regulation.

In sum, terrorist organizations must and do receive support from many sources in order to survive and carry on their activities. Some sources are calculated and some unwitting; some are active and some are passive. Of them all, state support is the most critical, and passive support by a state turning a blind eye for fear of reprisals is probably the most insidious. Since states can be held responsible for their acts, however, state support for terrorism is also the form of support most sensitive to international censure.

6

Strategy,
Tactics, and Victims

Let us now get down to the mechanics of terrorism: What types of acts do terrorist groups consider, how do they chose from among them, and who are the victims? Terrorism always has victims, if not physically then through severe damage or threat to people's psychological, social, political, or economic well-being. In most instances the victims are not the real target of the terrorist attack—that is the governing authorities the terrorists are seeking to intimidate—but rather symbolic targets or merely innocent bystanders who happened to be in the wrong place at the wrong time. If there is any moral injunction against terrorism, it is the inhumanity of creating victims. There is no one, including groups that regularly employ terrorism, who will dispute the inhumane nature of terrorist tactics.

Terrorism can be viewed as either an overall strategy for planning and carrying out individual terrorist acts or a tactic in a broader program to achieve political change. On the whole, it is more of a tactical than a strategic concept. Revolutionary theorists, from Mao Zedong to Carlos Marighella, the Brazilian urban guerrilla, have emphasized the tactical nature of terrorism in the context of armed struggle. Marighella also looked on terrorism as a means of provoking government repression, but maintained that it should not be viewed as an end in itself.[1] Even leftist groups that conduct terrorist activities in the absence of an insurgency, such as the Red Army Faction and Action Directe, adhere, at least in theory, to the notion that terrorism is but one tactic in revolutionary armed struggle.

Right-wing groups hold similar views. For neo-Nazis and Fascists, purifying the society and the political system is the strategic goal, and terrorism is but one tactic to achieve that goal. Anticommunists and religious fanatics share the same point of view. Islamic fundamentalists view the use of violence as only one aspect of the broader concept of *jihad*.

Terrorism can also be seen in a strategic context, however. Each group must choose a mix of specific terrorist operations that collectively are deemed the most advantageous in terms of effectiveness and risk. The mix could be called the terrorist strategy of that particular group, and the operations seen as tactics in that strategy.

Operational terrorist tactics include almost any violent act that intimidates noncombatants. Often threats are as effective as the act itself, particularly in situations in which the target audience feels powerless to stop it. The most common types of terrorism are armed attacks, including bombings, arson, murder, and physical injury, along with hijacking and kidnapping. The targets can be individuals, property, or both. Depending on the target audience and the need to maintain constituent support, a group might intentionally avoid loss of life. On the other hand, personal attacks can be aimed at specific persons or else at highly populated areas to maximize the number of casualties. Physical targets can include military installations (foreign or domestic), government offices, public transportation facilities, public utilities, and private property with symbolic value, such as "American" businesses attacked by Marxist groups.

Terrorists employ armed attacks for a variety of reasons. They may be seeking to instill a sense of fear and helplessness among civilians either to alienate them from the government or to make them lose faith in the government's ability to protect it. They may be seeking to instill a sense of impotence among government officials or to intimidate them as a means of neutralizing their active opposition to the terrorist group. They may be seeking to undermine the national economy by discouraging foreign investment, dissuading foreign tourists from visiting the country, or spurring capital flight by domestic investors. Economic targets would include key installations and infrastructure, public carriers, and transportation networks such as railroads and highways. The terrorists may be seeking to provoke harsh government reprisals to gain the sympathy of the population, or they may simply be seeking to create an international incident to publicize their political cause. Usually, specific attacks are planned for a combination of reasons.

Terrorists groups have made the general traveling public a prime target audience, seeking to intimidate it through fear of hijackings and sabotage into avoiding particular carriers, terminals, or even countries. The terrorist act can be aimed at the state owning the carrier or the state whose nationals either own it or are passengers on it. The ultimate target, however, is still the political authorities which the terrorists hope to force into meeting its demands—either long-term political objectives or such short-term demands as releasing a fellow member from custody. The stated demands of hijackers need not always be negotiable. They can be designed simply to gain maximum publicity. Because hijackings generally tend to be media events, they provide one of the best means for providing maximum media coverage of a group's political demands.

The spectacular hijacking of the Italian cruise ship *Achille Lauro* in October 1985 reaped tremendous publicity, which appeared to be the hijackers' main purpose, although the media focus on their murder victim, Leon Klinghoffer, almost totally undermined the image of brilliant, fearless warriors they tried to project.

Hijacking can involve any public conveyance but most often involves airliners. They are the most vulnerable and, assuming there is a country that will allow the plane to land, offer the hijackers the best opportunity to avoid capture and escape, should the attempt fail.

Surface transportation (buses and trains) provide easier targets for police and military forces to recapture. In 1975 and 1977, South Moluccan terrorists (an Indonesian separatist group) hijacked two Dutch trains to publicize their cause and demand freedom for jailed colleagues. They did get publicity, but the authorities refused to heed their demands or to allow them to escape. Dutch marines stormed the train and killed six terrorists (and two of the hostages).

The *Achille Lauro* hijacking underscored the difficulties of making a successful escape on the open seas. Ships move slowly and do not pose the same threat of imminent loss of life as an airliner running out of fuel. That removes the urgency of allowing it to enter a port and provides time for diplomatic pressure to mount on countries to refuse entry. Ships are also vulnerable to forcible recapture by military forces trained for the purpose.

Some airline hijackings are not, strictly speaking, terrorist acts in the political sense. In the 1960s and 1970s, airline hijacking became popular for people seeking asylum, avoiding real or imagined persecution, or who were simply seeking publicity. As countries have become less and less tolerant of such behavior, it has become rarer.

Both hijacking and kidnapping involve hostage-taking. Publicity is often a key motive because of the high drama associated with kidnapping, but, as in the case of the ELN in Colombia, it may also be an important source of revenue. The kidnapping of Americans and Europeans in Lebanon in the mid-1980s by Hizballah's Imad Mughniya was primarily aimed at trading the victims for Lebanese (and Iraqis) imprisoned in Kuwait for terrorism, including his brother-in-law.

Terrorist-associated kidnapping may also involve purely criminal elements. It is thought that many of those kidnapped in Lebanon were actually taken by professional criminals, and one victim, Peter Kilburn, may have been kidnapped by criminals for the sole purpose of selling him to the highest bidder.[2] Hostages may also be taken to avoid capture in an armed attack or a robbery attempt. The distinction is more important to the counterterrorist than to the terrorist because of special measures required in dealing with hostage barricade situations.

Ancillary terrorist tactics aimed at extracting financial rewards include extortion, blackmail, ransom, and robbery. They can be conducted in conjunction with kidnapping or hijacking, or with a threat of bodily harm. To maximize their psychological value, terrorist attacks are generally (although not always) accompanied by a public relations effort usually involving exploitation of the communications media to assure maximum publicity.

In June 1985, for example, shortly before the passengers of the hijacked TWA flight 847 were to be released, the media were invited to interview them in a small school in Beirut. The hijackers and the media both knew that many hostages, just before their release, tend to identify with their captors out of sheer relief.[3] Moreover, most of the passengers were still too intimidated to say anything negative about the terrorists. As a result, the whole world witnessed on television the sympathetic testimony of many of the passengers toward their captors. A week later the passengers developed a strong sense of outrage toward their captors, but by that time no one was there from the media to record it. The terrorists thus gained a media victory.

How a group engaged in terrorism decides upon its strategy or mix of operational tactics is a question that has occupied terrorism analysts for a long time. If any generalization is valid, it is that there seems to be no pattern at all: The mix of tactics is as varied as the number of groups. In some cases groups seem to emphasize certain tactics and eschew others for no apparent reason. For example, there is no compelling constraint for the Basque ETA against attempting to sabotage civil airliners; it has the technical, personnel, and financial resources to do so. Yet it has never shown any disposition to engage in this type of activity.

Several factors may influence if not totally dictate the choice of operational tactics. The most important are the operational environment, including physical, political, security, and economic factors and organizational strengths and weaknesses of a particular group.

The operational environment is the field upon which the terrorists play, and is thus a primary determinant of a terrorist group's strategy. The physical environment has to do with geographic and demographic conditions in the area in which the group is operating. The range of tactics most appropriate in a Salvadoran jungle differ markedly from those in the Northern Irish countryside. Rural and urban tactics also vary, so much, in fact, that the term "urban guerrilla" has entered the vocabulary as a distinct category of terrorist.[4] Demographic factors also have a pronounced effect on tactics. Seeking to win the constituent support of a large peasant or working class population in rural and urban Latin America presents a different set of tactical inducements and constraints from winning over a radical middle-class intellectual elite in Western Europe.

The degree of ethnic solidarity can also be important. The most radical Palestinian terrorist, for example, cannot ignore an overall Palestinian consensus for a negotiated peace settlement, no matter how committed he or she is to armed struggle. Action Directe, on the other hand, can ignore the fact that the vast majority of fellow ethnic Frenchmen oppose its ideology, aims, and tactics.

The political environment largely refers to the degree of political stability present in the area of operations. In countries with visible instability, such as in Central America, terrorist tactics are largely used in support of a broader insurgent effort. In Western Europe, on the other hand, where there is a high degree of political stability, terrorist tactics are generally carried out independently, in the absence of any insurgency.

Stability is not solely a function of public support (or apathy) toward a regime. Government security capabilities also help determine the degree of stability and have a significant impact on the type of terrorist tactics a group might choose.

In Lebanon, for example, where there is virtually no public security beyond that provided by Syria, Israel, and the various sectarian militias, terrorist tactics can be employed with little regard for secrecy and security. In countries with effective security services, on the other hand, elaborate precautions must constantly be taken to avoid detection and arrest. That would tend to rule out large, concerted terrorist campaigns and suggest, instead, either carefully planned attacks that take months or even years to plan or random attacks, which are less effective psychologically but also hard to detect in advance.

The hijacking of an airliner may take as long as eighteen months to two years to develop. In the aborted hijacking of Pan Am flight 73 in Karachi in 1986, the terrorists avoided the terminal and its metal detectors. They gained access to the aircraft by entering through a rear airport perimeter gate in a van painted to look like a security vehicle, wearing uniforms that looked like security uniforms at a time when such a van would normally be expected. In order to plan the attack, the terrorists had to infiltrate the country and hide in a safe house. They had to maintain surveillance of the airport and learn the movements of the airport security forces, a process that required weeks or even months; they had to obtain a van, paint it to look like a security vehicle, and then hide it until the day of the hijacking; and they had to find tailors to make facsimile security uniforms and then prevent them from informing. Finally, the coordinator of the attack, who did not enter the aircraft, had to develop a plan to flee the country in case the plan failed, as it did in this case. The hijackers were caught, and the coordinator was also arrested just as he was about to leave the country.

The urgency of the terrorist response in terms of time can also be important. With a year or two to plan, a group with good organizational skills and internal security can plan a spectacular attack, but such an attack is difficult to link to specific political events. One way around this is to keep planning attacks so there will always be one at an advanced stage when needed. In order to do so, however, a group must have extensive resources or else must be able to call upon a country like Libya for assistance. Moreover, at some point the attack reaches a stage where it must either go ahead or be aborted to avoid detection, and the decision cannot be changed.

Another way to link the attack to political events is to seek government reprisals for one attack while already planning an attack to be made "in response" to the reprisal. If a group needs to make a prompt response to some political situation, however, and has little or no lead time, it may have to settle for a less sophisticated approach. It may plan multiple attacks to make sure that at least one succeeds. That was the case with the Libyan terrorist campaign against U.S. targets in April 1986 in response to the U.S. bombing raid. Of five known attempts, only one, the attack on the Berlin disco, succeeded.[5] U.S. and local security forces were able to interdict planned attacks on U.S. military installations at Ankara and Izmir, the U.S. Consulate General in Paris, and another U.S. site in Frankfurt.

From the terrorist's standpoint, economic dislocations and maldistribution of income have more to do with the political than the economic environment, for they can be critical factors in undermining political stability. For a terrorist group, a favorable economic environment mainly refers to accessibility of financial resources. Although all terrorist tactics are relatively cheap, particularly when compared to other forms of political violence, some are more expensive than others, and the range of tactics available to a group is directly proportionate to its financial resources.

A group that operates on very limited resources must generally content itself with such unsophisticated tactics as gang-style killings, bombing offices or autos, or sending letter bombs. If it wishes to expand, it must seek a patron, who will probably impose his own target priorities on the group. Even some of the wealthier groups, such as the Abu Nidal Organization, have depended on patrons for financial and other logistical support. When the ANO broke with the PLO in 1974, it first sought Iraqi patronage, then Syrian, and finally Libyan.

The wealthier the group, the broader the range of operational tactics from which it can choose, and the broader the geographic range it can cover if it so desires. With ever more stringent airline and airport security, hijacking or sabotaging a civilian airliner is not only time-consuming but very costly compared to other tactics, and is now beyond the financial, to say nothing of the organizational, resources of many groups engaged in terrorist activities.

The need to raise money can directly influence terrorist tactics. Bank robbing and kidnapping for ransom has been a significant source of revenue for terrorist groups in Colombia, for example, and narco terrorism is becoming an even greater one both there and in Peru. In countries where public security is more effective, groups must resort to other means to raise money.

The choice of tactics and their effectiveness are also greatly influenced by the organizational strengths and weaknesses of the terrorist group. Beyond saying that terrorism is mainly a small group activity, there is virtually no overall organizational pattern that can be observed among individual groups. Some are small independent groups numbering less than a dozen, while others are members of larger political organizations such as the PLO, or insurgency organizations such as the Salvadoran FMLN, both numbering in the thousands. Where security is tight, a cell structure is the most common form of organization, with individual members knowing only those in their own cell and only one member communicating with the cell structure next highest in the chain of command.

Organizational strengths and weaknesses generally are not attributable to organizational structure. Rather, they result primarily from the quality of leadership and personnel and the support provided by constituencies and state patrons. Quality leadership means more than charisma to motivate the members. Successful groups also require managerial and organizational skills that are vital in covert operations. One of the reasons that the Palestinian leader Khalil al-Wazir (Abu Jihad) was murdered by Israel was his brilliant organizational skills. Abu Nidal has also been considered a genius in organizing and implementing intricate and sophisticated terrorist attacks.

The level and variety of a group's technical skills also play an important role in the tactics it chooses and their effectiveness. Areas of technical expertise needed by terrorist groups cover a wide range. Bomb and weapons technology includes knowledge of electronics, explosives, and small arms; logistical expertise includes knowledge of communications, manufacture of forged documents, surveillance techniques, auto mechanics, and special driving skills; security expertise includes surveillance techniques, detection of electronic and other devices, and the proper use of cover techniques. The level and combination of skills available to a group will greatly determine what tactics it chooses.

As they take into account all these variables and begin to develop strategies, most terrorist groups develop a recognizable *modus operandi* (m.o.). For example, the 1986 hijacking of Pan American flight 73 was first linked to Abu Nidal because it fitted his group's m.o. The m.o. of the 17 November Organization assassinations in Greece is a three-man hit team riding motor scooters and often using the same weapon. In addition, most sophisticated explosive devices leave traceable "signatures" from which forensic investigators can trace the device back to its originator. The initial linkage of the bombing of a synagogue in Istanbul with Abu Nidal was based on the signature of the bomb, and the bomb placed in TWA flight 840 from Rome to Athens in April 1986 bore the signature of a Palestinian leader, Abu Ibrahim.

One might wonder why groups involved in terrorism continue to use tactics or employ devices that are traceable to themselves. It is in part because some groups want the act traced to them even if they deny it, as a subtle means of psychological intimidation. In addition, however, groups appear to become creatures of habit. If they have an expert in explosives or some other device, for example, they will continue to use his services, and he will teach others his methods, perpetuating the use of the tactic.

The danger that a terrorist group might acquire a nuclear device or even biological or chemical agents is highly unlikely, but the implications of such an eventuality are so catastrophic that the threat must be taken seriously by government officials charged with protecting national security. The options open to a group contemplating nuclear, biological, or chemical terrorism are either to steal such a weapon or to construct its own. Stealing a nuclear device or chemical or biological agents would require breaching the elaborate security measures installed to prevent such an act. In the case of a nuclear device, a stolen weapon would have to be disarmed to bypass all the devices designed to prevent unauthorized tampering and then rearmed, or its components would have to be rebuilt into a new device. Constructing a nuclear device from scratch would require fissionable materials, which themselves would have to be obtained. Chemical and biological agents would be relatively easier to obtain but would still require expertise to handle.

Recruiting the requisite expertise to steal, handle, or construct such weapons, particularly nuclear devices, is also a constraint. Whether it is even possible for a terrorist group to build a nuclear device is a subject of debate within the nuclear community, but at any rate the number of nuclear weapons specialists is not great, and most can be accounted for in government installations and academic institutions. Those with both the skills and the motivation to participate in nuclear terrorism, therefore, represent an even smaller number for counterterrorist forces to keep under surveillance.

Aside from stringent government security measures to prevent such weapons from falling into the wrong hands, and the difficulties in recruiting the expertise to steal, construct, or even handle them, the greatest constraints against nuclear, biological, or chemical terrorism rest with the terrorists themselves and relate to political expediency and political morality.

Doomsday weapons are capable of killing thousands, even millions of people and do not discriminate between friend and foe. Killing, however, is not a primary aim of most terrorists. Terrorism is a psychological tactic; body count is not vitally important and could even be a negative factor if a group's constituency were to become so appalled that it withdrew even tacit support. Moreover, most terrorist groups rationalize their activities by claiming that the ends justify the means. Mass murder is difficult to justify no matter what the ends.

At the very least, the terrorists would hope the mere threat to use such a device would produce the desired results, although having gone that far, they might feel compelled to use it if the threat fails, blaming their opponents for the consequences. As a media event, such a threat might indeed be gripping, but were it carried out, the catastrophe would totally overshadow the terrorist's cause and serve to escalate the alienation of the group's supporters even more.

One other way in which a terrorist group could engage in nuclear terrorism is to attack a nuclear power installation in the hope that the public would blame the government for the incident. Such a tactic, however, would leave no means of avoiding a disaster, whereas simply possessing a weapon could be used to threaten the established authority; once accomplished, the terrorist groups would lose all further control over events.

If a nuclear, biological, or chemical threat ever does materialize, it would probably be with aid of a country providing financial, logistical, and technical support. It is such a scenario that gave rise to deep concern over the chemical plant being constructed in Libya. States supporting terrorism are subject to political and military reprisals of other states, however, and would be well advised to think twice before taking such a risk.

Of all the tactics a terrorist organization could adopt, the most inhumane involve physical acts against innocent victims. In order to rationalize such tactics, many terrorists assert that there are no innocent victims, that armed struggle is a moral imperative against an oppressive social class, ethnic group, or religious community. Just as the public at large stereotypes and dehumanizes members of terrorist groups, so terrorists tend to stereotype and dehumanize their victims. The victims are human, however, and one may assume they are also innocent. Besides they include not only the immediate victim but his or her family and loved ones as well.

For those who survive a terrorist attack, notably hijack and kidnap victims, responses to the intense stress experienced both during and after the incident are complex and are still not fully understood. We know that victims go through the whole range of emotional responses to stress—helplessness, despair, rage, impotence, guilt—and that the responses to stress can be both conscious and unconscious. Guilt is a major response. It can arise over why the victim allowed himself or herself to get caught, why he or she was spared when others were tortured or executed or was released when the others were not, or how difficult it was for family members to cope without him or her.

Psychological defense mechanisms, which are generally unconscious means of coping with stress, come into play in terrorist situations. In the initial stage of a terrorist incident, many victims frequently manifest a psychological defense mechanism of "denial," a partial or total blocking out of the experience and the emotions and memory associated with it.[6] For example, a hostage on the hijacked Dutch train in 1977 initially refused to lie on the floor in case of a shootout because it would get her dress dirty; a passenger on an airliner hijacked in Jordan by PFLP initially refused to believe that a hijacking was taking place.[7] Victims often fantasize that it is all a dream and that soon they will wake up.

Another initial reaction is the irrational conviction of imminent rescue. Victims will grasp at the slightest hint to reinforce their belief that whatever they are going through will soon be all over. As time passes, other defense mechanisms can come into play: intellectualizing the crisis, humor, becoming occupied with busywork, and taking stock of one's life.

If the incident is not quickly resolved, personal communication between the victim and the captor can create a psychological bond that can be positive, depending in part on the treatment the victim receives and the degree to which the victim perceives that he owes his life to his captor. This bonding, in which the victim unconsciously incorporates the characteristics of the feared person, is a form of "reaction formation" in which the victim identifies with the aggressor. By psychologically transforming oneself from a threatened person to a person who makes the threat, the victim can reduce anxiety.[8]

This phenomenon has been called the "Stockholm syndrome," after a 1973 bank robbery in Stockholm, Sweden, in which bank employees were held hostage for more than five days. Contrary to expectations, the hostages identified with their captors more than with the police and even after their rescue bore the captors no hatred. Thomas Strentz, who has written about the Stockholm syndrome, sees it as regression to an infantile identification with the aggressor similar to that sometimes experienced by abused children.[9] The hostage is like a small child who is totally dependent on the captor for his or her continued survival and is terrified of the outside world. Over time a hostage can develop the notion that, "if only the police would go away and allow the terrorist to go free, I can also go free." As captivity becomes prolonged, a related experience is the conviction that the authorities are incompetent, uncaring, or unwilling for some conspiratorial reason to free the hostages. One of the hostages of the Dutch train hijacking retained his resentment toward the authorities for several years.[10]

The nature, causes, and even existence of the Stockholm syndrome are still being debated. It certainly does not happen to all victims, and thus far no single type or mix of personality types has been identified to make a subject more inclined to experience it. It is undeniable, however, that victims have identified with their captors too often to dismiss it as a mere aberration.

A similar identification can also affect the terrorists, as they get to know victims personally and the barrier of dehumanization breaks down. Indeed, when a personal bond is established between a terrorist captor and a hijack or kidnap victim, it becomes increasingly difficult for the terrorist to continue to mistreat him or her. In another example from the 1975 Dutch train hijacking, the terrorists spared a Dutch journalist chosen to be executed after hearing him open his heart to a fellow hostage in a last message to his family. He no longer appeared to them as a faceless symbol or a threatening hero, but as a somewhat flawed but very human being.[11] In a similar vein, when the British Ambassador to Uruguay, Sir Geoffrey Jackson, was held for 244 days by Tupamaro terrorists in the early 1970s, his magnetic personality was such that they had to change his guards regularly and isolate him for fear he would convince his guards of the superior justice of his cause over theirs.[12]

Defense mechanisms, because they are not based on the reality of the situation, do not necessarily increase the victim's chances for survival. In the case of denial, it can even be dangerous. In the initial stages of an incident, when the victims are still dehumanized by the terrorists, if a victim refuses to accept the real danger he is in and attempts to do something "heroic," he or she may be killed.

As the reality of the situation sinks in, the victim is compelled to try to cope with the situation. Though similar in some respects to defense mechanisms, coping generally refers to more conscious, deliberate methods to reduce the stress created by a given situation. It is a process that develops as victims learn more and more of the aims and personalities of their captors.

The essence of captivity is the loss of freedom and loss of one's destiny. All of life's choices, including the choice to live, are made by the captors. The meaning of life is also obscured. Unlike POWs or political prisoners, terrorist victims can usually find no coherent answer to "Why me?" As human beings, they have no intrinsic value; they are simply symbolic enemies or human collateral to bargain for some political demand.

Few generalizations can be made about terrorist captivity. The conditions and duration differ widely from case to case. For longer periods, a common reaction appears to be pure boredom. With all personal decisions made by the captors, it is easy to sink into a state of extreme passivity. In some cases this can create a sense of pseudo-security at great variance from the "razor's edge" state many victims' families imagine they are going through. Some captives have tried to counteract this passive state through mental games and physical exercise. Books, if allowed by their captors, can also be a source of strength, as in the case of some of the Lebanese hostages who were allowed by their captors to have Bibles.

In the initial stages of a terrorist incident, the most effective coping strategy is to acknowledge the loss of personal control to one's captor. This serves two purposes: It reinforces the reality of the situation, and it reduces the chances that the terrorists will act precipitately against the hostage.[13] Moreover, in order to relinquish control, the victim must be aware of, and thus to some extent in control of, his or her own emotional responses. That enables the victim to remain passive and still maintain self-esteem. Westerners, particularly Americans, have tremendous resistance to passivity. Doing something wrong is better than doing nothing at all. In a terrorist hostage situation, doing nothing at all may be the best thing one can do.

Whatever one does, however, it is vital to maintain self-esteem. When captivity is prolonged, maintaining self-esteem may be decisive for psychological and physical survival. Even risking loss of life may be preferable to loss of self-esteem; in fact, they may come down to the same thing, particularly if loss of life becomes the only way to maintain self-esteem.

Other coping strategies include keeping mentally occupied in gathering information. Such information has helped to improve the victim's ability to respond to captors as more is learned about them. Trying to establish bonds with the captors has also been an effective means of coping, making it more difficult for the captor to treat the victim as dehumanized abstraction. One of the Teheran Embassy hostages, kept in isolation during the entire ordeal, regularly engaged in political and religious discussions with his captors.

Seeking to create a group affiliation with other victims, if possible, can also be stress-reducing. It produces a feeling that "we are all in this together." In Lebanon the hostages captured by Hizballah were allowed to have prayer meetings together, led by one of their number who was a minister. Those meetings apparently strengthened their collective will to survive.

Finally, many victims, particularly of prolonged captivity, who get through their ordeals fairly well, have attributed it to having early on becoming convinced that they would survive for some specific reason or purpose. The reasons are varied. In the case of some POWs, it has simply been the determination to prevail over their captors' attempts to break them. Others have been convinced that their government, their family, or even humanity at large would not abandon them.

It is still too early to predict the long-term physiological and psychological effects of terrorist incidents on the victims. As terrorist incidents have multiplied in recent years, research on actual terrorist victims has also increased. Research on related types of captive situations, including research on POWS, inmates of concentration camps, prison inmates, and victims of violent crimes such as rape, has also been useful.

Terrorist victims probably respond to their ordeal in a manner similar to the way victims of violent crimes do, particularly in their overriding sense of isolation. They commonly develop a deep-seated sense of isolation out of a feeling of guilt that they did not do everything possible to escape, and shame at being humiliated and defiled.[14] The feeling of isolation is also characteristic of many returning POWs. For the terrorist victim, when defense mechanisms like denial fail to relieve anxiety during the incident, a trauma-related anxiety syndrome develops that can last for several years.[15] Friends and relatives are surprised, saddened, and frustrated that the victim's feelings of guilt and shame do not just go away when it is explained to him or her that they are not justified.

Not everyone who experiences hostage captivity is irrevocably scarred. The months or years in captivity may be taken as an opportunity for the captive to review his basic values and direction and come out of captivity the stronger for it. Following his captivity in Lebanon, the Reverend Benjamin Weir, an American missionary, appeared to have weathered his ordeal exceptionally well. Indeed, he was subsequently elected Moderator of the General Assembly (chief executive) of the Presbyterian church. Research has shown that older, more highly educated, and more mature individuals with firmly ingrained values, a sense of humor, and a commitment to a cause are more likely to cope with the stresses of captivity.[16]

Victimization in terrorist incidents also extends to the families of the victims. If the victim is a hostage, not knowing the condition or the fate of a family member or loved one can be particularly stressful. As with the victim, the incident is all the more acute when the period of captivity is prolonged and indefinite. We are still learning about the problems families of terrorist victims go through. Most of the research on families coping with stress due to the captivity of a family member centers on prisoners of war, although studies of the Iran embassy hostages in 1979–80 have also been made.[17] The Lebanon hostage situation in the mid-1980s also contributed to our understanding.

A family's initial reaction is generally shock, followed by emotions similar to those the victim: rage, fear, grief, and guilt. The strength of the reaction is often affected by how the families are originally told of the incident. Insensitive or "bureaucratic" communications by harried public officials, for example, can focus subsequent feelings of anger and suspicion on the government. This is an area in which most governments, including that of the United States, have been notably weak. At an early stage there is an insatiable desire for information, down to the smallest detail, and for the psychological well-being of the family member, every effort should be made to meet that desire no matter how trivial it may seem.

There is also an initial tendency for a family member to blame someone, often oneself. Later, the blame shifts from self to victim. "He should not have been there." "Why did she do this to me?" If the captivity is prolonged, blame, anger, and hostility later shift to authority figures. Usually this begins with lessening confidence in the foreign government authorities at the scene, but generally it soon spreads to the embassy at the scene and ultimately to one's own government at home. In the United States, the State Department often becomes the villain. American hostage families have expressed the feeling that if only the President or Secretary of State could hear the "true facts," which they are convinced are being withheld by the professionals, the hostages could be freed.

As time passes, the desire for information is accompanied by the need for contact, not only with government officials working on the case but in support groups with other victims' families. In some instances the need is to compensate for being "forgotten people." Families of terrorist victims also often find themselves celebrities overnight, and their support groups can expand to become political activist groups with an agenda far beyond finding mutual psychological support. Where fatalities are involved, support groups can also have a negative impact by keeping the emotions of the families fresh and inhibiting them from getting on with their lives. In other cases notoriety can cause some families to seek anonymity and isolate themselves from former friends and acquaintances.

In the United States, the Lebanon hostage families created a strong support group in the mid-1980s, and a similar group was formed by the families of the Pan Am flight 103 victims in 1988. The former group quickly became politicized and actively sought contact with higher and higher officials until it saw the President, apparently in the hope that the higher the contact, the better the chances of motivating the government to obtain the release of the hostages. This fitted right in with the aims of the captors, who were convinced that hostage family pressure would eventually enable them to obtain their demands of a hostage swap for Lebanese prisoners held in Kuwait.

Also over time, the original motive of wanting one's loved ones free can be joined by more personal secondary motives, such as fame (being on TV talk shows), importance (having media pundits ask one's opinion of national policy), and even monetary gain (from articles and interviews). The more these appetites are fed, the greater they can become, and the rationalization that all is excused by the goal of seeking rescue tends to deflect criticism. In some instances the release of the hostage has actually been met with resentment by family members who had become used to their celebrity status.

It is also possible for employers to exhibit characteristics similar to those of families. In the case of the Reverend Weir, for example, the bureaucracy of the board of missions of the Presbyterian Church (UP-

USA) maintained a hostile and suspicious attitude toward the U.S. government throughout his captivity and apparently harbored suspicions after his release that the government might try to "brainwash" him for some unspecified reasons.[18]

Reuniting former terrorist captives with their families can also present problems. Family members may have had to adopt new roles or take additional responsibilities, and they can find reverting to previous roles difficult or even impossible. Returning victims, on the other hand, often expect nothing to have changed and find it difficult to cope with the new, more mature, more responsible, and more independent family. Some families idealize the captive to an extent that he or she cannot possibly live up to. Without proper communication, pent-up rage and guilt by both the former captive and the family can also be a problem.

On the other hand, families as well as individuals can come through a terrorist crisis stronger than ever before. Long-established families that communicate freely, are high achievers, have religious-moral orientations, and have children and a flexible family structure appear to cope most successfully.[19]

In reviewing terrorist tactics and strategy, one is struck by the rationality with which most terrorist groups decide their operational priorities, carefully weighing internal strengths and weaknesses and external environmental factors. Their ultimate aim is the psychological intimidation of the government authorities they oppose, as well as the political constituencies of those authorities. Since the victim is seldom the ultimate target, the link between terrorist tactics and strategy and terrorist victims is most often pure caprice, but it is a caprice based on callous disregard for human life and dignity. It is the victims, more than any other factor, that makes terrorism a politically and morally unacceptable form of behavior.

7

Meeting the Threat

The decade of the 1990s has dawned in an atmosphere of great optimism and hope for reduced international tensions and a greater chance for world peace. And yet the admonition of many critics of Cold War politics, that most of the world's problems are not simply byproducts of global politics, is no less true now that global tensions appear to be diminishing than it was at the height of the Cold War. Terrorism, in particular, is far too complex a phenomenon to be vitally affected by the course of East–West relations, no matter how much those relations have influenced the politics of violent dissent. The sanctions against terrorism are too weak, the means to commit terrorist acts are too available, and the political, economic, and social motivations for committing them are too compelling for one to conclude that terrorism will simply fade away. It has become a regular feature of the contemporary international political landscape and is likely to remain so for the foreseeable future, no matter what changes ultimately occur in superpower relations. The terrorism issue is likely to remain high on the international public policy agenda for the 1990s.

A basic assumption of this book has been that in order to combat terrorism effectively, one must seek first to understand the phenomenon. Having looked at definitions and descriptions, motivations, groups and supporters, tactics, strategies, and victims of terrorists and terrorist activities, it now remains to address the fundamental question, how do we combat it?

In addressing any policy problem, most of us prefer to look for definite solutions. Terrorism is not a finite problem that can be solved once and for all, however, nor is it a condition that can be totally eradicated. No sooner is it brought under control in one area than it breaks out in another. The ease and availability of terrorist tactics and the continuing political, economic, and social conditions that spawn terrorism virtually assure a continuation of the threat no matter what type of policy is adopted.

Prescriptive solutions help to alleviate the frustration that terrorist attacks on innocent victims invariably create, but they do little more than that. Unfortunately, frustration, anger, and revenge form a very poor basis for formulating a policy response. The results are generally simplistic and, while emotionally satisfying, are seldom successful in the long run. Rhetoric and exaggerated threats of retaliation beyond logical capabilities are self-defeating. Concentrating on short-term aspects of the problem, prescriptive solutions rapidly become out of date. Groups, leaders, and causes change; only the overall threat remains constant.

Terrorism as a separate, generic policy issue is a relatively new phenomenon. Formerly, terrorist activities were seen as a subcategory of some other policy issue. Palestinian terrorism, for example, was a considered a subcategory of the Arab-Israeli problem; terrorism in Northern Ireland was viewed as an extension of bitter relations between Britain and Ireland. With the passage of time and the spread of terrorism, those and other terrorist situations have increasingly been seen as subcategories of international terrorism. As a result, the need is for a global antiterrorism policy, not an upgrading of uncoordinated attempts to deal piecemeal with terrorism on a regional basis.

In order to deal in an objective, coherent, and consistent manner with the many disparate, disjointed, and changing elements that make up the terrorism problem, such a policy must be based on a comprehensive framework. Creating such a framework requires an analysis of both the policy components—the broad operating principles and the various types of measures that make up the policy—and the policy process, the administrative dynamics of the policy.

One of the main difficulties in formulating an antiterrorism policy is the inherent contradiction between the need for a consistent long-term approach and the necessity of dealing with individual situations on their own terms as they arise. To bridge this gap, antiterrorism policy should include a number of general principles, encompassing as broad a range of policy considerations as possible, as a basis of maintaining an effective overall policy direction.

Perhaps the most important principle of all is that antiterrorism policy must be long-term in scope. Terrorism is a continuing problem, and to be successful, governments must be committed to a long-term effort to contain it and reduce it to manageable proportions. Spectacular responses, such as the highly publicized Israeli hostage rescue mission at Entebbe, Uganda, in 1976 and the similar West German mission in Mogadishu, Somalia, the following year, are sometimes appropriate in certain crises, but the ultimate success of antiterrorism policy will depend primarily on its record over the long run.[1]

Policy must also be adaptable to a variety of geopolitical circumstances. Terrorist acts fall into three categories: attacks by domestic groups within their own country; attacks by groups in a foreign country; and attacks outside the country on a country's nationals, properties, or interests. The latter two are certainly international in scope, and the first usually is also, to the degree that it affects the interests of host countries in terms of regional political stability or the safety of foreign nationals. The development of terrorism as a transnational enterprise is what has made it a separate unit of policy concern in the first place. To be effective, antiterrorism policy must address both domestic and international manifestations of the problem.

The point has been made repeatedly that terrorism is not a homogeneous problem. Some groups, such as the Red Army Faction, engage almost exclusively in terrorism and display no inclination or aptitude for political organization. Other groups, such as the Palestinian Liberation Organization, are involved in both violent and nonviolent political activities. Still others, such as the Salvadoran FMLN, conduct terrorism as a part of broader guerrilla warfare tactics. Some groups, such as Peru's Sendero Luminoso, conduct their activities solely within a single country, while others, such as the Japanese Red Army, conduct operations in many countries.

Obviously, no single tactic or set of tactics will succeed in combating so many different manifestations of terrorism, and any policy framework, to be effective, must be broad enough to accommodate an infinite number of tactical considerations. As a general policy principle, no antiterrorism tactic by itself is a panacea, and no tactic should be automatically ruled out.

No successful antiterrorism policy can be formulated or implemented in a vacuum. Counterterrorism is only one of many legitimate interests governments must pursue, and not necessarily the most crucial policy issue facing them in terms of political, social, and economic costs to society. A country's response to terrorism must be tempered by recognition of competing national policy interests. For example, following the Rome and Vienna airport attacks in December 1985 and the corroboration of Libya's role in them, the United States initially ruled out force and reacted with an economic embargo. Its European allies did little to back up the embargo, not out of tacit support for Libya's terrorist policies, but because of the economic and commercial costs they would have incurred in halting trade with Libya. Had the United States attempted to force the Europeans into declaring an embargo on Libya, it could have seriously threatened commercial relations with its trading partners and perhaps even its whole free trade policy, so no attempt was made. The effectiveness of antiterrorism policy must come at the cost of dealing effectively with other equally compelling issues, and those costs must be carefully considered if the policy is to gain the support it needs to be successful.

Another very important ingredient of a successful antiterrorism policy is a special emphasis on international cooperation. In the past the tendency has been for countries to deal unilaterally with terrorist threats involving their own nationals and installations and to cooperate with other countries only when those interests were served. For example, the Lebanese hostage situation has at one time or another involved more than thirty foreign nationals from at least nine different countries. Despite occasional exchanges of information and views, however, each government has worked more or less independently to seek the freedom of its own nationals, almost as if there were a contest to see which one would be the most successful.[2]

Unilateral actions are sometimes the most appropriate response, but they are an insufficient basis for overall policy. The international scope of terrorism requires both commitment and cooperation by all countries. If a country fails to act because a given incident is "someone else's problem," or else acts unilaterally in cases involving its nationals regardless of the impact on other countries, the threat of terrorism will not be mastered.

Any policy that focuses on terrorist groups rather than terrorist acts is virtually certain to make international cooperation more difficult. Even close allies will differ on the legitimacy of specific political groups that use terrorist tactics. For example, to Israel the PLO is a terrorist group, but to much of the rest of the world it is a recognized political organization, some of whose members commit acts of terrorism. To British authorities, the IRA is a terrorist group, but many Irish-Americans reject that designation. On the other hand, most terrorist acts are unarguably criminal, including murder, arson, kidnapping, hijacking, and piracy. Emphasizing the criminality of their acts allows us to avoid value judgments on the political legitimacy of groups engaged in terrorism.

There has been a great deal of discussion about how to deal with terrorists and about whether governments even should. Some governments have felt compelled to bargain over terms with terrorists for the release of hostages or in response to other threats. Both the United States and France bargained with Iran for the release of their nationals held hostage in Lebanon. Others have refused to have any dealings at all with certain groups that have engaged in terrorism; such is the position of Israel with regard to the PLO leadership. As a general rule, a government should always be willing to talk directly with groups involved in terrorism if some good can come of it. The peaceful resolution of any conflict requires dialogue, and dialogue by itself does not necessarily confer approbation or bind a party in advance to any unacceptable concessions.

The question of how to deal with terrorists is more complicated. There is a general consensus that no concessions should be given to terrorists. That principle has been ignored by some countries, and others have used it as an excuse not to negotiate with groups seeking redress of legitimate grievances. The question really comes down to what concessions, if any, a government should be prepared to make. Again as a general rule, governments should be willing to negotiate with terrorist groups to resolve terrorist situations or even broader political problems only if the groups can claim no advantage or reward as a result of their terrorist acts. If terrorism can be seen to be successful, others will always be encouraged to try it.

Terrorism involves the public at large through fear and intimidation. For an antiterrorism policy to be effective, therefore, it must also involve the general public. Not only must there be a general consensus supporting the policy, but special provisions must be made to safeguard the lives and properties of citizens worldwide, including an ongoing dialogue between government officials and the companies and individuals most at risk.

In addition to broad principles, there are a number of specific operational measures that also amount to antiterrorism policy components. They include political measures, law enforcement measures, and low-intensity conflict countermeasures.

The political nature of terrorism distinguishes it from comparable forms of criminal activity and, more importantly, determines in great part the character of the policy response. Even when the government response may be primarily economic or military, the policy requires a political decision. Because there are so many competing interests to be weighed, the guiding principle behind any antiterrorism policy must be expediency: to get the most benefit for the least cost. One must distinguish, however, between political expediency and political opportunism. In order to achieve sufficient international commitment and cooperation, for example, political measures must gain international acceptance. Geoffrey Levitt, in his work on the international legal aspects of terrorism, has suggested four basic characteristics for a collective response: consistency, clarity, credibility, and consensus.[3]

Maintaining a consistent antiterrorism policy is as important as it is difficult. Expediency dictates different responses for the same type of offense, for a country is not likely to take the strong punitive measures against a friendly state that it might take against an antagonist. For example, in October 1985, when Italy refused a U.S. request to extradite Abu al-Abbas, the mastermind of the *Achille Lauro* hijacking, and allowed him to slip quietly out of Italy to Yugoslavia, other U.S.-Italian interests dictated that the U.S. response be muted. Nevertheless, if there is to be international cooperation, governments must be consistent in how they categorize terrorist offenses, not calling them one thing in one case and something else in another. Whether, and to what degree, a country condemns the actor, there should be no exceptions in condemning the act.

While expediency dictates the type of response to a terrorist act, it does not justify using the universally negative image of terrorism as the rationale for responses not really related to terrorism. For example, there have been those who would seize on almost any pretext to brand the Soviet Union as a major supporter of terrorism, not because of its support for terrorism *per se,* but out of general antipathy for an antagonist on the world stage. Fighting communism is an important and laudable free world policy objective, but to do so under the guise of fighting terrorism is questionable, because it makes it harder to persuade communist countries to reduce their support for terrorism, and because it complicates efforts to obtain their active cooperation against terrorism. Political responses to terrorism should be clearly linked to terrorist activity and not to other policy concerns, no matter how compelling those other concerns might be.

Extravagant claims about declaring war on terrorism or ending terrorism are generally counterproductive. Despite President

Reagan's uncompromising stand against terrorism at the beginning of his first term—stimulated in part by the Iran hostage crisis under President Carter—his second administration was never able to resolve the Lebanon hostage issue. There are only so many resources a government can justify expending on a terrorism situation, and not all situations can be resolved quickly or favorably. Moreover, the occasions when the public is most aware of antiterrorist policies—during large-scale crises—are the times when those policies have shown the greatest evidence of having failed, for a crisis is, almost by definition, the result of a failure of preventive measures.

To be credible, antiterrorism policy should reflect what is reasonably possible to accomplish with international cooperation. Terrorists must know that while the international community is not able to eradicate terrorism or to resolve every crisis successfully, it can over the long run make the costs of conducting terrorist acts prohibitively high. In the absence of any form of international political discipline, collective action must be based on consensus. It is equally important for unilateral responses to be taken within a collective framework. In other words, an international consensus should be created to support such actions. Actions taken in the absence of a consensus, such as the U.S. boycott of Libya in 1986, in which the Europeans would not participate, are not likely to succeed. Conversely, the greatest achievements in international cooperation against terrorism have been accomplished through consensus by the Summit Seven countries (the United States, Canada, Great Britain, France, West Germany, and Italy).[4]

In some respects, the U.S. attack on Libya in April 1986 was the exception that proved the rule. While it was a unilateral act taken without the consensus of its main allies (although Britain was highly supportive), it created the climate for a consensus among those allies of the need to take more concrete measures against terrorism, which was reflected in the Tokyo Economic Summit a few weeks later.[5] Because the need for creating and maintaining a consensus is so important, ongoing consultation with close allies is imperative. If a country's response to a terrorist situation is too mild, it can encourage more terrorism; if it is too harsh, it can undermine international cooperation.

Three types of political measures are involved in counterterrorism policy: long-term political measures, immediate diplomatic measures, and public affairs measures.

The ultimate goal of long-term political measures is to alleviate the types of broad political problems that encourage terrorist behavior.

Unfortunately, most of the political problems breeding terrorism appear to defy solution. That is in large part why various groups adopted terrorism in the first place, as a tactic of last resort when more legitimate tactics failed. It is not realistic, therefore, to place too high expectations on efforts to find solutions to such problems. Conversely, it would be simplistic to assume that finding a solution to an underlying political problem would automatically bring an end to terrorism. The Middle East, for example, is too politically volatile to expect all terrorism to cease even if the Arab-Israeli problem were settled. In fact, the prospects of imminent settlement could encourage a surge of terrorism by diehards on both sides. Moreover, the religious confessional strife and daily acts of terrorism in Lebanon vividly show that the Arab-Israeli problem is not the only political problem giving rise to terrorism in the region. Still, the intractability of such problems is no reason to abandon serious efforts to solve them. If their solution is a long-term necessity, so is antiterrorism policy in general. And without addressing the underlying political problems, there will be no progress in seeking to reduce the incidence of terrorism in politically ravaged areas.

Tactical diplomacy is the bread and butter of any foreign policy. In the case of antiterrorism policy, its goals should be to encourage, maintain, and increase international cooperation against terrorism and to isolate terrorist groups and states supporting them until they are induced to cease. Efforts at greater international cooperation should be both bilateral and multilateral. Bilateral diplomacy generally focuses on the mutuality of interests and priorities between two states, with the diplomat using a combination of pressure and persuasion to increase bilateral cooperation against terrorism. Multilateral efforts focus on international organizations and forums such as the United Nations, and regional organizations such as the Organization of American States, the South Asia Association for Regional Cooperation (SAARC), the Association of Southeast Asian Nations (ASEAN), the South Pacific Forum, and the European Community.

One of the more effective international groups in the past decade has been the Summit Seven. Since 1978 it has repeatedly addressed itself to terrorism in declarations that have augmented international treaties dealing with terrorist crimes.[6] Indeed, the Tokyo Economic Summit in May 1986, which closely followed the American raid over Libya, was given over almost entirely to the subject of international terrorism, and the director of the U.S. State Department's Office of Counter-Terrorism, Ambassador Robert Oakley, was summoned from Washington to attend.

Isolating terrorist groups and states supporting terrorism is the primary goal of international cooperation. Many countries are too intimidated to take measures, unilaterally or multinationally, to deprive terrorist groups of mobility, safe haven, and sources of income. Ironically, the lack of terrorist activity in a country can at times be more intimidating than its presence. A number of smaller European countries that thus far have not been targeted by terrorist groups are fearful that they might be if they were to tighten their security procedures and cooperate more openly with their neighbors in interdicting suspected terrorist movements. It is the role of diplomacy to convince such countries that in the long run one cannot buy immunity from terrorism by turning one's back on it.

Isolating states supporting terrorism is even more difficult. Competing economic and political interests usually influence one or more key countries not to cooperate or to make only token efforts at cooperation against specific states supporting terrorism. It is all the more imperative, therefore, that diplomatic efforts to isolate such states be linked to concrete and specific terrorist activities rather than to general political antipathy, and that the punishment fit the crime. The object is not simply to punish states for supporting terrorism but to compel them to cease their support. To the degree that punitive policies create a martyr complex or challenge the "honor" of a country, they are likely to have an effect opposite to the one intended.

Providing and sharing technical assistance is another form of tactical antiterrorism diplomacy. In recent years the United States has instituted a program for training and sharing antiterrorism technology and expertise. While the technical benefits of such assistance programs are certainly valuable, perhaps even more valuable is the greater professional cooperation that results from personal contacts with foreign counterparts.

Despite the importance of public support for efforts to combat terrorism, most democratic countries have a mixed record in promoting their policies, even when they have the desire to do so. The problem stems largely from the fine line between educating the public, which is permissible, and propagandizing, which is not. It is ironic that in countries with free market economies, where the private sector excels at marketing products, the public sector has such a hard time marketing antiterrorism policies.

The first requirement, to use Levitt's criteria, is to formulate a clear, consistent, and credible public policy that can be used in explaining the varied and often seemingly contradictory responses to different terrorist situations. Such a formulation, for example, could state that it is the country's policy, working in cooperation with like-minded civilized states, to employ all the available and appropriate means—political, economic, and the use of force—to increase the costs of conducting international terrorism to the point where groups and states sponsoring them can no longer afford to do so, and to seek to deny any benefit or gain from terrorism to any group engaged in it or any state supporting it. By using such a formulation as a constant point of reference, individual policy and crisis management decisions could be more easily explained and accepted. Even where public opposition arises, it can be based on a more accurate understanding of what the policy-makers faced, which would be invaluable in creating long-term support for antiterrorism policy.

Having a constant point of reference would also help in dealing with the media. It has been noted that policy-makers and the media have very different perspectives regarding the use of information before the public. The former are primarily interested in explaining and justifying responses to generally very complicated situations, whereas the media are primarily interested in telling—and selling—a story. Complexities and nuances generally detract from a story. By using a clear, consistent public policy frame of reference, the policy-maker can supply the conceptual simplicity that the reporter requires without resorting to simplistic polemics that ill-serve the decision-maker, the media, and the public alike.

Another facet of public affairs is the warning process, a truly vital though thankless task for which governments must take the main responsibility. After virtually every significant terrorist incident, there are those who charge that officials responsible for public safety were derelict in their duties by not adequately publicizing existing indications that an attack was imminent. In nondemocratic countries, this often results in public outcries demanding the heads (literally or otherwise) of those officials; in democratic countries, such outcries can be accompanied by demands for additional legislation to ensure better warning procedures.

Adequate warning procedures constitute an invaluable aspect of antiterrorism policy. In the United States they include a variety of responses. All threats are evaluated by the intelligence community to determine the level of credibility. If a threat is specific and credible, and cannot be countered, warnings will be issued to the appropriate individuals, facilities, or companies and to responsible foreign government officials. Even where the threat to U.S. carriers and passengers is not specific as to timing, airline, or flight, the Federal Aviation Administration can issue an Aviation Security Bulletin to carriers and to U.S. diplomatic posts to seek the cooperation of local security officials. Most threats are aimed against official Americans and facilities, not at the public at large, and the volume is high. Specific threats against U.S. diplomatic personnel and facilities average about two every three days, for example.

If there is a threat to the public at large, the State Department issues a travel advisory. There are two types, a "caution," which describes unusual situations and travel conditions, and a "warning," which describes conditions involving the potential for physical violence and danger. Such advisories were already in effect in Lebanon, Colombia, and Peru when a number of kidnappings and deaths occurred in those countries in the past few years.

In the final analysis, whether or not to warn the public and with what degree of urgency are basically a matter of judgment, not procedure. Too zealous a policy of warning the public of potential threats could result in the short run in excessive anxiety and panic. In the long run it could inure the public to the warning process altogether, opening the government to charges of crying wolf. The economic costs of false alarms to international business, airline travel, and tourism could also be high. On the other hand, failure to inform the public of potential threats could result in unconscionable and preventable bodily injury and loss of life. To ensure the best results, governments should be held accountable for the warning process, but the public should be made to realize that it is not an exact science.

In addition to the more traditional public affairs aspects of antiterrorism policy, a strong effort must be made to maintain a sympathetic and sensitive relationship with the families of victims, both during crises and in the period following. Such an effort is important not merely for the public relations benefits but because of the humanitarian need to offer comfort to those engulfed in personal tragedies. Crisis periods are among the most difficult periods for showing such sensitivity, given the trying and harrowing conditions in which crisis managers are forced to work, but in the days and weeks following a crisis people turn their attention to other problems. For those reasons, care should be taken that sympathetic people who are professionally trained to deal with the public in such circumstances are not only always on call but kept fully informed as the crisis unfolds so that they can provide as much information and, more to the point, as much comfort as possible to victim families. This is an area in which many governments, including that of the United States, have been notably lacking.

Law enforcement measures form one of the most important weapons in the antiterrorism arsenal. In the absence of a legal definition of terrorism, no one can be convicted of terrorism *per se*, only of criminal acts. A primary goal of any antiterrorism policy, therefore, should be to depoliticize terrorist acts and treat them as purely criminal acts. By treating terrorism as a law enforcement problem, one can seek to avoid the conflicting political interests that inevitably dilute political responses.

There are two principal types of law enforcement apparatus to consider in creating an antiterrorism policy framework: domestic law enforcement and international law. Virtually all terrorist acts are criminal acts that come under the jurisdiction of domestic law enforcement agencies. Those agencies have as their primary responsibility the maintenance of law and order within a country, which means to investigate crimes and to bring criminals to justice. They usually have specialized units (SWAT teams and hostage negotiators) to handle terrorist crises. Once the terrorist is captured, it is the responsibility of the judicial system to see that he or she gets a fair trial under due process of law (assuming there is due process in the country where he is caught).

Technically, there is little or no difference legally between terrorist crimes and any other violent crimes. Nevertheless, because of their political content and international scope, detecting and apprehending those who commit terrorist acts present a very special set of problems. Law enforcement agencies must work more closely with other police departments, with intelligence services, and with the military than might otherwise be the case. If terrorist activities result in a large-scale breakdown of civil order, for example, the military may have to be brought in to help pacify the population.

Application of domestic law to international cases has caused difficulty. One problem is legal coverage. Many countries have had to supplement their criminal statutes to cover unforeseen contingencies. For example, when a number of Americans were killed in the brutal terrorist attacks on the Rome and Vienna airports in December 1985, the FBI had no jurisdiction to intervene overseas, because under U.S.

law murder of private American citizens is a state crime, not a federal crime. The U.S. Congress has since passed legislation expanding federal jurisdiction to cover this and other terrorist crimes.

Another problem has to do with sovereignty and jurisdiction. When terrorists commit crimes against a country's nationals and property abroad, national law enforcement agencies cannot operate outside national boundaries without the permission of host governments. There is also the question of under whose legal jurisdiction the crime should be prosecuted. When the *Achille Lauro* returned to Egypt, jurisdiction over the hijackers could have gone to Egypt, where they were apprehended; to Italy, which owned the ship; or to the United States, because the murder victim was American. The question of jurisdiction is particularly acute for the United States, since the vast majority of terrorists attacks against Americans occur outside its borders. For the United States, therefore, international antiterrorism cooperation is as crucial for law enforcement as for diplomacy.

In the absence of an international enforcement mechanism, compliance with international law is largely a political matter, requiring international consensus and commitment. In some respects, therefore, international law can be seen as a medium for increasing and maintaining international cooperation against terrorism. There is no single convention proscribing terrorism. Rather, a series of multilateral conventions have been concluded over the years committing the signatories to take criminal jurisdiction over specified crimes associated with terrorism. They include the Hague Convention of 1970, which covers aircraft hijacking; the Montreal Convention of 1971, which addresses aircraft sabotage; the 1975 Convention on Prevention and Punishment of Crimes Against Internationally Protected Persons (mainly referring to diplomats); the 1979 Convention Against the Taking of Hostages; and the 1979 Convention on Physical Protection of Nuclear Materials. In March 1988 the Convention for the Suppression of Unlawful Acts Against the Safety of Maritime Navigation was initialed in Rome. These conventions are far from comprehensive, and many countries have yet to ratify them. Collectively, however, they provide a sound basis for international legal sanctions against terrorism, particularly when augmented by the declarations of the Summit Seven.

Another important instrument is the bilateral treaty. One of the most important aspects of international cooperation from the law enforcement point of view is the ability to extradite accused terrorists to stand trial for their crimes. Extradition is an accepted feature in antiterrorism conventions and declarations, and the Bonn Declaration of the Summit Seven states, "In cases where a country refuses extradition or prosecution of those who have hijacked an aircraft and/or do not return such aircraft, the heads of state and government are jointly resolved that their governments should take immediate action to cease all flights to that country." The Venice Declaration of 1987 applied the same conditions to aircraft sabotage.

A key feature of antiterrorism policy, therefore, should be to expand the number of extradition treaties with other countries and to obtain their commitment to uphold their own judicial findings of extraditability for terrorist crimes in cases they do not wish to prosecute. With such treaties, and with a dedicated effort to treat as many terrorist acts as possible as crimes rather than political acts, it should be possible to reduce the number of terrorists who can avoid being brought to justice.

Most extradition treaties include an exemption for political offenses, and terrorists regularly invoke that exemption in order to avoid prosecution. A case in point was an incident involving Northern Irish terrorists who fled to the United States and claimed political exemption to avoid extradition to Britain. In order to close this loophole, the United States and Britain negotiated a supplemental treaty to the effect that political exclusion clauses should not impede extradition for violent crimes to democratic countries that respect due process of law and provide for a fair trial. It took several years for the treaty to be ratified by the U.S. Senate because of strong opposition from Irish-American constituents.

Mutual legal assistance treaties are another form of bilateral cooperation that can aid in combating terrorism. Such a treaty is intended to enable law enforcement authorities from one country to obtain evidence from another country in a form admissible in court and provides for assistance at all stages of the law enforcement process, including investigations. This can be very important to law enforcement officials, who are obligated to make investigations of possible crimes even if the subjects are never extradited. If the investigation is postponed until jurisdiction and the decision to prosecute is determined, the case may be too old for evidence to be gathered. The United States has such treaties with Switzerland, Italy, the Netherlands, and Turkey, and treaties with Belgium, Canada, Mexico, Thailand, and Great Britain are awaiting ratification.[7]

In addition to these formal legal instruments, two other forms of legal measures are important to antiterrorism policy. One is the informal working relationships that law enforcement officials develop with their overseas counterparts and with such international bodies as Interpol. Professional bonds have always existed among law enforcement officials and can be greatly strengthened with encouragement from the highest political levels. This cooperation is all the more important when the countries involved have different legal systems, as between the common law of the United States and Britain and the civil law of the rest of Western Europe. The two systems have different rules of evidence and trial procedures, and, of course, the different countries have different statutes regarding the same offenses. Coordinating different legal systems is an important goal in any antiterrorism policy framework.

The other law enforcement measure against terrorism is for a country or its nationals to become litigants directly involved in judicial proceedings in another country, as in the trial of the Lebanese terrorist George Ibrahim Abdallah in Paris. The U.S. government and the widow of Lieut. Col. Charles Ray, one of the victims of Abdallah's group, became civil parties to the case. Abdallah ultimately received a life sentence for the murder of Ray and an Israeli diplomat. Similarly, the U.S. government assisted passengers in the TWA hijacking and the parents of the U.S. Navy diver Robert Strethem, who was murdered, to become civil parties in the pretrial stage of the prosecution of the terrorist Muhammad Ali Hammadi in West Germany. Hammadi also received a life sentence.

Terrorism is often seen by military analysts as a new kind of warfare that must be countered in kind. It has been demonstrated that terrorism is too broad a phenomenon to be included wholly within the concept of warfare. Although some manifestations of terrorism are closely associated with guerrilla warfare, others are not. One military analyst makes the distinction between "local internal terrorism," which he describes as the low-intensity stage of guerrilla warfare, and "nonterritorial terrorism," which is not associated with an insurgency.[8] This approach, while adding an element of precision, tends to confuse the issue when it comes to deciding on a response. In looking at the component parts of an antiterrorism policy, terrorism should be considered low-intensity conflict whether or not it is associated with guerrilla warfare. But the tactical response to it, whether political, law enforcement, or military, should be kept distinct from counterinsurgency measures.

The most important military measures in combating terrorism deal with hostage rescue operations. Many countries have special units to deal with hostage barricade situations, some under police services and others under military services, but all basically military.[9] These units are frequently, but not always, a part of larger special operations structures. The training and doctrine of each unit is held secret to deprive potential opponents of any advantage. One problem, though, is that each country has adopted slightly different methods, so joint operations with units of other countries is out of the question. Nevertheless, a degree of cooperation does exist among the units of friendly countries.

Political interests are a major constraint in hostage rescue operations. For example, the United States strives to cooperate fully with the host government of a country where a crisis is occurring, either offering to undertake the rescue operation itself or providing advice and consultation to the host government. Operating in an unfriendly environment, such as the aborted Iran rescue mission in 1979, bears a much higher potential political cost as well as a higher risk of human casualties.

A second military response to terrorism is a retaliatory raid such as the U.S. bombing of Libya on April 15, 1986. Evaluating such a raid on the basis of purely military criteria is irrelevant, because no military mission is involved. Such raids are basically psychological and political, aimed at convincing the government involved that the price of continuing to support terrorist activities is prohibitive. By political standards, the Libya raid must be judged a success. Not only was Colonel Qadhafi at least temporarily constrained from further acts of terrorism, but the raid persuaded the West Europeans and Japan to increase antiterrorism cooperation.

The possible benefits of reprisal raids should not overshadow the political risks, however. Such a raid is intended as a deterrent. But if it fails, or if a combatant is captured and paraded publicly, it can have just the opposite effect. In demonstrating U.S. determination against terrorism, the Libya raid probably just made up for the psychological losses of the aborted Iran hostage rescue mission. Even more important, the political risks of a reprisal raid must be carefully weighed. The use of force is an extreme measure, and to justify its use to one's friends and allies it can only be used under extreme circumstances or provocation.

A third possible response is to restore or maintain civil order. It was mentioned above that this is primarily a police function, but situations can arise that are beyond the capabilities of a civilian police force, and then martial law becomes a necessity. Such was the case when the British sent military units to keep the peace in Northern Ireland. However, using the military for this function can bear its own risks. The military is generally neither trained nor equipped to win over the loyalty of the public. That is usually a police function.

Security measures provide a static defense against terrorist attacks. Alone they cannot stop terrorism, but they can discourage targeting specific sites and personnel. The spectacular rise in terrorism in the last two decades has necessitated an upgrading of security measures for possible targets, both persons and property. Government officials and high-ranking corporate officers, both prime targets overseas, routinely learn defensive driving and other protective measures; sensitive or symbolic physical installations, such as embassies and military installations, are designed to resist attack.

As an example of the increased importance of security, the U.S. State Department's former Office of Security, which was involved largely in internal security of the Foreign Service—investigating security violations, conducting background investigations, and the like—is now the Bureau of Diplomatic Security, with an annual budget of hundreds of millions of dollars earmarked for the protection of officials and installations abroad. Other national security related agencies and departments that could make likely targets at home or abroad have also upgraded their security personnel and procedures. Multinational corporations with worldwide business interests have done likewise.

Providing adequate security for American embassies and consulates overseas creates a special problem. Their function is to be open to the general public, overseas Americans as well as foreigners, but the more accessible they are, the less secure from terrorist attack. The best that can be achieved, therefore, is a compromise of accessibility and security that will please neither the diplomat nor the security officer. Besides, securing every embassy and consulate from terrorist attack would cost billions of dollars, far more money than is available. Decisions must be made about which sites to fortify and to what extent, knowing full well that if millions are spent building a more secure embassy where there is no visible threat, the decision will be subject to harsh criticism. If, on the other hand, there is an attack at an unlikely site, there will be even stronger criticism for not having spent millions. With both human lives and national pride at stake, these decisions are exceedingly difficult to make.

Among the most important security measures for any antiterrorism policy must be to create and maintain close communication with the private sector. That includes not only airline officials and other passenger lines, but businessmen working and regularly traveling overseas. American businessmen abroad are a prime target of anti-American terrorism, and many companies have greatly increased their own security capabilities as a result. It is imperative for the private and public sectors to work closely on this common problem if both are to be successful, and a special effort should be made to coordinate the many agencies and departments in the government that could make such a collaboration a success.

Of all the components of antiterrorism policy, intelligence measures are perhaps the most important. No policy can be successful if one does not know who the enemy is and where and when he is most likely to strike. Since terrorist operations are covert, efforts to obtain this information must also be largely covert. The importance of intelligence to political, law enforcement, military, and security measures cannot be overstated. Even in diplomacy, intelligence that bears upon responsibility for or complicity in terrorist acts is a key element in making a case for singling out groups or states for punitive policy responses.

There is almost no debate on the need to place a high priority on intelligence collection against terrorism-related targets. Because lives are at stake, the timely acquisition of tactical intelligence on planned or suspected terrorist attacks is vital if adequate countermeasures are to be effective. Terrorism is a long-term problem, however, so other types of information are equally important: biographical data, organizational structures and plans, operational strengths and weaknesses, modus operandi, technical skills, and terrorist sympathizers and contacts.[10] There is nothing unique about terrorism that would require special collection methods. Nevertheless, the clandestine nature of terrorist organizations, their organization into small groups or cells, their maintenance of security procedures, and the availability of safe havens for them make terrorist groups an especially difficult target for intelligence collection.

With stiff competition for limited resources, there must be a commitment at the highest level to antiterrorism intelligence gathering, even at the cost of less collection against other important targets. Terrorists often seek publicity for their acts and may even leave a "signature" at the scene of the crime, yet they assiduously avoid leaving evidence behind that can lead to their capture or conviction. As a result, most of the raw intelligence and criminal evidence implicating terrorists is circumstantial and extremely difficult to collect. That simply underscores the importance of obtaining as much raw intelligence as possible against terrorist groups. Expert intelligence analysis to formulate a plausible and convincing explanation for what has happened or is likely to happen in the future is no less necessary. Since the intelligence is usually fragmentary at best, this can be a difficult process.

The primary intelligence consumers in one's own government are the policy-makers who must decide how to respond to a terrorist threat or situation. There is a natural tension between intelligence officers and policy-makers. The intelligence collector is concerned with protecting sources and methods of collection, and the analyst is concerned with interpreting the situation as accurately as possible. The policy-maker, on the other hand, is often part of an advocacy process, hence uses information to build a case for choosing one course of action or response over others. The value of the information and analysis often depends on how widely they can be used. U.S. policy-makers had an interest in letting the world know about Libya's direct involvement in the 1986 Berlin disco bombing, but the intelligence community did not want to divulge it for fear of exposing the source of the information.

There is another source of tension. Intelligence analysts do not like to state unequivocal conclusions without conclusive evidence, whereas policy-makers do not like to deal in uncertainties and probabilities. When there is political pressure to take strong action, the policy-maker is tempted to restate the analyst's best and most educated guess as gospel or, conversely, to exploit the analyst's equivocation to say no compelling evidence exists when it is politically expedient to do nothing. In the interests of sound policy, however, there should be a clear understanding on the policy-maker's part about the nature of the intelligence information and the bases for the analyst's conclusions.

Judicial and law enforcement agencies both collect and consume intelligence. Prosecutors generally have to make a case linking a group to a specific act based on an interpretation of pieces of raw intelligence and circumstantial evidence gathered by criminal investigators. That is not to say that a conclusive case cannot be made on circumstantial evidence alone, but it makes the job that much more difficult.

Law enforcement agencies generally look on the information gathered quite differently from intelligence services, however. Information gathered by criminal investigators must conform to rules of evidence and must be available to be used openly in a court of law to convict a criminal. Intelligence information need not conform to the rules of evidence and, in order to protect collection sources and methods, can seldom be introduced in court. Nevertheless, since law enforcement agencies are also charged with public security, they have become major consumers of terrorism intelligence.

Because of the international scope of terrorism and the recent rise in the number of terrorist incidents around the world, intergovernmental intelligence sharing on terrorist activities has also gained importance. Increased sharing of information following cooperative measures taken in the wake of the U.S. raid on Libya, for example, has played a great part in the reduction of terrorist incidents in Europe in the past few years.

Terrorism is covert action generally conducted by fanatical and ruthless people, and there are circumstances in which countering it with covert action should be considered. One must never forget, however, that covert action is a high-risk tactic. If it fails because of faulty intelligence or miscalculation, if official involvement is discovered with no plausible denial, or if captives are taken, the terrorist can gain a huge psychological advantage. Moreover, democratic governments must always institute adequate safeguards to ensure that covert action is not abused. The United States, for example, has banned political assassinations, no matter how tempting such an expedient option might appear to be. Covert action is a short-term tactic and must always be viewed within the long-term perspective of counterterrorism policy. It is no quick-fix solution to terrorism.

Since long before anyone perceived the need for a comprehensive antiterrorism policy, the individual policy components—diplomacy, law enforcement, investigations, intelligence, and the use of force—have all been the responsibility of some particular agency, ministry, or department of government in virtually every country in the world. Those responsibilities are jealously guarded, and attempts to reassign them always result in bureaucratic turf wars and rivalries. A few years ago a close ally of the United States declined to have combined diplomatic, police, military, and intelligence discussions with the Americans, not because the various representatives would not talk to their American counterparts but because they would not talk in each other's presence. One of the most important elements of a policy framework, therefore, is to ensure internal cooperation and coordination of the many agencies involved. Before a government can successfully cooperate with other governments, it must learn to cooperate with itself.

There is no single formula for organizing a government to combat terrorism. Government organization and policy processes vary greatly from country to country, as do the nature of the terrorist threat and public perceptions of the threat. In small countries with relatively small bureaucracies, coordination can be effected on a more personal basis. Large countries with large bureaucracies, however, must reorganize slowly and carefully to prevent their many agencies from working at cross purposes. Whatever the organizational arrangements, there must be a recognized division of labor among bureaucratic entities dedicated to policy formulation, coordination, and implementation. Bureaucratic accommodation is absolutely vital to the success of the policy.

There are a number of ways to establish ongoing policy coordination. One way would be to create a department, ministry, or agency to carry out all antiterrorism policy, headed by a sort of antiterrorism "czar." Though this idea has never gained acceptance in the U.S. government, it was privately favored by several members of the vice president's antiterrorism task force in the mid-1980s. Theoretically, it has the advantage of reducing bureaucratic infighting, but in practice it would probably raise the level of infighting to a higher political level, where it could be even more debilitating to the policy process. It would also create a tremendously wasteful overlapping of related responsibilities with other departments, ministries, and agencies that few governments could afford.

A more pragmatic approach would be to create a government-wide system for antiterrorist policy coordination, headed by someone at the senior working level to monitor the activities of all government agencies involved in countering terrorism and to make sure that they are not working at cross purposes. The senior coordinator could be assisted by a coordinating committee made up of senior representatives from foreign affairs, defense, intelligence, finance and economics, justice and law enforcement, and other involved agencies, such as customs, immigration, civil aviation, Coast Guard, border patrol, drug enforcement, and nuclear energy.

The United States has already developed a structure of that sort. The State Department Office of Counter-Terrorism was established in the 1970s. The director is the coordinator for all antiterrorism policy at the senior working level. He chairs a Policy Planning Committee on Terrorism, which serves as the senior working-level coordinating group and has several subcommittees to look into special problems requiring interagency cooperation. The choice of the State Department as the lead agency reflects the predominantly overseas nature of the terrorist threat to Americans. Other countries have a proportionately larger domestic threat, in which case a ministry of interior might be more appropriate. Israel's coordinator is attached to the Prime Minister's office.

One of the greatest benefits of a policy coordination approach is the degree to which personal relationships that develop through regular contact help smooth over potential frictions among the various agencies. An essential element of an effective comprehensive policy is the willingness of politicians and professionals to work together in placing general policy goals ahead of narrow bureaucratic rivalries.

For crisis management situations as well as for higher political deliberations, the direct involvement of senior political officials in the antiterrorism policy process becomes absolutely essential. In crisis periods time is often the worst enemy. Governments must be able to make quick decisions regarding whether to dispatch a hostage rescue force or hostage negotiators, whether to request extradition, and so on. Most hostage rescue forces around the world are primed to depart for the scene of the incident within a few hours of first hearing of the incident. Communications must also be maintained at an appropriately high level at home and with one's diplomatic representatives and foreign governments overseas in the event that the crisis involves foreign nationals or occurs abroad.

For this purpose the United States has also created a senior political level antiterrorist coordinating group, which includes the National Security Adviser, the Under Secretary of State for Political Affairs, the Deputy Director of the FBI, and representatives from the Defense Department and the CIA. The exact bureaucratic structure for coordinating those officials is subject to change with each new administration, but the basic representation remains the same.

There is also a need to create procedures for crisis management at the working level. In the United States the principal departments and agencies involved generally maintain around-the-clock task force operations linked by secure communications to each other and to the White House. Those groups monitor the crisis, maintaining communications with American diplomatic and military commands nearest the crisis site, informing senior officials as the crisis unfolds, informing and making contact with victims' families, and coordinating announcements and statements for the press. The ultimate test of antiterrorism policy for any country is not the high drama but how well the process works on a quiet day-to-day, long-term basis.

Evaluating the policy process is in some respects like painting a picture of a moving train. By the time you have created an accurate picture of it, the scene has changed and you obliged to begin again. Antiterrorism policy is a comparatively new concept, and governments are still in the process of rearranging their policy-making and bureaucratic structures to cope with it. A great deal of progress has been made, but as the severity of the problem grows, a great deal more must be done. To succeed, adequate resources and high standards of professionalism are certainly needed. More than that, however, ultimate success will depend on patience, dedication, and a long-term commitment.

No study of this kind is entirely complete without a look at the future. At no time since World War II, however, has it been more difficult to predict what the future might hold in store. The momentous political changes occurring in the Soviet Union and Eastern Europe raise the distinct possibility that the relatively stable bipolar world we have known for the past four and a half decades might be coming to an end, and with few signs of what the new order might look like. In 1992 European economic integration might change the whole international economic landscape as well, with incalculable political and social consequences. At the same time some of the seemingly insoluble political and economic problems that have given rise to so much terrorism—the Arab-Israeli problem, the Northern Ireland problem, maldistribution of wealth and political power in Latin America—show almost no signs of constructive change. Economically, the poor countries are getting poorer, with the terms of trade for most single-commodity export countries worse now than they were right after World War II and unchecked population growth wiping out the modest economic gains those countries might have made in recent years. Narco-terrorism, which is supporting a growing terrorist infrastructure in Colombia and Peru, shows every sign of increasing in intensity in the years to come.

A key question is what effect the easing of the Cold War might have on terrorism. Will the Soviet Union cease to support "wars of national liberation" at the levels it has previously? If so, will its clients, such as Cuba and Nicaragua, continue their efforts to spread armed struggle and communist revolution without Soviet help, or will they follow Moscow's lead and seek a political accommodation with the West? Will terrorist organizations cease to pursue their activities just because a major source of supply has been cut off, or will their desperation over being abandoned make them all the more fanatical? How will right-wing groups be effected by global political economic changes?

Welcome as an easing of Cold War tensions is, the direct effect on terrorism is not likely to be so great as one might hope. One result will be to demonstrate that the rest of the world has never been quite the extension of East–West rivalries that the superpowers have so long assumed they were. Most terrorist organizations, including Marxist groups, and most states supporting them are far more preoccupied with their own local problems than they are with where they fit into superpower calculations. If a lessening of Cold War tensions results in a growing disinclination of both superpowers to support an insurgency, neither antagonist would be fatally disadvantaged. Narco-terrorists, who have become financially independent of outside sources of support, would be even less affected by global power politics. Moreover, there is no certainty that a multipolar world will be any more stable than the bipolar world has been with its balance of terror. It might be harder, not easier, to address some of the more intractable political problems fueling terrorist activity.

Much of today's terrorism is based on ethnic, national, and religious causes far removed from the Cold War, and even the left-wing insurgency movements are driven by local social, economic, and political inequities far more than by Marxist ideology. The conditions giving rise to their activities are not likely to change as a result of an easing of global tensions.

This rather somber projection is not to say that the same terrorist leaders, groups, and state supporters will necessarily continue to be predominant. In time Colonel Qadhafi, Ahmad Jabril, and Abimael Guzmán will disappear; Libya will no longer support terrorism; and such groups as the PFLP-GC and Sendero Luminoso will either be crushed or will disband (with or without attainment of their aims). But there is every likelihood that old leaders will be replaced by new leaders, and that old groups will be replaced by new ones. So long as there are political, economic, and social inequities, and so long as there are individuals who will gravitate toward violence in reaction to those inequities, there will be terrorism. Its low cost, availability, and psychological effectiveness are all too tempting for it simply to go away.

APPENDIX

Profiles of Leading Terrorist Groups

Literally hundreds of groups throughout the world are engaged in terrorist acts. One of the most comprehensive data bases of terrorist groups, compiled by Ariel Merari and Anat Kurz of the Jaffee Center of Strategic Studies of Tel Aviv University, lists more than 600. Coming up with a formula for choosing which of these groups should be included among the following profiles was virtually impossible. In the absence of any acceptable standard criteria for what constitutes a terrorist group, the task was of necessity subjective and often arbitrary.

Good arguments can be made for the inclusion of many groups that were left out. Consideration was given to about twenty additional active groups, mainly from Central and South America. Conversely, there are bound to be arguments over some of the choices that were included. In any case, it was the considered view of the author that the roughly eighty groups that appear below have been among the most active terrorist organizations over the last twenty years, though some are presently dormant.

The reader will also note some inconsistencies from profile to profile and the frequent use of the terms "not known" and "not available." Information about nearly all terrorist groups is sketchy and occasionally contradictory. That which appears in these profiles and in the text is derived from many sources, and an attempt has been made to verify it from more than one source. In some cases, however, adequate verification was not possible. The profiles nonetheless represent a collation of the best available information.

Action Directe (AD)

Full name/English translation: L'Action Directe (Direct Action)
Year founded and country of origin: 1979, France
Ideology/ethnic–national identification: New Left, Marxist-Leninist, anarchist
Leaders: Jean Marc Rouillan, Nathalie Menigon, Joelle Aubran, and Georges Cipriani (all arrested in 1987), Frédéric Oriach (arrested in 1982), Regis Schlicter, André Olivière
Membership: 50–250; middle-class French
Base(s) of Operations: Paris, Lyons, southern France
Operational areas: Paris, southern France, Belgium,
Targets: Domestic and foreign personalities; political and economic targets; murdered George Besse, Chairman of Renault, 1986
Organizational structure and links: Cell structure; broke into domestic and international wings in 1982; linked to other New Left groups (RAF, Red Brigades, etc.), as well as LARF and other Palestinian groups
Publications: None known

Abu Nidal Organization (ANO)

Full name/English translation: Majlis al-Thawri al-Fatah (Fatah Revolutionary Council; has also used Black June, Black September, Revolutionary Organization of Socialist Muslims)
Year founded and country of origin: Broke off from al-Fatah in 1974 over latter's moratorium on international terrorism
Ideology/ethnic–national identification: Palestinian nationalist, pan-Arabist
Leaders: Sabri al-Banna (Abu Nidal)
Membership: Estimated 50 hard core; 1,000 followers
Base(s) of operations: Libya, Syria, Lebanon, Eastern Europe, Western Europe, India, Pakistan, Central and South America
Operational areas: Middle East, Western Europe, South Asia
Targets: Israelis, moderate Palestinians, al-Fatah, Egyptians, Americans, Turks, Western Europeans; responsible for Rome and Vienna airport attacks in 1985, Pan Am airline hijacking in Karachi in 1986, attack on a synagogue in Istanbul in 1986, and attacks in Khartoum Sudan in 1988 killing five Britons and wounding five Americans

Organizational structure and links: Tightly knit, semimilitary cell structure of three to seven persons linked in self-contained 40-member units with each cell training for a specific operation; uses dormant agents; tactical links to West European terrorist groups and some non-Fatah Palestinian groups
Publications: No regular periodical known

African National Congress (ANC)

See *Umkhonto we Sizwe (MK)*

Alfaro Vive ¡Carajo! (AVC)

Full name/English translation: Alfaro Vive ¡Carajo! (Alfaro Lives, Expletive! *Carajo* is a strong expletive in Spanish with no precise translation into English. Its use by the group could be a play on words with *caraje:* courage); also known as Eloy Alfaro Popular Armed Forces
Year founded and country of origin: c. 1983, Ecuador
Ideology/ethnic—national identification: Marxist (Maoist or Albanian); favors "social reform," opposes oligarchy and imperialism, including foreign, particularly U.S., interests
Leaders: Most of senior leadership was arrested or killed in 1986–87; current leadership unknown
Membership: 50–200, middle-class students
Base(s) of operations: Quito and Guayaquil
Operational areas: Urban areas of Ecuador, particularly Quito and Guayaquil
Targets: Economic targets, police, kidnapping
Organizational structure and links: Personalized leadership and cell structure; links with M-19, MRTA, Cuba, and Nicaragua
Publications: None known

All-India Sikh Students' Federation

Full name/English translation: All-India Sikh Students' Federation
Year founded and country of origin: Early 1980s, India
Ideology/ethnic—national identification: Marxist, Sikh separatist

Leaders: Not known
Membership: Not known
Base(s) of operations: Punjab, India
Operational areas: India
Targets: Not available
Organizational structure and links: Political front organization used as recruiting ground for Sikh terrorists
Publications: None known

Arab Liberation Front (ALF)

Full name/English translation: Jibhat al-Tahrir al-'Aribiya (Arab Liberation Front)
Year founded and country of origin: 1969, Iraq
Ideology/ethnic–national identification: Palestinian nationalist, Ba'thist
Leaders: Abd al-Rahim Ahmad, Asad Aka, Jamil Shahada, Abd al-Majid al-Rifai
Membership: 500
Base(s) of operations: Baghdad
Operational areas: Middle East
Targets: Israel
Organizational structure and links: Member organization of the PLO; under Iraqi operational control
Publications: *al-Thawra al-Arabi (The Arab Revolution)*

Arab Nationalists' Movement (ANM)

Full name/English translation: Harakat al-Watiniyin al-Arabiyin (Movement of Arab Nationalists)
Year founded and country of origin: c. 1949, Beirut, Lebanon
Ideology/ethnic–national identification: Palestinian Nationalist, Marxist
Leaders: Included George Habbash, Naif Hawatamah, Ahmad al-Khatib (Wadi Haddad, deceased, was also a founding member)
Membership: Not known
Base(s) of operations: Lebanon, Occupied Territories, Kuwait, South Yemen

Operational areas: Not available
Targets: Not available
Organizational structure and links: Not operationally involved in terrorism, many of its members belong to radical Palestinian groups, including PFLP, PFLP-GC, PFLP-Special Command, LARF; South Yemen regime is of ANM origin
Publications: None known

Armenian Secret Army for the Liberation of Armenia (ASALA)

Full name/English translation: Armenian Secret Army for the Liberation of Armenia; also uses 9th of June Organization, 3rd of October Movement, Armenian Red Army
Year founded and country of origin: 1975, Lebanon
Ideology/ethnic–national identification: Armenian nationalist; Marxist-Leninist
Leaders: Monte Melkonian (Revolutionary Movement branch), Alex Ynikomeshian, _____ Keshishian, (Hagop Hagopian, Militant branch, killed March 1988)
Membership: 40 plus
Base(s) of operations: Beirut, Damascus, Cyprus, Athens, Paris, Los Angeles
Operational areas: North America, Western Europe, Turkey, Cyprus, Lebanon, Syria, Iran
Targets: Turkish diplomats, officials, and interests; French and Swiss diplomats
Organizational structure and links: Highly centralized cell structure; uses special units for special operations and often uses cover names
Publications: *Hay Bakar, Gamk* (Paris-based Armenian paper)

Babbar Khalsa

Full name/English translation: Babbar Khalsa
Year founded and country of origin: early 1980s, Punjab, India
Ideology/ethnic–national identification: Sikh separatist, emphasizes Sikh religious indoctrinations, particularly *sant sipahi* (the saint-

soldier), based on the life of the tenth Sikh guru, Gorbind Singh (d. 1709)
Leaders: Not known
Membership: Not known
Base(s) of operations: India, United States, Canada
Operational areas: Punjab, Canada, United States
Targets: Indian political and economic targets
Organizational structure and links: Highly centralized, cell structure
Publications: None known

Bhindranwale Tiger Force of Khalistan

Full name/English translation: Bhindranwale Tiger Force of Khalistan
Year founded and country of origin: Early 1980s, India
Ideology/ethnic–national identification: Sikh separatist
Leaders: Gurbachan Singh Monochahal
Membership: Not known
Base(s) of operations: Punjab, India
Operational areas: India
Targets: Indian government officials and Hindus
Organizational structure and links: Not known
Publications: None known

Black Order

Full name/English translation: Ordine Nero (Black Order)
Year founded and country of origin: 1974, Italy; successor to New Order Organization, banned in 1973
Ideology/ethnic–national identification: Neo-Fascist, Italian national-ist
Leaders: Mario Affatigato, Pierluigi Concutelli
Membership: 300
Base(s) of operations: Italy
Operational areas: Italy
Targets: Jews, leftist personalities and property
Organizational structure and links: Not known
Publications: None known

Black September Organization (BSO)

Full name/English translation: Munathamat Sabtambir al-Aswad (Black September Organization)
Year founded and country of origin: 1970 by al-Fatah
Ideology/ethnic–national identification: Palestinian nationalist; pan-Arabist
Leaders: Salah Khalaf
Membership: 15–30
Base(s) of operations: PLO camps in Lebanon
Operational areas: Israel and the Arab world
Targets: Israel, United States
Organizational structure and links: Terrorist wing of al-Fatah, 1970–74
Publications: See al-Fatah

Chukaku-Ha

Full name/English translation: Chukaku-Ha (Central Core Faction, Middle Core or Nucleus Faction), League of Revolutionary Communists–National Committee
Year founded and country of origin: 1963, Japan
Ideology/ethnic–national identification: New Left, Marxist-Leninist
Leaders: Hidimitsu Horiguchi, Shirai Roo, Kitakooji Toshi, Fujiwara, Takuji Mukai, Higeo Yamamori
Membership: c. 200 hard core, 3,000 followers; students and workers
Base(s) of operations: Tokyo
Operational areas: Tokyo, Osaka
Targets: Government facilities, particularly Tokyo International Airport at Narita and Kansai Airport, Osaka
Organizational structure and links: Cell structure; has shown no interest in cooperating at home or abroad
Publications: Weekly *Zensen* (*Advance* or *Progress*)

Communist Combatant Cells (CCC)

Full name/English translation: Cellules Communistes Combattantes (Communist Combatant Cells)
Year founded and country of origin: 1984, Belgium

Ideology/ethnic–national identification: New Left Marxist-Leninist, anarchist
Leaders: Pierre Carette (arrested 1985)
Membership: small
Base(s) of operations: Brussels
Operational areas: Belgium
Targets: Government, economic, and NATO facilities (no known attacks since the arrest of Carette in 1985)
Organizational structure and links: Small, independent cells; links with other European New Left groups, ETA, LARF; prefers no injuries
Publications: *Subversion*

Dal Khalsa

Full name/English translation: Dal Khalsa (the name of the Sikh irregular army of the eighteenth and nineteenth centuries)
Year founded and country of origin: 1978, Punjab, India
Ideology/ethnic–national identification: Sikh separatist
Leaders: Jajgit Singh Chauhan
Membership: Not known
Base(s) of operations: India, Great Britain, Canada, United States
Operational areas: Punjab, India
Targets: Hijacked an Indian Airliner in 1981; claimed credit for 1986 murder of General A. S. Vaidya, Army Chief of Staff during Operation Blue Star, 1984 attack on Sikh militants
Organizational structure and links: Probably has links to Chauhan's London-based National Council of Khalistan and to Sikh groups in Canada and the United States
Publications: None known

Dashmesh Regiment

Full name/English translation: Dashmesh "Tenth" Regiment (named after the Tenth Sikh guru, Gorbind Singh, d. 1708)
Year founded and country of origin: 1982, Punjab, India
Ideology/ethnic–national identification: Sikh separatist
Leaders: Current leadership unknown; probably founded under the aegis of the late Sikh militant leader, Sant Jarnail Singh Bhindranwale, or by Major General Shahbeg Singh and Surrinder Singh Gil

Membership: 200
Base(s) of operations: Punjab, India
Operational areas: All India, and possibly international
Targets: Prominent personalities, railways, and airlines (two attacks on Air India in 1985)
Organizational structure and links: Structure unknown; links to other Sikh extremist groups
Publications: None known

al-Da'wa (The Call)

Full name/English translation: al-Da'wa al-Islamiya (the Islamic Call)
Year founded and country of origin: 1960s, Iraq
Ideology/ethnic-national identification: Shi'a fundamentalist, opposed to secular Iraqi regime; wish to spread Iranian-style Islamic revolution throughout Muslim world; include Iraqis, Kuwaitis, Lebanese
Leaders: Spiritual founder, Sayyid Muhammad Baqir al-Sadr (executed by Iraqi regime in 1980); founder, Muhammad Baqir al-Hakim; spokesman, Muhammad Mahdi al-Asafi
Membership: Not known
Base(s) of operations: Najaf, Iraq; Tehran, Iran; Beirut, Lebanon
Operational areas: Iraq, Kuwait, Lebanon
Targets: Kuwaiti, American, French, Iraqi
Organizational structure and links: associated with the Supreme Assembly of the Islamic Revolution, the "Iraqi government in exile" in Tehran, and ties to the Kurdish National Union in Iraq, the Iranian government, and Hizballah in Lebanon
Publications: *al-Muqatilun (The Warriors)*

Democratic Front for the Liberation of Palestine (DFLP)

Full name/English translation: Jibhat al-Dimuqratiya lil-Tahrir Filistin (Democratic Front for the Liberation of Palestine); also known as the Popular Democratic Front for the Liberation of Palestine
Year founded and country of origin: 1969 by Palestinians
Ideology/ethnic–national identification: Marxist-Leninist; Palestinian nationalist, pan-Arabist

Leaders: Naif Hawatamah, founder; Yasir Abid Rabbu, Qais Sammari (Abu Layla), Abd al-Karim Hammad (Abu Adnan), Issam Abd al-Latif (Abu al-Abbad), Rifat Salah, Khalid Abu Abd al-Rahim, Yasir Khalid, Abu Hasum, Jamil Hillul, Mamduh Nufal
Membership: 500
Base(s) of operations: At large (elements in Lebanon, possibly Syria)
Operational areas: Lebanon and Israel
Targets: Israeli people and property
Organizational structure and links: Organized on quasi-Marxist–military lines with a central committee and politburo and four infantry battalions, an artillery battalion, central military intelligence and special forces; has links to the USSR, the PLO and at times to Syria but is fiercely independent; rejected the Reagan and Fez (Arab) Peace Plans in 1983 and Arafat's "Hussein Initiative" with Jordan but refused to support Syrian-backed anti-Arafat PLO rebels in 1983–84
Publications: *al-Huriyah (Freedom)*

Eelam Revolutionary Organization of Students (EROS)

Full name/English translation: Eelam Revolutionary Organization of Students
Year founded and country of origin: 1975, Great Britain
Ideology/ethnic–national identification: Tamil separatist (Sri Lanka)
Leaders: Rajanayagam (London), V. Balakumar (Madras)
Membership: Not known; draws support from ethnic Indian plantation workers in the hill country of north-central Sri Lanka
Base(s) of operations: London, India (Madras), Sri Lanka
Operational areas: Sri Lanka
Targets: Property; prefers sabotage to assassination or robbery
Organizational structure and links: Not known
Publications: None known

Eelam People's Revolutionary Liberation Front (EPRLF)

Full name/English translation: Eelam People's Revolutionary Liberation Front

Year founded and country of origin: 1970s, Sri Lanka
Ideology/ethnic–national identification: Tamil separatist
Leaders: K. Panmanabha
Membership: Not known; draws support from ethnic Indian plantation
    workers in the hill country of north-central Sri Lanka
Base(s) of operations: Northern Sri Lanka
Operational areas: Sri Lanka
Targets: Sinhalese persons and property; kidnapped but later released
    a U.S. AID official and his wife in 1984
Organizational structure and links: Not known
Publications: None known

Ejército Guerrillero de los Pobres (EGP)

Full name/English translation: Ejército Guerrillero de los Pobres
    (Guerrilla Army of the Poor)
Year founded and country of origin: 1975, Guatemala
Ideology/ethnic–national identification: Marxist
Leaders: Cesar Montes, Ricardo Ramirez de León (Rolando Moran)
Membership: Around 1,500
Base(s) of operations: Guatemala, possibly Mexico
Operational areas: Mainly active in the northwest highlands, Gua-
    temala City, and Quiche Province
Targets: Politicians, government officials
Organizational structure and links: Divided into three "fronts"; joined
    URNG in 1982; has links with Nicaragua
Publications: None known

Ejército de Liberación Nacional (ELN)

Full name/English translation: Ejército de Liberación National (Na-
    tional Liberation Army)
Year founded and country of origin: 1964, Colombia
Ideology/ethnic–national identification: Marxist-Leninist, pro-Cuban
Leaders: Manuel Perez Martinez, Nicolas Rodrigues Bautista (Dario)
Membership: 1,700
Base(s) of operations: Colombia

Operational areas: Santander, Arauca, and Antioquia Departments of Colombia; Venezuela
Targets: Oil companies (foreign and domestic), ranchers; involved in assassinations, kidnappings, bank robberies, bombings, armed attacks
Organizational structure and links: Structure not known; links to Cuba and Nicaragua
Publications: None known

Ejército Popular de Liberación (EPL)

Full name/English translation: Ejército Popular de Liberación (Popular Liberation Army)
Year founded and country of origin: 1967, Colombia
Ideology/ethnic–national identification: Marxist-Maoist
Leaders: Francisco Caraballo, Javier Robles, Jario Clavo
Membership: 750–1,000
Base(s) of operations: Colombia
Operational areas: Santander, Antioquia, Córdoba, and Cesar Departments of Colombia
Targets: Government and security personnel and facilities, foreign business personnel and facilities, banks; engages in kidnapping, assassination, extortion, bank robberies, armed attacks, and bombings
Organizational structure and links: Not known
Publications: Not known

Ejército Revolucionario del Pueblo (ERP)

Full name/English translation: Ejército Revolucionario del Pueblo (Revolutionary Army of the People)
Year founded and country of origin: 1972, El Salvador
Ideology/ethnic–national identification: Marxist-Maoist; "people's revolutionary warfare"
Leaders: Joaquin Villalobos
Membership: Not known
Base(s) of operations: El Salvador
Operational areas: El Salvador

Targets: Government and prominent right-wing personalities and properties; has a reputation for assassinations and kidnapping

Organizational structure and links: Member organization of the Farabundo Marti National Liberation Front (FMLN); also controls a political front organization, the Popular Leagues of 28 February (LP-28)

Publications: None known

Epanastikos Laikos Agonas (ELA)

Full name/English translation: Epanastikos Laisos Agonas (Revolutionary Popular Struggle)

Ideology/ethnic–national identification: Marxist; New Left

Leaders: Not known

Membership: 50 plus

Base(s) of operations: Athens, Thessaloniki (Greece)

Operational areas: Athens, Greece

Targets: Greek political and commercial interests, U.S. and Israeli interests

Organizational structure and links: Loosely coordinated autonomous cells; has claimed ties to Action Directe and RAF but no evidence of formal ties; possible ties to Marxist Palestinian groups

Publications: None known

Euzkadi Ta Azkatasuna (ETA)

Full name/English translation: Euzkadi Ta Azkatasuna (Basque Homeland and Freedom)

Year founded and country of origin: 1959, northeast Spain and southwest France

Ideology/ethnic–national identification: Basque separatist; Marxist; seeks to establish an independent Marxist Basque state

Leaders: José Antonio Urruticoechea-Bengoechea (Josu Ternera, arrested January 1989), Mugica Garmendia, Echeveste Eugenio Domingo Iturbe Abásolo (exiled by France to Gabon in 1986 and now presumed dead), Santiago Arrospide Sarasola (Santi Potros, arrested by the French, 1987), Javier Mariator Francisco Larreategui Cuadro

(Atxulo), José Javier Zjabaleta Elosegui (Waldo), Eloy Uriarte Díaz de Gereno (Señor Robles, or Le Robles)
Membership: Around 200 hard-core, most leading a "double life," with several dozen involved in terrorism
Base(s) of operations: Basque regions of Spain and France
Operational areas: Madrid, Barcelona, the Basque area
Targets: Government officials and security services, industrialists and industrial property, U.S. and French commercial properties
Organizational structure and links: ETA has split several times in its history; current terrorist group is technically ETA-M (Militar). Has (mainly ideological) links to Cuba and Nicaragua as well as to the Provisional IRA, European New Left groups, and Marxist Palestinian groups
Publications: None known

al-Fatah

Full name/English translation: Harakat al-Tahrir al-Filistini (Palestinian Liberation Movement; *Fatah* means "conquest" in Arabic and is also a reverse acronym of its Arabic name, i.e., FTH as it is spelled in Arabic)
Year founded and country of origin: 1959, by Palestinians
Ideology/ethnic–national identification: Palestinian nationalist
Leaders: Yasser Arafat (Abu Amar), Salah Khalaf (Abu Iyad), Faruq al-Qadumi (Abu Lutf), Hani al-Hasan
Membership: 6,000
Base(s) of operations: Tunisia, Lebanon, Syria, Iraq, Algeria, North Yemen, South Yemen, Libya, Occupied Territories, Greece
Operational areas: Israel, Occupied Territories, Middle East, Western Europe
Targets: Currently a moratorium on terrorism, formerly Israelis, Americans, rival Palestinian groups, property
Organizational structure and links: Ten-man Central Committee, 40-man Revolutionary Council; terrorism carried out by separate terrorist units: Force 17, "Col. Hawari" Group, now-defunct Black September (not to be confused with ANO alias); member organization of the Palestinian Liberation Organization (PLO)
Publications: *Filistin al-Thawra (Revolutionary Palestine)*

al-Fatah–Abu Musa Faction

In 1982, Sa'd Musa (Abu Musa), with the help of Syria, tried to oust Arafat from *al-Fatah*. The effort failed, and Abu Musa's group is now little more than a surrogate of Syria.

Fifteen May Organization

Full name/English translation: Munathamat Khamista'shar Mayo (Fifteen May Organization)
Year founded and country of origin: 1980, after breakup of PFLP-Special Operations Group following the death of its leader, Wadi Haddad, in 1978
Ideology/ethnic–national identification: Palestinian nationalist
Leaders: Husayn al-Amri (Abu Ibrahim)
Membership: Small, exact number not known
Base(s) of operations: Iraq
Operational areas: Middle East
Targets: Expert on bombings, including aircraft
Organizational structure and links: PFLP-SC, possibly al-Fatah (Col. Hawari)
Publications: None known

Force 17

al-Fatah terrorist organization headed by Muhammad Ahmad Natur (Abu Tayib; see *al-Fatah*)

Frente Farabundo Martí para la Liberación Nacional (FMLN)

Full name/English translation: Frente Farabundo Martí Para la Liberación Nacional (Farabundo Martí National Liberation Front)
Year founded and country of origin: 1980 by El Salvadoran groups meeting in Cuba
Ideology/ethnic–national identification: Marxist, pro-Cuban, anti-United States

Leaders: Joaquin Villalobos (René Cruz), Jorge Shafik Handal (Simon),
Leonel Gonzales (Salvador Sanchez), Eduardo Sancho Castaneda
(Ferman Cienfuegos), Francisco Jovel (Roberto Roca), Fabio Cast-
illo, Salvador Cayetano Carpio (Commandante Marcial)—represent-
ing five member organizations
Membership: About 7,500
Base(s) of operations: El Salvador, with key officials in Nicaragua
Targets: Government officials and installations, economic facilities,
rural mayors
Organizational structure and links: FMLN is an umbrella organization
created at the insistence of Cuba and made up of five Marxist groups:
Ejército Revolucionario del Pueblo (ERP), Frente Popular Libera-
ción (FPL), Fuerzas Armadas de Resistance Nacionales (FARN),
Fuerzas Armadas Liberaciones (FAL), and Partido Revolucionario
Trabajadores de la America Central (PRTC); Democratic Revolution-
ary Front (FDR) is its political front party
Publications: None known

Frente Patriótico Manuel Rodriguez (FPMR)

Full name/English translation: Frente Patriótico Manuel Rodriguez
(Manuel Rodreguez Patriotic Front)
Year founded and country of origin: 1983, Chile
Ideology/ethnic–national identification: Utopian urban Marxist group
dedicated to the overthrow of the Chilean government
Leaders: Roberto Torres, Claudio Enrique (arrested)
Membership: About 1,000
Base(s) of operations: Carrizal Bajo, Chile
Operational areas: Urban areas of major Chilean cities
Targets: local economic sites, American officials, Mormon Church
Organizational structure and links: Probably splintered into two fac-
tions; links with Cuba
Publications: None known

Frente Popular Liberación (FPL)

Full name/English translation: Frente Popular Liberación (Popular
Liberation Front)

Year founded and country of origin: 1974, El Salvador
Ideology/ethnic–national identification: Marxist
Leaders: Salvador Cayetano Carpio (Commandante Marcial)
Membership: Not known
Base(s) of operations: El Salvador
Operational areas: El Salvador
Targets: Government personnel, economic targets, mayors
Organizational structure and links: Member organization of Farabundo
   Martí National Liberation Front FMLN)
Publications: None known

Front de la Libération de la Corse (FLNC)

Full name/English translation: Front de la Libération de la Corse
   (Front for the Liberation of Corsica)
Year founded and country of origin: 1976, Corsica
Ideology/ethnic–national identification: Marxist, separatist Corsican,
   nationalist
Leaders: Alesandro Pantalon, Lorant Cobili, Marcel Lorenzoni
Membership: 30 activists, 200 supporters
Base(s) of operations: Corsica
Operational areas: Corsica, France
Targets: Tourist industry, police stations, banks, courthouses, tax of-
   fices, business establishments, French Gendarmes and barracks
Organizational structure and links: Links with Action Directe, IRA,
   PLO groups, ETA
Publications: *U Ribellu (The Rebel)*

Fuerzas Armadas Liberaciones (FAL)

Full name/English translation: Fuerzas Armadas Liberaciones (Armed
   Forces of Liberation)
Year founded and country of origin: 1979, El Salvador
Ideology/ethnic–national identification: Marxist
Leaders: Jorge Shafik Handal
Membership: Several hundred
Base(s) of operations: El Salvador
Operational areas: El Salvador

Targets: Government troops, installations, mayors
Organizational structure and links: Guerrilla organization of the Communist Party of El Salvador; member of FMLN
Publications: None known

Fuerzas Armadas Rebeldes (FAR)

Full name/English translation: Fuerzas Armadas Rebeldes (Rebel Armed Forces)
Year founded and country of origin: 1962, Guatemala
Ideology/ethnic–national identification: Marxist
Leaders: Jorge Soto García (Pablo Monsanto)
Membership: About 400–500
Base(s) of operations: Guatemala City
Operational areas: Guatemala City, El Petén Department, Lake Izabel (far north)
Targets: Government forces
Organizational structure and links: Joined the Guatemelan National Revolutionary Union (URNG) in 1982
Publications: None known

Fuerzas Armadas Revolucionarias de Colombia (FARC)

Full name/English translation: Fuerzas Armadas Revolucionarias de Colombia (Revolutionary Armed Forces of Colombia)
Year founded and country of origin: 1966, Colombia
Ideology/ethnic–national identification: Marxist
Leaders: Manuel "Dead Shot" Marulanda Velez (Pedro Antonio Marín Tiroijo), Jacobo Arenas, Raúl Reyes
Membership: 4,000–5,000 guerrillas
Base(s) of operations: La Uribe, Meta Department, Colombia
Operational areas: Central and southern Colombia
Targets: Domestic and foreign personnel and installations; engages in bombings, kidnappings, armed assaults, and robberies
Organizational structure and links: Patriotic Union (UP) is the political front party; links with drug traffickers and with Cuba and Nicaragua
Publications: None known

Fuerzas Armadas de Resistencia Nacional (FARN)

Full name/English translation: Fuerzas Armadas Resistencia Nacional (Armed Forces of National Resistance)
Year founded and country of origin: 1975, El Salvador
Ideology/ethnic–national identification: Marxist
Leaders: Ernesto Jovel, Fernán Cienfuegos
Membership: Not known
Base(s) of operations: El Salvador
Operational areas: El Salvador
Targets: Government troops, officials, installations, mayors
Organizational structure and links: Broke off from the ERP; member of the FMLN
Publications: None known

Hizballah

Full name/English translation: Hizballah (Party of God); also uses cover name Islamic Jihad
Year founded and country of origin: 1962 in Lebanon during Israeli invasion
Ideology/ethnic–national identification: Lebanese Shi'a fundamentalists, seeking to create an Iranian-style Islamic republic of Lebanon under Shi'a control
Leaders: Spiritual leader, Imam Muhammad Husayn Fadlallah; Imad Mughniya, Abbas al-Musawi, Husayn al-Musawi, Subhi al-Tufayli
Membership: 4,000–6,000
Base(s) of operations: Baalbek, Bekaa Valley, Brittal, West and South Beirut, Maydun, al-Luwiza, and Janta, Lebanon
Operational areas: Bekaa Valley, southern Lebanon, Beirut, Lebanon; Western Europe (France, Italy, West Germany, Denmark, Sweden) and Africa (Ivory Coast)
Targets: Americans and other Europeans in Lebanon and elsewhere; Israelis and the Multinational Force in Lebanon; Kuwaitis, Saudis, Iraqis in the Arab world
Organizational structure and links: No hierarchy; loosely organized confederation of groups plus Shi'a clerical leadership; tactical links to various radical Lebanese groups. External links to Iran both directly

and through Iranian Revolutionary Guard in Lebanon, and al-Da'wa; sometimes cooperates with and sometimes in opposition to Amal (Lebanon), Syria, and various PLO groups

Publications: *al-Ahad (The Alliance), Sawt al-Islam* (Voice of Islam) radio station

Irish National Liberation Army (INLA)

Full name/English translation: Irish National Liberation Army
Year founded and country of origin: 1974, Ireland (split off from the Official IRA)
Ideology/ethnic–national identification: Irish nationalist, Marxist-Trotskyist, Roman Catholic; dedicated to rejoining Northern Ireland to the Irish Republic
Leaders: None currently known
Membership: Not known
Base(s) of operations: Dublin, Ireland
Operational areas: Northern Ireland, England, France, Germany
Targets: British and Northern Irish security forces, Protestants, British public facilities
Organizational structure and links: Currently dormant; supposedly functioned as "military wing" of the Irish Republican Socialist Party; internal power struggle between two factions: the Army Council and the General Headquarters
Publications: None currently known

Irish Republican Army (IRA or OIRA)

Full name/English translation: Official Irish Republican Army
Year founded and country of origin: Originally founded in Ireland in 1916; became known as the Official Irish Republican Army after the Provisional Irish Republican Army split off in 1969
Ideology/ethnic–national identification: Irish nationalist, Marxist, Roman Catholic; wants to rejoin Northern Ireland to the Irish Republic
Leaders: None currently known
Membership: Not known; large number of sympathizers
Base(s) of operations: Ireland

Operational areas: Northern Ireland
Targets: Followers now emphasize political action
Organizational structure and links: Largely dormant; military organization; political wing is Sinn Fein ("We Ourselves" in Gaelic)
Publications: None currently known

Islamic Jihad

See *Hizballah*

Janatha Vimukthi Peremuna (JVP)

Full name/English translation: Janatha Vimukthi Peremuna (Peoples' Liberation Front)
Year founded and country of origin: 1965, Sri Lanka
Ideology/ethnic–national identification: Sinhalese ethnic chauvinism, ethnic Buddhism, Marxism
Leaders: Not known
Membership: 2,000–4,000
Base(s) of operations: Sri Lanka
Operational areas: Colombo area of Sri Lanka
Targets: Tamils and moderate Sinhalese officials favoring a settlement with the Tamils
Organizational structure and links: Leader Rohan Wijerwee was killed under mysterious circumstances in November 1989; current status of organization unknown
Publications: Not known

Japanese Red Army (JRA)

Full name/English translation: Nippon Sekigun (Japanese Red Army)
Year founded and country of origin: 1971, Japan
Ideology/ethnic–national identification: New Left Marxist; anarchist; sympathizers with the Arab armed struggle against Israel
Leaders: Fusaka Shigenobu
Membership: 25–30

Base(s) of operations: Lebanon, Arab Middle East
Operational areas: Middle East, Western Europe, Far East
Targets: Pro-Western government installations and officials, particularly American and Israeli
Organizational structure and links: Broke off from the Japanese Red Army Faction (Sekigun-ha); closely associated with PFLP; also has links with European New Left groups; possibly uses cover name, Anti-Imperialist International Brigades
Publications: *Solidarity*

Justice Commandos of the Armenian Genocide (JCAG)

Full name/English translation: Justice Commandos of the Armenian Genocide
Year founded and country of origin: 1975, Lebanon
Ideology/ethnic–national identification: Armenian nationalism; seeks an independent Armenia from territory in Turkey and Iran but excluding Soviet Armenia
Leaders: Patchek (or Katchik) Arabaian, Carl Bursamian, Sirkis Inkuadosian, Varujan Kilician
Membership: Not known
Base(s) of operations: Los Angeles, Beirut
Operational areas: Los Angeles, Boston, Philadelphia; Belgrade, Yugoslavia; Beirut, Lebanon; Athens, Greece
Targets: limited to Turkish officials and installations
Organizational structure and links: Trains one-time teams that disband after the operation
Publications: *Yeruan*

Khalistan Commando Force

Full name/English translation: Khalistan Commando Force
Year founded and country of origin: Early 1980s, Punjab, India
Ideology/ethnic–national identification: Sikh separatist
Leaders: Founded by a General Labh Singh, killed in 1988
Membership: Not known but believed among the largest Sikh separatist groups
Base(s) of operations: Punjab, India

Operational areas: Punjab, India
Targets: Indian officials, Hindus, general population
Organizational structure and links: Not known
Publications: None known

Khalistan Liberation Force

Full name/English translation: Khalistan Liberation Force
Year founded and country of origin: Early 1980s, Punjab, India
Ideology/ethnic–national identification: Sikh separatist
Leaders: Founded by a shadowy figure called "Brahma," killed in 1988
Membership: Not known
Base(s) of operations: Punjab, India
Operational areas: Punjab, India
Targets: Indian officials, Hindus, general population
Organizational structure and links: Not known
Publications: None known

Kommando Jihad (Indonesia)

Full name/English translation: Kommando Jihad (Holy Struggle Commandos)
Year founded and country of origin: Early 1980s, Indonesia
Ideology/ethnic–national identification: Santri Sunni Muslim fundamentalist
Leaders: Muhammad Imron Zain
Membership: Not known
Base(s) of operations: Santri areas of Indonesia along the coasts
Operational areas: Same
Targets: Hijacking, armed attacks
Organizational structure and links: Not known
Publications: None known

Lebanese Armed Military Faction (LARF)

Full name/English translation: Lebanese Armed Revolutionary Faction
Year founded and country of origin: 1979, Lebanon (following the

breakup of PFLP-Special Operations Group after the death of its leader Wadi Haddad the previous year

Ideology/ethnic–national identification: Marxist, Palestinian nationalist, Arab nationalist, Lebanese nationalist

Leaders: George Ibrahim Abdallah

Membership: 20–30, mainly from Qubayyat and Andaqat, two villages in northern Lebanon

Base(s) of operations: Lebanon, formerly France and Italy

Operational areas: Lebanon, formerly also France and Italy

Targets: U.S. and Israeli diplomats, French officials

Organizational structure and links: PFLP, New Left groups, ASALA

Publications: None known

Liberation Tigers of Tamil Ealam (LTTE)

Full name/English translation: Liberation Tigers of Tamil Eelam

Year founded and country of origin: 1972, Sri Lanka (did not turn to violence until 1975)

Ideology/ethnic–national identification: Tamil separatism

Leaders: Veluppillai Prabakaran, leader, and Anton Balasingam, spokesman

Membership: 2,000

Base(s) of operations: Jafna Peninsula, Sri Lanka

Operational areas: Northern Sri Lanka

Targets: Sinhalese population and officials

Organizational structure and links: Links with Indian Tamils

Publications: None known

Mano Blanco

Full name/English translation: Movimiento de Acción Nacionalista Organizado (MANO); Mano means "hand" in Spanish, and the group became known as "Mano Blanco" (White Hand)

Year founded and country of origin: 1966, Guatemala

Ideology/ethnic–national identification: Right-wing extremist; anti-Communist

Leaders: Not known

Membership: Not known

Base(s) of operations: Guatemala
Operational areas: Izqual and Zacapa Provinces
Targets: "Communists," Jesuits, "Liberal" priests, communist guer-
rillas
Organizational structure and links: Not known
Publications: None known

May 15 Organization

See *Fifteen May Organization*

Movement of Arab Nationalists

See *Arab Nationalists' Movement*

Movimiento 19 de Abril (M-19)

Full name/English translation: Movimiento de 19 Abril (Movement of
19 April), generally known as M-19
Year founded and country of origin: 1974, Colombia
Ideology/ethnic–national identification: Marxist, nationalist, xeno-
phobic
Leaders: Pabón Rosemburg, Navarro Antonio Wolf, Carlos Gómez
Pizarro
Membership: Estimated several hundreds to 2,000
Base(s) of operations: Velle del Cauca, Tolima Caldas, Quindio Depart-
ments, Putumayo Province, Colombia
Operational areas: Bogotá, Cali, Medellín, Bucaramanga, and other
major cities; most of the major provinces
Targets: Oil facilities, diplomats (U.S. and Ecuadorian), banks, wealthy
ranchers, military posts
Organizational structure and links: Divided into columns with head-
quarters elements in urban areas, and subdivided into cells, which
are responsible for day-to-day operations; linked to FARC and to
drug traffickers; also links to leftist groups in Bolivia, Ecuador, and
Perú and to Cuba and Nicaragua
Publications: None known

Movimiento de la Izquierda Revolucionario (MIR)

Full name/English translation: Movimiento de la Izquierda Revolucionario (Movement of the Revolutionary Left)
Year founded and country of origin: 1965, Chile
Ideology/ethnic–national identification: Marxist, pro-Castro
Leaders: Andrés Pascal Allende, Hernán Aguilo Donoso, Manuel Cabienes Donoso, Nelson Gutierrez
Membership: 300–400
Base(s) of operations: Chile
Operational areas: Chile
Targets: Economic targets; prefers bombings
Organizational structure and links: Cell structure; close ties to Cuba
Publications: None known

Moviemiento Patria Libre (MPL)

A small Columbian Marxist group; see *Simón Bolívar National Guerrilla Coordinator*

Movimiento Revolucionario Tupac Amarru (MRTA)

Full name/English translation: Movimiento Revolucionario Tupac Amaru (Tupac Amaro Revolutionary Movement)
Year founded and country of origin: 1982–83, Perú
Ideology/ethnic–national identification: Pro-Castro Communists
Leaders: Ernesto Montes Aliaga, Jose Carazas Ybar (in prison), Cirilo Javier Huamani (in prison), Wilder Rojas Sánchez (in prison), Luis Varese Scotto (in prison)
Membership: 50–200
Base(s) of operations: Lima, Cuzco
Operational areas: Lima, Cuzco, Huancayo, Chimbote, Arequipa, Chicolayo, and Frujillo
Targets: Government, economic, and diplomatic targets
Organizational structure and links: Personalized leadership and cell structure; links to M-19 of Colombia
Publications: *Venceremos (We Shall Win)*

Mussolini Action Squads

Full name/English translation: Mussolini Action Squad
Year founded and country of origin: 1968, Italy
Ideology/ethnic–national identification: Neo-Fascist
Leaders: Not known
Membership: Not known
Base(s) of operations: Italy
Operational areas: Italy
Targets: American and other foreign interests, Jews, left-wing politicians
Organizational structure and links: Not known
Publications: None known

National Council of Khalistan

Full name/English translation: National Council of Khalistan
Year founded and country of origin: 1979, London
Ideology/ethnic–national identification: Sikh separatist
Leaders: Dr. Jagjit Singh Chauhan (self-exiled in London)
Membership: Not known
Base(s) of operations: London, United States, Canada, West Germany, Pakistan
Operational areas: North America, Western Europe, Punjab
Targets: The National Council is less operational than Dal Khalsa, which Chauhan also started, and apparently serves as a conduit for propaganda, financing, and recruiting
Organizational structure and links: Member of the Panthic Committee
Publications: None known

Orden

Full name/English translation: Organización Democrática Nacionalista (Democratic Nationalist Organization); the acronym ORDEN also means "order" in Spanish
Year founded and country of origin: Mid-1960s, El Salvador
Ideology/ethnic-national identification: Right-wing nationalist, extremist; started out as a government-created rural auxiliary paramilitary group

Leaders: Many over the years
Membership: Not known; at one time reached 100,000
Base(s) of operations: San Salvador
Operational areas: Rural areas
Targets: Left-wing leaders and reformers, including Catholic nuns and
    lay workers, Archbishop Oscar Romero (1980), Marxist guerrillas
Organizational structure and links: Organized along military lines
Publications: None known

Organización Revolucionaria de Personas Armadas (ORPA)

Full name/English translation: Organización Revolucionaria de Per-
    sonas Armadas (Revolutionary Organization of People Under Arms
Year founded and country of origin: Early 1970s, Guatemala
Ideology/ethnic–national identification: Marxist
Leaders: Rodrigo Asturias Amado (Gaspar Ilom)
Membership: Not known
Base(s) of operations: Guatemala
Operational areas: Southwest Guatemala
Targets: Government officials, security forces, installations
Organizational structure and links: Member of URNG, links to Cuba
Publications: None known

Palestine Liberation Front (PLF)

Full name/English translation: Jibhat Tahrir Filistin (Palestine Libera-
    tion Front)
Year founded and country of origin: 1977, broke off from PFLP-GC
Ideology/ethnic–national identification: Palestinian nationalist
Leaders: Muhammad Abu al-Abbas, Abu Ahmad Hajji Yusuf al-Mak-
    dah, Abd al-Fatah al-Ghanim
Membership: Not known
Base(s) of operations: Tunis, Lebanon (?), Syria (?)
Operational areas: Europe and the Middle East
Targets: Israelis, Americans, moderate Arabs
Organizational structure and links: Abu al-Abbas broke off from PFLP-
    GC in 1977; in 1983, he broke off from his own group and affiliated

his PLF with al-Fatah (this groups murdered Leon Klinghofer aboard the *Achile Lauro*); the rest of PLF also split
Publications: None known

Palestine Liberation Organization (PLO)

Full name/English translation: Munathamat Tahrir Falistin (Palestine Liberation Organization)
Year founded and country of origin: 1964, Jordan
Ideology/ethnic–national identification: Palestinian nationalist
Leaders: Yasser Arafat (and leaders of member Palestinian groups)
Membership: 15,000 active; supported by virtually the entire Palestinian population
Base(s) of operations: Tunis, Lebanon, a number of "embassies" throughout the world
Operational areas: Worldwide
Targets: Operational activities are carried out by member organizations rather than the PLO as such
Organizational structure and links: The PLO is an umbrella organization of member groups, most of which have engaged in occasional terrorism and some of which use terrorism as the tactic of preference. In late 1988 it declared a moratorium on terrorism, but it is not clear how long and to what degree that policy will remain in force. The organization itself consists of the Palestine National Congress (PNC), represented by the member groups, the Central Committee, and the Executive Committee, which runs the organization's daily operations. The PLO has financial, diplomatic, and political activities to coordinate the policies of the member groups
Publications: WAFA News Agency, *Sawt al-Filistin* (Voice of Palestine) radio

Palestinian Popular Struggle Front (PPSF)

Full name/English translation: Jibhat al-Kifah al-Sha'bi al-Filistini (Palestinian Popular Struggle Front)
Year founded and country of origin: 1967, Jordan
Ideology/ethnic-national identification: Palestinian nationalist, Marxist, pan-Arabist

Leaders: Samir Ghusha, Khalid abd al-Majid, Ibrahim Halali Fattani (Abu Naif), Mahmud Ibrahim (Abu Ziyad)
Membership: 100–200
Base(s) of operations: Syria, Lebanon, Sweden
Operational areas: Lebanon, Western Europe
Targets: Israel, United States
Organizational structure and links: Central committee, political bureaus; remnants of the old Palestine Liberation Army (PLA), military wing of the pre-1967 PLO; joined the Rejection Front in 1979 along with PFLP, PFLP-GC, and PLF; links to PFLP-GC, ASALA, Syria, and Libya; reportedly pressed for money and willing to hire out for terrorist jobs
Publications: *Nidal al-Sha'b (Struggle of the People)*

Partido Revolucionario de los Trabajadores (PRT)

A small Colombian Marxist group; see *Simón Bolívar Coordinator*

Partido Revolucionario Trabajadores de la America Central (PRTC)

Full name/English translation: Partido Revolucionario Trabajadores de la America Central (Revolutionary Party of Central American Workers)
Year founded and country of origin: Late 1970s, El Salvador
Ideology/ethnic–national identification: Marxist/Trotskyist
Leaders: Fabio Castillo (in exile)
Membership: Not known
Base(s) of operations: El Salvador
Operational areas: El Salvador
Targets: Government officials, security forces, economic targets, foreign interests
Organizational structure and links: Cell structure; member of FMLN; has a political front, Movimiento Liberación Popular (MLP)
Publications: None known

People's Liberation Organization of Tamil
Eelam (PLOTE)

Full name/English translation: People's Liberation Organization of
  Tamil Eelam
Year founded and country of origin: 1980, Sri Lanka
Ideology/ethnic–national identification: Tamil separatist
Leaders: Uma Maheswaran
Membership: Not known, large number of Muslim Tamil speakers
Base(s) of operations: Northern and eastern Sri Lanka
Operational areas: Northern and Eastern Sri Lanka
Targets: Sinhalese officials, but avoids civilian casualties
Organizational structure and links: Broke away from Liberation Tigers
  of Tamil Eelam
Publications: None known

Popular Front for the Liberation of Palestine
(PFLP)

Full name/English translation: Al-Jibha al-Sha'biya lil-Tahrir Filistin
  (The Popular Front for the Liberation of Palestine)
Year founded and country of origin: 1967, Jordan
Ideology/ethnic–national identification: Palestinian nationalist; Marx-
  ist
Leaders: Dr. George Habbash (founder), Fuad Abu Ahmad, Ahmad
  Abd al-Rahim, Abd al-Rahim Fallah, Ali Abu Mustafa, Bassam Taw-
  fiq Abu, Sahrif, Abu Mahir al-Yaman
Membership: 300–1,200
Base(s) of operations: Lebanon, Syria
Operational areas: Israel, Occupied Territories, Arab states
Targets: Israelis, Americans, Jews
Organizational structure and links: Central Committee, Political Bu-
  reau, six operational "battalions;" member of the PLO; links with
  European New Left groups, PIRA, Japanese Red Army, and South
  Yemen, Syria, Libya, USSR, North Korea, and German Democratic
  Republic
Publications: *al-Hadaf* (*The Objective*)

Popular Front for the Liberation of Palestine– General Command (PFLP-GC)

Full name/English translation: Al-Jibha Sha'biya lil-Tahrir Filistin–al-Qadiya al-Ama (Popular Front for the Liberation of Palestine–General Command)
Year founded and country of origin: 1968, Jordan
Ideology/ethnic–national identification: Palestinian nationalist, Marxist
Leaders: Ahmad Jabril (founder), Talal Naji, Abu Abid, Abu Tamam, Abu Firaz, Abu Riyad, Abu Zaim Fadl Shururu
Membership: 600
Base(s) of operations: Syria, Lebanon
Operational areas: Israel, Lebanon, Jordan, Western Europe
Targets: Israelis, Americans, moderate Arabs
Organizational structure and links: Cell structure; member of the PLO; links with PFLP, Abu Musa's breakaway al-Fatah organization
Publications: *Ila al-Amam*

Popular Front for the Liberation of Palestine–Special Command (PFLP-SC)

Full name/English translation: Al-Jibha al-Sha'biya lil-Tahrir Filistin–al-Qadiya al-Khasa (Popular Front for the Liberation of Palestine–Special Command)
Year founded and country of origin: 1979, Lebanon
Ideology/ethnic–national identification: Palestinian nationalist, Marxist, pan-Arabist
Leaders: Salim Abu Salim
Membership: 20–30, Palestinians and Europeans
Base(s) of operations: South Yemen
Operational areas: Middle East, Western Europe, Africa
Targets: Israelis, Americans, moderate Arabs
Organizational structure and links: Formed from remnants of Wadi Haddad's PFLP–Special Operations Command, after his death in 1978; Haddad broke away from PFLP in 1974; links to New Left groups, Libya, Iraq, and South Yemen
Publications: None known

Provisional Irish Republican Army (PIRA)

Full name/English translation: Provisional Irish Republican Army (also known as Provos)

Year founded and country of origin: 1969, Ireland and Northern Ireland

Ideology/ethnic–national identification: Irish nationalist, seeks to re-join Northern Ireland with the Irish Republic, Catholic, leftist

Leaders: Gerry Adams, Martin McGuinnes

Membership: 200–400 hard core, 600 regular fighters and about 2,500 sympathizers

Base(s) of operations: Ireland, Northern Ireland, Netherlands, Sweden

Operational areas: Ireland, Northern Ireland, Britain, West Germany, Netherlands, Belgium

Targets: British and Northern Irish (Protestant) public officials, police and military services and general population, NATO installations, economic targets

Organizational structure and links: Military organization, with small independent units (6 to 10 members); Women's Section (Gunmann Nam Ban); Youth Section (Fianna Na H'Eirenann); political wing is Provisional Sinn Fein. Broke off from the IRA, which had turned too much to political action rather than armed struggle and was too Marxist for some PIRA extremists

Publications: *An Phoblacht*

Red Army Faction

Full name/English translation: Rote Armee Fraktion (Red Army Faction); also known as the Baader-Meinhof Group from the names of two founders, Andreas Baader and Ulrike Meinhof

Year founded and country of origin: 1968 in West Germany

Ideology/ethnic–national identification: New Left Marxist, anarchist

Leaders: Most of the original leadership is dead, the new leaders include Barbara Mayer, Inge Viett, Wolfgang Grams, Horst Meyer, Suzanne Albrecht, Tomas Simon, Birgit Hogefeld and Silke Maier-Witt

Membership: West Germans; 20–40 hard core, 100–200 sympathizers

Base(s) of operations: West Germany (seek safe haven in Scandinavia after attacks)

Operational areas: West Germany, Belgium, Spain

Targets: West German officials and installations; U.S. officials, installations, and commercial facilities; NATO installations and personnel

Organizational structure and links: Cell structure on three levels: underground who carry out most violent attacks including murder, militants who carry out sabotage but lead normal lives, and sympathizers who provided logistic support

Publications: *Konkret* (Meinhof wrote for it in the 1970s); *Zusammen Kampfen (Common Struggle)*

Red Brigades (BR)

Full name/English translation: Brigate Rosse (Red Brigades)

Year founded and country of origin: 1969, Italy

Ideology/ethnic—national identification: New Left Marxist, anarchist

Leaders: Most of the leadership is in jail; Scarfio Gregorio is the new Rome BR leader

Membership: 50–70 hard core

Base(s) of operations: Rome, Milan, Naples, Genoa, Tuscany region

Operational areas: Italy

Targets: U.S. military officials and installations; Italian officials and politicians (e.g., Christian Democrats), municipal judges, industrialists, multinational companies and executives

Organizational structure and links: Cell structure; currently two factions: First Position and Second Position; most militant subgroup is the "Fighting Communist Party"; a new cell, "14 December Brigade," was founded in December 1988

Publications: *Politica E Rivoluzione (Politics and Revolution); Il Proletariato Non Si É Pentito (The Proletariat Has Not Repented)*

Red Hand Commandos

Full name/English translation: Red Hand Commandos

Year founded and country of origin: 1972–73, Northern Ireland

Ideology/ethnic—national identification: Northern Irish Protestant sectarian; status quo

Leaders: Not known

Membership: Not known, made up of blue-collar toughs and criminal elements

Base(s) of operations: Northern Ireland
Operational areas: Northern Ireland
Targets: Northern Irish Catholics, IRA, PIRA
Organizational structure and links: Not known
Publications: None known

Revolutionary Cells (RZ)

Full name/English translation: Revolutionaere Zellen (Revolutionary
  Cells)
Year founded and country of origin: 1973, West Germany
Ideology/ethnic–national identification: New Left Marxist, anarchist,
  anti-American, anti-Zionist
Leaders: Weinrich Johannes, Rudolph Raabe, Sonja Suder, Christian
  Gauger, Rudolf Schindler, Sabine Eckle
Membership: 100–200
Base(s) of operations: West Berlin, West Germany, Frankfurt
Operational areas: West German cities, West Berlin
Targets: U.S. installations and officials, NATO installations, high-tech
  companies, local officials and offices
Organizational structure and links: Semi-independent cells with little
  central direction; each cell contains 2 to 10 people
Publications: *Revolutionaere Zellen* (*Revolutionary Wrath* or *Revolu-
  tionary Rage*)

Revolutionary Organization of 17 November

Full name/English translation: Epanastaiki Organosi 17 Noemvri (Rev-
  olutionary Organization of 17 November), named for a student upris-
  ing on November 17, 1973, at the Athens Polytechnic Institute
Year founded and country of origin: 1975, Greece
Ideology/ethnic–national identification: Marxist, anti-American; pri-
  mary goal of the group is to force Greece out of NATO and expel the
  American military, political, and economic presence
Leaders: Not known
Membership: Not known; thought to be very small (as few as 2 or 3 and
  up to maybe 20)
Base(s) of operations: Athens, Greece

Operational areas: Athens, Greece

Targets: Greek and U.S. officials, Turkish diplomats, Greek and U.S. military and commercial sites; prefers bombings and assasinations (typically shootings from motor scooters)

Organizational structure and links: Not known; no apparent outside links

Publications: *Noemvri (November)*

al-Sa'iqa

Full name/English translation: Al-Sa'iqa (means "Thunderbolt" in Arabic)

Year founded and country of origin: 1968, Syria

Ideology/ethnic–national identification: Palestinian nationalist, pan-Arabist

Leaders: Issam al-Qadi, Sami al-Attari, Diab Ahmad Hasan, Abu Hajja Farhan, Sayid Muhammad al-Bari, Tariq Ibrahim Shafa'Amri, Salah Hilmi

Membership: 1,500–2,000

Base(s) of operations: Syria, Lebanon

Operational areas: Western Europe, southern Lebanon

Targets: Israelis, Jews, moderate Arabs

Organizational structure and links: al-Saiqa was formed under the direction of Syria and is virtually a Syrian surrogate; links to PLO, al-Fatah–Abu Musa Faction

Publications: *Al-Tali'a (The Vanguard)*

Sekigun-Ha (Japanese Red Army Faction)

Full name/English translation: Nipon Sekigun-ha (Japanese Red Army Faction)

Year founded and country of origin: 1969, Japan; broke off from the League of Communists

Ideology/ethnic–national identification: New Left Marxist

Leaders: Not known

Membership: Not known

Base(s) of operations: Japan

Operational areas: Japan

Targets: Japanese officials and installations

Organizational structure and links: Mainly known as the organization from which Fusako Shigenobu and her Japanese Red Army broke off in 1971; Baader and Meinhof took the name Red Army Faction from this group
Publications: None known

Sendero Luminoso (Shining Path)

Full name/English translation: Pardido Comunista del Perú en el Sendero Luminoso de José Carlos Mariategui (Communist Party of Peru in the Shining Path of José Carlos Mariategui)
Year founded and country of origin: 1969–70 in Peru; began terrorist operations in 1980
Ideology/ethnic–national identification: An original blend of Peruvian Marxist-Maoist ideology and Indian chauvinism
Leaders: Manuel Abimael Guzmán (Comrade Gonzolo), founder; Maximillian Durán (in jail), Mezzich César, Carlota Tello Cutti (Carla)
Membership: Not known; estimated 20,000 members; 5,000 are fighters
Base(s) of operations: Ayacuchu, Upper Huallaga Valley, Lima
Operational areas: 15 of Peru's 24 departments
Targets: Domestic political, security, and military officials and installations; foreign and domestic banks, firms, and embassies (mainly U.S. but also Japanese, British, and Soviet)
Organizational structure and links: Central Committee which oversees six regional committees (north, south, east, central, metropolitan, and a base committee for Ayacuchu)
Publications: Published a 110-page document of its ideology and tactics: "To Develop People's War and Reach World Revolution"

Simón Bolívar National Guerrilla Coordinator

Full name/English translation: Coordinadora Guerrilla Nacional Simón Bolívar (Simón Bolívar National Guerrilla Coordinating Board or Simón Bolívar National Guerrilla Coordinator)
Year founded and country of origin: 1987, Colombia
Ideology/ethnic-national identification: Marxist
Leaders: Leaders of member groups

Membership: No appreciable membership except that of member organizations
Base(s) of operations: Colombia
Operational areas: Colombia
Targets: No operational activities; those are done by member organizations
Organizational structure and links: Organized as a coordinating group for six member organizations: FARC, M-19, ELN, EPL, MPL, and PRT. The last two, the Free Fatherland Movement and the Workers' Revolutionary Party, are quite small
Publications: None known

Tamil Eelam Liberation Organization (TELO)

Full name/English translation: Tamil Eelam Liberation Organization
Year founded and country of origin: 1983, Sri Lanka
Ideology/ethnic—national identification: Tamil separatist
Leaders: Thangathurai (killed in 1983), Sri Sabaratnam (killed by LTTE in 1986)
Membership: None known
Base(s) of operations: Northern Sri Lanka
Operational areas: Northern Sri Lanka
Targets: Sinhalese officials, rival Tamil groups (e.g. LTTE)
Organizational structure and links: Not known; group was decimated in a struggle with LTTE in 1986
Publications: None known

Ulster Defense Association (UDA)

Full name/English translation: Ulster Defense Force
Year founded and country of origin: 1971, Northern Ireland
Ideology/ethnic—national identification: Northern Ireland Protestant sectarian, status quo
Leaders: None currently known
Membership: Not known
Base(s) of operations: Northern Ireland
Operational areas: Northern Ireland
Targets: Northern Irish Catholics, PIRA

Organizational structure and links: Largely reverted to street gangs on the fringe of the law with a potential for attracting a large following; a vigilante group that is more reactive than proactive
Publications: None known

Ulster Freedom Fighters

Full name/English translation: Ulster Freedom Fighters
Year founded and country of origin: 1972–73, Northern Ireland
Ideology/ethnic–national identification: Northern Irish Protestant sectarian; status quo
Leaders: Not known
Membership: Not known
Base(s) of operations: Northern Ireland
Operational areas: Northern Ireland
Targets: Northern Irish Catholics, PIRA
Organizational structure and links: Currently dormant; formed from street gangs with little cohesion; suspected of carrying out terrorist acts for the UDA, which denies the allegations; possibly was a cover name for the UDA
Publications: None known

Ulster Volunteer Force (UVF)

Full name/English translation: Ulster Volunteer Force
Year founded and country of origin: 1912; revived in 1966, Northern Ireland
Ideology/ethnic–national identification: Northern Ireland Protestant sectarian; status quo
Leaders: Founded by Gusty Spence (no longer active)
Membership: 500 at its height (1960s, 1970s)
Base(s) of operations: Northern Ireland
Operational areas: Northern Ireland
Targets: Northern Irish Catholics, PIRA; "officially" renounced terrorism in 1976, but group has little discipline
Organizational structure and links: Currently dormant; was a grass-roots blue-collar organization that included criminal elements and with no intellectual or middle-class political leadership
Publications: None known

Umkhonto We Sizwe (MK) (Military Wing of ANC)

Full name/English translation: Umkhonto We Sizwe (Spear of the Nation)
Year founded and country of origin: 1912, South Africa
Ideology/ethnic–national identification: Black nationalist, Marxist, anti-Apartheid
Leaders: Not known
Membership: Not known
Base(s) of operations: South Africa, Mozambique, Tanzania, Angola, Zimbabwe, Zambia
Operational areas: South Africa
Targets: Security forces, black policemen
Organizational structure and links: MK is the military arm of the African National Congress
Publications: (ANC) *Sechaba*, published in Addis Ababa, Ethiopia

Unión Guerrera Blanco (UGB)

Full name/English translation: Union Guerra Blanca (White Fighting Union)
Year founded and country of origin: 1976, El Salvador
Ideology/ethnic–national identification: Right wing extremist; anti-Communist
Leaders: Not known, close ties to military and security forces
Membership: Not known
Base(s) of operations: El Salvador
Operational areas: El Salvador
Targets: Leftist guerrillas, sympathizers
Organizational structure and links: Not known
Publications: None known

Unión Revolucionaria Nacional de Guatemala (URNG)

Full name/English translation: Unión Revolucionario Nacional de Guatemala (Guatemalan National Revolutionary Union)

Year founded and country of origin: 1982, Guatemala
Ideology/ethnic–national identification: Marxist, pro-Castro
Leaders: Leaders of member groups
Membership: No separate membership
Base(s) of operations: Guatemala
Operational areas: Guatemala
Targets: Operations are carried out by member groups
Organizational structure and links: A coordinating group organized at
    insistence of Cuba; not so effective as El Salvador's FMLN; political
    arm is the Guatemalan Committee for Patriotic Unity (CGUP)
Publications: None known

Notes

CHAPTER 1
The Nature of Terrorism Today

1. Walter Laqueur and Yonah Alexander, *The Terrorism Reader: A Historical Anthology,* revised edition (New York and Scarborough, Ontario: Meridian, 1987), presents an excellent selection of writings on when political violence is justified, beginning with Aristotle's "The Origin of Tyranny."

2. See Alex Schmid, *Political Terrorism: A Research Guide* (New Brunswick, N.J.: TransAction Books, 1984), cited in Walter Laqueur, "Reflections on Terrorism," *Foreign Affairs,* Fall 1986, p. 88.

3. Several variations of this definition have appeared in various U.S. government documents. This version, developed in 1980, was quoted in James Adams, *The Financing of Terror: How the Groups That Are Terrorizing the World Get the Money to Do It* (New York: Simon & Schuster, 1986), p. 6. The 1987 version in the annual State Department publication *Patterns in Global Terrorism* (Washington: Government Printing Office, August 1988), defines terrorism as, "premeditated, politically motivated violence perpetrated against non-combatant targets by subnational groups or clandestine state agents, usually intended to influence an audience. 'International terrorism' is terrorism involving the citizens or territory of more than one state."

4. For a good discussion of the distinctions between terrorism and other forms of violence—anarchism, guerrilla warfare, and criminal activity—see Schmid, *Political Terrorism,* pp. 6–158.

5. For an interesting look at terrorism as a last resort, see J. N. Knutson, "Social and Psychodynamic Pressures Toward a Negative Identity: The Case of an American Revolutionary Terrorist," in Yonah Alexander and J. M. Gleason, eds., *Behavioral and Quantitative Perspectives on Terrorism* (New York: Pergamon Press, 1981), pp. 143–44.

6. The term "group" is used here in a social-psychological context rather than an organizational context. While the terms "terrorist group" and "terrorist organization" are generally more or less indistinguishable, it is possible for a terrorist group to be a suborganizational entity. For example, Force 17 is the group within the Palestinian organization al-Fatah that generally conducts acts of terrorism.

7. See Laqueur and Alexander, *The Terrorism Reader*, p. 7.

8. Brian M. Jenkins, "The Terrorist Mindset and Terrorist Decisionmaking" (Santa Monica, Calif.: Rand, June 1979), p. 5.

9. Geoffrey Levitt describes two approaches for defining terrorism. The deductive approach seeks a generic definition, and the inductive approach "makes no effort at abstraction, but covers a particular kind of [criminal] conduct that will trigger a given legal result without regard to political intent." He concludes that whereas the inductive approach does not focus on terrorism *per se* as would the deductive approach, it has the advantage of being politically neutral and thus makes possible cooperative legal efforts by a "disparate and fractious international community." See Geoffrey Levitt, "Is Terrorism Worth Defining?" *Ohio Northern University Law Review*, XIII, no. 1 (1986): 97–115.

10. Stephen Sloan, *Beating International Terrorism: An Action Strategy for Preemption and Punishment* (Maxwell Air Force Base, Ala.: Air University Press, December 1986), p. 4.

11. In the British tradition, the police, in countering domestic terrorist threats, are guided by the principle of "minimum force" in seeking to resolve the problem with a minimum of violence, whereas the military overseas are guided by the principle of "maximum force," that is, applying the maximum force necessary to obtain a military objective. See Paul Wilkinson, *Terrorism and the Liberal State* (London: Macmillan, 1977); Grant Wardlaw, *Political Terrorism: Theory, Tactics and Countermeasures* (Cambridge: Cambridge University Press, 1982); and Sloan, *Beating International Terrorism*.

CHAPTER 2
Understanding Terrorist Behavior

1. Martha Crenshaw, "The Causes of Terrorism," *Comparative Politics*, 13 (July 1981): 390.

2. Emma Goldman, "The Psychology of Political Violence," in Walter Laqueur and Yonah Alexander, eds., *The Terrorism Reader: A Historical Anthology*, revised edition (New York and Scarborough, Ontario: Meridian, 1987), p. 194.

3. For an excellent review of the state of research on terrorist psychology, see Martha Crenshaw, "The Psychology of Political Terrorism," in Margaret

G. Hermann, ed., *Political Psychology: Contemporary Problems and Issues* (San Francisco and London: Jossey-Bass, 1986), pp. 379–413.

4. Boris Savinkov, *Memoirs of a Terrorist*, J. Shaplen, trans. (New York: A. & C. Boni, 1931).

5. Saadi Yacef, *Souvenirs de la bataille d'Alger* (Paris: Julliard, 1962).

6. Menachem Begin, *The Revolt*, S. Katz, trans. (Los Angeles: Nash, 1977).

7. Brian M. Jenkins, *The Terrorist Mindset and Terrorist Decisionmaking: Two Areas of Ignorance* (Santa Monica, Calif.: Rand Corporation, June 1979).

8. Charles A. Russell and Captain Bowman H. Miller, USAF, "Profile of a Terrorist," *Military Review*, August 1977, pp. 21–34, cited in Jenkins, *Terrorist Mindset*, p. 1.

9. See Jerrold M. Post, "Terrorist Psycho-Logic: Terrorist Behavior as a Product of Psychological Forces," paper prepared for the Interdisciplinary Research Conference on "The Psychology of Terrorism: Behaviors, World-Views, States of Mind," Woodrow Wilson Center for Scholars, Washington, D.C., March 1987.

10. Ibid., pp. 9 ff. For a more detailed explanation of splitting, see O. Kernberg, *Borderline Conditions and Psychological Narcissism* (New York: Jason Aronson, 1975), and H. Kohut, *The Analysis of Self* (New York: International University Press, 1983).

11. See Charles A. Russell and Bowman H. Miller, "Portrait of a Terrorist," in Lawrence Freedman and Yonah Alexander, eds., *Perspectives on Terrorism* (Wilmington, Dela.: Scholarly Resources, 1983), pp. 45–60.

12. Crenshaw, "Psychology of Political Terrorism," p. 388.

13. See Post, "Terrorist Psycho-Logic," p. 5, and Crenshaw, "Psychology of Political Terrorism," pp. 388–89. Both cite a number of writers who discuss risk-takers and stress-seekers.

14. Crenshaw, "Psychology of Political Terrorism," p. 388.

15. *Ibid.*, pp. 386–87.

16. O. Demaris, *Brothers in Blood* (New York: Scribner, 1977), p. 220.

17. Martha Crenshaw, "The Subjective Reality of the Terrorist: Ideological and Psychological Factors in Terrorism," in R. O. Slater and M. Stohl, eds., *Current Perspectives on International Terrorism* (New York: St. Martin's, 1986).

18. Erikson's concept is developed in *Childhood and Society*, 2d ed. (New York: Norton, 1963), and *Identity: Youth and Crisis* (New York: Norton, 1968). See Crenshaw, "Psychology of Political Terrorism," pp. 391–95.

19. Crenshaw, "Psychology of Political Terrorism," pp. 391–95, and Post, "Terrorist Psycho-Logic," pp. 6–8.

20. The terms "terrorist group" and "terrorist organization" have been used more or less interchangeably thus far in this study. There is a distinction, however. "Terrorist organization" connotes an emphasis on institutional arrangements, and "terrorist group" connotes an emphasis on group dynamics. Since the following section is largely about group dynamics, the term "terrorist group" will be used, except when referring to specific organizations.

21. Crenshaw, "Psychology of Political Terrorism," p. 389.

22. See Clark R. McCauley and Mary E. Segal, "Social Psychology of Terrorist Groups," Chapter 10 in C. Hendrick, *Review of Personality and Social Psychology*, vol. 9, (Beverly Hills, Calif.: Sage Publications, 1988). Post first noted the similarity between cult conversion and terrorist recruitment. See Jerrold M. Post, "Notes on a Psychodynamic Theory of Terrorist Behavior," *Terrorism: An International Journal*, 7, no. 3 (1984): 241–56.

23. Post, "Terrorist Psycho-Logic," p. 8.

24. For a discussion of rewards of terrorist group membership, see McCauley and Segal, "Social Psychology of Terrorist Groups."

25. See Post, "Terrorist Psycho-Logic," p. 14.

26. From various interviews published in *Der Spiegel*, 1972 and 1980, quoted in *ibid., pp. 13–14.*

27. See, for example, Parker W. Borg, *International Terrorism: Breaking the Cycle of Violence,* Occasional Paper No. 8 (Washington, D.C.: Center for the Study of Foreign Affairs, U.S. Department of State Foreign Service Institute, June 1987).

28. I. L. Janis, *Victims of Group-Think* (Boston: Houghton-Mifflin, 1972), quoted in Post, "Terrorist Psycho-Logic," p. 18.

CHAPTER 3
Terrorism in the Struggle for National Identity

1. In its database on terrorism, the Jaffee Center for Strategic Studies at Tel Aviv University lists more than 600 organizations and groups worldwide. For a detailed and short description of guerrilla and terrorist groups, see Peter Janke and Richard Sim, *Guerrilla and Terrorist Organizations: A World Directory and Bibliography* (New York: Macmillan, 1983).

2. See William B. Quandt, Fuad Jabber, and Ann Mosely Lesch, *The Politics of Palestinian Nationalism* (Berkeley: University of California Press, 1973), pp. 7–8.

3. The classic account of the rise of Arab national aspirations is found in George Antonius, *The Arab Awakening: The Story of the Arab National Movement* (Philadelphia: J. B. Lippincott, 1939).

4. Both the McMahon Correspondence and the Balfour Declaration were so vaguely worded that the precise commitments made by the British have been the subject of intense debate. Balfour himself admitted, however, that the pledges to the Arabs and the Jews were irreconcilable. See Quandt, Jabber, and Lesch, *Politics of Palestinian Nationalism*, pp. 8–9.

5. John W. Amos II, *Palestinian Resistance: Organization of a Nationalist Movement* (New York: Pergammon Press, 1980), p. 6, and Aaron David Miller, "The Palestinians," Ch. 14 in David E. Long and Bernard Reich, eds., *The Government and Politics of the Middle East and North Africa*, 2d ed., (Boulder, Colo.: Westview, 1986), p. 286.

6. There is a long-standing debate as to whether the refugees fled from fear of Israeli atrocities, as some Arabs claim, or their departure was the responsibility of the Arab states, which told them to do so, as some Israelis claim.

7. Ariel Merari and Shlomi Elad, *The International Dimension of Palestinian Terrorism*, Jaffee Center for Strategic Studies, Tel Aviv University, Study No. 6, (Jerusalem: The Jerusalem Post, and Boulder, Colo.: Westview Press, 1986), p. 89.

8. Khalil was murdered by terrorists in Tunis in April 1988. See *Middle East Journal*, 42, no. 4 (Autumn 1988): 639. The assassination is generally believed to have been an Israeli operation.

9. Amos, *Palestinian Resistance*, pp. 45–47.

10. *Ibid.*, p. 53, and Riad el-Rayyes and Dunia Nahas, *Guerrillas for Palestine* (London: Croom Helm, 1976), p. 16.

11. ANO has used many cover names, including Black June, Arab Revolutionary Brigades, Revolutionary Organization of Socialist Muslims, and Black September (not to be confused with the earlier BSO of Salah Khalif).

12. The acronym is from "the Arab Nationalist Movement," a more widely used but inaccurate translation of the Arabic, Harikat al-Watiniyin al-Arabiyin.

13. In addition to Habbash, there were a number of other Palestinian Christians who joined the ANM, including Nayif Hawatamah and Wadi Haddad. Denied the universalism of Islam as an ideological basis for their political militancy, it is easy to see how they were attracted to secular Arab nationalism and socialism. For a history of the ANM through 1968, see Walid Kazziha, *Revolutionary Transformation in the Arab World* (New York: St. Martin's Press, 1975).

14. The groups joining with Habbash were Nayif Hawatamah's the Vengeance Youth, the Heros of the Return, and Ahmad Jabril's Palestinian Liberation Front (not an ANM-derived organization).

15. This group should not be confused with Ahmad Jabril's pre-1967 group of the same name, which became a part of the original PFL.

16. Originally called the Popular Democratic Front for the Liberation of Palestine.

17. See Laurent Gally, *The Black Agent: Traitor to an Unjust Cause*, trans. Victoria Reiter (London: Andrea Deutsch, 1988).

18. For an analysis of Gush Emunim terrorism, see Ehud Sprinzak, "Fundamentalism, Terrorism and Democracy: The Case of the Gush Emunim Underground," Occasional Paper no. 4, Woodrow Wilson Center for Scholars, Smithsonian Institution, Washington, D.C., September 1986.

19. Historic Ulster included nine northern countries—Antrim, Down, Armagh, Derry, Tyrone, Fermagh, Donegal, Monaghan, and Cavan. Only the first six were included in Northern Ireland. See John Darby, ed., *Northern Ireland: The Background to the Conflict* (Syracuse, N.Y.: Appletree Press, 1983), p. 13.

20. The names Irish Republican Army and IRA had been used in various uprisings for years, but the organization as it known today stems from the Irish Volunteers and was first called the IRA in the Easter Uprising. See J. Bowyer Bell, *The Secret Army: A History of the IRA 1916–1970* (London: Anthony Blond, 1970), p. 15, note 3.

21. Timothy Patrick Coogan, *The IRA* (New York: Praeger, 1970). According to Bell, it was founded in 1906 by uniting the Dungannon Clubs and Cumann na Gaedheal, two separatist organizations, and absorbing another, the National Council, in 1908. See Bell, *Secret Army,* p. 8.

22. See J. Bowyer Bell, *The Gun in Politics: An Analysis of the Irish Political Conflict, 1916–1986* (New Brunswick, N.J.: TransAction Books, 1987), p. 165.

23. The Ulster Special Constabulary was created by the British in 1920, largely from the Protestant Ulster Volunteer Force, to augment the Royal Irish Constabulary (later Royal Ulster Constabulary) in Northern Ireland during the Irish Rebellion. It was divided into three sections: A Section was full time, B Section was part time, and C Section was reserve. The B Section, or "B Specials" as they were called, served as a semisanctioned Protestant militia and was a symbol of oppression to the Catholics until it was disbanded in March 1970. See Edgar O'Ballance, *Terror in Ireland* (Novato, Calif.: Presidio Press, 1981), pp. 46, 134.

24. Barry White, "From Conflict to Violence," in Darby, *Northern Ireland*, p. 187.

25. See Bell, *Gun in Politics*, pp. 182–86.

26. They are Alaua, Guiposcoa, Navarra, and Vizcaya.

27. See John L. Sullivan, *ETA and Basque Nationalism: The Fight for Euskadi, 1890–1986* (London: Routledge, 1988), p. 2.

28. *Ibid.,* p. 144.

29. Cheovadurai Manogaran, *Ethnic Conflict and Reconciliation in Sri Lanka* (Honolulu: University of Hawaii Press, 1987), p. 2.

30. The Citizenship Act of 1948 made about 975,000 Indian Tamils stateless, while 135,000 received Sri Lankan citizenship. Over the years, India and Sri Lanka have negotiated the status of those remaining, with India granting citizenship to some 505,000 and Sri Lanka to about 470,000. See Manogaran, *Ethnic Conflict*, p. 206, n. 68.

31. The official rationale was to rid the country of a vestige of colonialism by ending the use of English as an official language. This worked a disproportionate hardship on the Tamil middle class, however, as English was its principal second language, not Sinhala. Moreover, despite earlier promises, no accommodation was made for Tamil to be used as an official language in the northern and eastern provinces.

32. Manogaran, *Ethnic Conflict*, p. 56. The clause referring to Buddhism declares that "it shall be the duty of the state to protect and foster Buddhism." See Government of Ceylon (Sri Lanka), *Constitution of Sri Lanka*, p. 4.

33. For a detailed description of Tamil organizations, see D. B. S. Jeyeraj, "How Strong Are the Boys?," *Frontline*, March 23–April 5, 1985, quoted in Manogaran, *Ethnic Conflict*, p. 206, n. 59. Much of the following material comes from these sources.

34. *Time Magazine*, December 19, 1988, p. 42.

35. Rajiv A. Kapur, *Sikh Separatism: The Politics of Faith* (London: Allen & Unwin, 1986), p. 2.

36. For a discussion of the role of the caste system among Sikhs, see W. H. McLeod, *The Evolution of the Sikh Community: Five Essays* (Oxford: Clarendon Press, 1976), ch. 5, "Caste in the Sikh Panth."

37. See Satinder Singh, *Khalistan: An Academic Analysis* (New Delhi: Amar Prakashan, 1982), pp. 45, 79–80; and Kapur, *Sikh Separatism*, p. 234, n. 98.

38. Personal communication from Director-General of Police (ret.) K. S. Dhillon, State Academy of Administration, Bhopal, India, April 3, 1989.

39. Credit for the attacks was taken by the Committee for Solidarity with Arab and Middle Eastern Political Prisoners (CSPPA), which has never been heard from again. See Gally, *Black Agent*, (note 17 above), pp. ix–x.

CHAPTER 4
Doctrinal Terrorism

1. Charles A. Russell and Captain Bowman H. Miller, USAF, "Profile of a Terrorist," *Military Review*, August 1977, pp. 21–34. For a discussion of terrorist profiles, see Chapter 2.

2. For a detailed account of its early period, see Jillian Becker, *Hitler's Children: The Story of the Baader-Meinhof Gang* (Philadelphia: J. B. Lippincott, 1977).

3. *Ibid.*, p. 15.

4. Peter Janke and Richard Sim, *Guerrilla and Terrorist Organizations: A World Dictionary and Bibliography* (New York: Macmillan, 1983), p. 19.

5. U.S. Department of Defense (DOD), *Terrorist Group Profiles* (Washington, D.C.: Government Printing Office, 1988), p. 67.

6. Bonnie Cordes, Bruce Hoffman, Brian M. Jenkins, Konrad Kellen, Sue Moran, and William Sater, *Trends in International Terrorism, 1982–1983* (Santa Monica, Calif.: Rand Corporation, August 1984), p. 37.

7. *Ibid.*, p. 34.

8. Laurent Gally, *The Black Agent: Traitor to an Unjust Cause*, trans. Victoria Reiter (London: Andre Deutsch; New York: Bantam Books, 1988), p. x.

9. Cordes *et al.*, *Trends in International Terrorism*, p. 28.

10. See Gally, *Black Agent*, particularly ch. 11 and 13.

11. DOD, *Terrorist Group Profiles*, pp. 115–16.

12. It was first known as the Arab Chapter of Sekigun-Ha until November 1971, when it broke all ties. It was then known briefly as the Arab Red Army before settling on the Japanese Red Army. Sekigun-Ha subsequently allied with another group, *Keihin Ampo Kyoto* (the Keihin Anti-Treaty League), to form the United Red Army. The Japanese Red Army and the United Red Army appear to have renewed contact in the late 1980s). Based on Government of Japan, National Police Agency, *White Paper on Police, 1988* (Tokyo: The Japan Times, 1988), and personal notes of Dr. William R. Farrell.

13. *Washington Post*, February 23, 1989, p. A26.

14. *Time*, January 30, 1989, p. 40.

15. See Kenneth Thompson, "Guatemala: From Terrorism to Terror," *Conflict Studies*, no. 23 (London: Institute for the Study of Conflict, May 1972).

16. Colonel Alvaro Puentes Salavarrieta, "Terrorism in Colombia," paper presented at a conference on International Terrorism in the Decade Ahead, sponsored by the Office of International Criminal Justice of the University of Illinois at Chicago, August 22–24, 1988, pp. 6–7.

17. Mariategui's writings include *Siete Ensayos de la Realidad Peruana* ("Seven Essays on Peruvian Reality"), cited in Gabriela Tarazona-Sevillano, "The Personality of Shining Path and Narcoterrorism," paper

prepared for the Standing Group on Terrorism, Center for Strategic and International Studies, Washington, D.C., February 29, 1988, p. 2.

18. The name comes from an eighteenth-century Peruvian Indian revolutionary executed by the Spanish, in whose memory the Uruguayan Tupamaros were also named.

19. Cordes *et al.*, *Trends in International Terrorism*, p. 40.

20. Dennis Pluchinsky, "Political Terrorism in Western Europe: Some Themes and Variations," in Yonah Alexander and Kenneth Myers, eds. *Terrorism in Europe* (London and Canberra: Croom Helm, 1982), p. 46.

21. Cordes *et al.*, *Trends in International Terrorism*, p. 40.

22. See Kenneth F. Johnson, "On Guatemalan Political Violence," *Politics and Society*, Fall 1973, p. 71; for a conspiratorial viewpoint, see Allan Nairn, "Behind the Death Squads: An Exclusive Report on the U.S. Role in El Salvador's Official Terror," *The Progressive*, 48, no. 5 (May 1984): 1, 20–29.

23. See William M. LeoGrande and Carla Anne Robbins, "Oligarchs and Officers: The Crisis in El Salvador," *Foreign Affairs*, 58 (Summer 1980): 1088.

24. The popular interpretation of *jihad* in the West, holy war, is inadequate. *Jihad* means the personal and communal struggle to live a Godly life and establish and maintain a just (i.e., Islamic) social and political order. The latter may include war in defense of Islam.

25. For a brief discussion of Ibn Taymiya's views, see John Alden Williams, ed., *Islam* (New York: George Braziller, 1961), pp. 205–10.

26. Ishak Musa Husaini, *The Moslem Brethren* (Beirut: Khayats, 1956), p. 140. A definitive history of the Brethren to the end of the 1960s is Richard P. Mitchell, *The Society of Muslim Brothers* (New York: Oxford University Press, 1969).

27. Adeeb Dawisha, *The Arab Radicals* (New York: Council on Foreign Relations, 1986), p. 88.

28. *Ibid.*

29. *Takfir* in Arabic can mean atonement or expiation, or it can mean the charge of heresy or excommunication. There is some confusion about which meaning the group had in mind. *Hijra* means emigration and generally refers to the Hijra or flight of Muhammad from Mecca to Medina in A.D. 622, which marks the beginning of the Muslim (or "Hijriya") calender, a lunar calender with years eleven days shorter than solar years and usually designated A.H.

30. John Esposito, "Islamic Revivalism," *The Muslim World Today* Occasional Paper no. 3, American Institute for Islamic Affairs, School of International Service, American University, Washington, D.C., 1985, pp. 5–6.

31. Guy Scarboti, "The Extremists Exorcised," *Far Eastern Economic Review,* April 10, 1981, p. 28.

32. Shi'as are split into a number of branches, the most prominent being the Imamis or "Twelvers," who recognize twelve Imams in the line after Ali; the Isma'ilis, who recognize seven Imams; and the Zaydis of North Yemen, who traced the Zaydi Imamate from Ali through his great grandson, Zayd bin Ali, and who recognized Imams up to the Yemeni revolution of 1962. The Alawi sect, which dominates Syrian politics, is an offshoot of Imamism but is not universally recognized as such by either Sunnis or Shi'as.

   Modern militant Shi'a fundamentalism deals mainly with the Imamis. They make up most of the population of Iran, where Imamism is the official religion, a majority population of Iraq and Bahrain, and most of the Shi'a population of the rest of the Gulf, Lebanon, and the Indian subcontinent. Discussion will be limited to them unless otherwise specified.

33. Muhammad Husayn Tabataba'i *Shi'ite Islam* (Albany: State University of New York Press, 1975), p. 211.

34. Hanna Batatu, "Iraq's Underground Shi'a Movements: Characteristics, Causes and Prospects," *Middle East Journal*, 34, no. 4 (Autumn 1981): 579.

35. Dawisha, *Arab Radicals*, pp. 91–92, 122–23.

36. Fouad Ajami, *The Vanished Imam: Musa Sadr and the Shia of Lebanon* (Ithaca, N.Y.: Cornell University Press, 1986), pp. 47–48.

37. Dawisha, *Arab Radicals*, pp. 121–24.

38. Martin Kramer, "Hezbollah: The Moral Logic of Extraordinary Means," paper delivered to the Interdisciplinary Research Conference on the Psychology of Terrorism: Behaviors, World Views, States of Mind, sponsored by the Woodrow Wilson International Center for Scholars, Washington, D.C., March 16–18, 1987, p. 3.

39. In Shi'a Islam, only mujtahids are qualified to issue fatwas.

40. Kramer, "Hezbollah," pp. 16–22.

CHAPTER 5
Support for Terrorism

1. For a discussion of problems confronting democratic states facing terrorist threats, see Paul Wilkinson, *Terrorism and the Liberal State*, 2d ed. (London: Macmillan, 1987).

2. Israel has never officially admitted carrying out the assassination.

3. See James Adams, *The Financing of Terror: How the Groups That Are Terrorizing the World Get the Money to Do It* (New York: Simon & Shuster, 1986.)

4. The book most often cited in propounding this view is Clair Sterling, *The Terror Network: The Secret War of International Terrorism* (New York: Holt, Reinhart & Winston, 1981). In fact, the book itself does not argue for a conspiracy theory nearly so strongly as some of those who cite it. Sterling attempted to document the many groups employing violent tactics supported by the Soviet Union.

5. David C. Martin and John Walcott, *Best Laid Plans: The Inside Story of America's War Against Terrorism* (New York: Harper & Row, 1988), p. 325.

6. Adams, *The Financing of Terror, p. 239.*

7. *Ibid.*, ch. 6.

8. Sterling, *Terror Network.*

9. Technically, the term "narcotic" refers to opium-derived and synthetic substances that are physiologically addictive. In common parlance, the terms "drugs" and "narcotics" are used interchangeably and generally also refer to cocaine, marijuana, and other synthetic substances. See James A. Inciardi, *The War on Drugs: Heroin, Cocaine, Crime and Public Policy* (Palo Alto, Calif.: Mayfield Publishing, 1986), pp. 50–51.

10. See Mark S. Steinitz, "Insurgents, Terrorists and the Drug Trade," in Walter Laqueur and Yonah Alexander, eds., *The Terrorism Reader: A Historical Anthology*, rev. ed. (New York and Scarborough, Ontario: Meridian, 1987), pp. 327–37.

11. U.S. Congress, House of Representatives, Committee on Foreign Affairs, *U.S. Narcotics Control Programs in Peru, Bolivia, Colombia, and Mexico: An Update*, Report of a Staff Study Mission to Peru, Bolivia, Colombia, and Mexico, November 19 to December 18, 1988 (Washington, D.C.: Government Printing Office, February 1989), p. 23.

12. *Ibid.*, p. 10.

13. *Ibid.*

14. *Ibid.*, p. 24.

15. See the statement by a former president of CBS news quoted in Grant Wardlaw, *Political Terrorism: Theory, Tactics and Counter-Measures* (Cambridge: Cambridge University Press, 1982), p. 81.

CHAPTER 6
Strategy, Tactics, and Victims

1. See Carlos Marighella, *Minimanual of the Urban Guerrilla* (n.p. [United States]: New World Liberation Front, 1970).

2. Kilburn was murdered in 1986. His murderers are thought to have been Libyans who "bought" him for that purpose in retaliation for the American raid on Libya in April 1986. Two British subjects were also murdered at

the same time, probably in response to allowing the raids to be staged in part from the United Kingdom.

3. The tendency is often called "Stockholm syndrome," after a hostage incident in Stockholm. The nature and even existence of Stockholm syndrome is subject to debate and will be discussed more fully below in discussing victims.

4. Marighella, *Minimanual of Urban Guerrilla*.

5. Other attacks were attempted against the American Consulate in Paris and U.S. military installations in Ankara and Izmir, but all failed.

6. Jared Tinklenberg, "Coping with Terrorist Victimization," in Frank M. Ochberg and David A. Soskis, eds., *Victims of Terrorism* (Boulder, Colo.: Westview Press, 1982), p. 62.

7. *Ibid.*, p. 63.

8. *Ibid.*, p. 64.

9. Thomas Strentz, "The Stockholm Syndrome," in Ochberg and Soskis, *Victims of Terrorism*, p. 152.

10. Frank M. Ochberg, "A Case Study: Gerard Vaders," in Ochberg and Soskis, *Victims of Terrorism*, pp. 26, 31.

11. Ochberg and Soskis, *Victims of Terrorism*, p. 17.

12. Sir Geoffrey Jackson, *Surviving the Long Night* (New York: Vanguard, 1973), p. 49.

13. Tinklenberg, "Coping with Terrorist Victimization," p. 67.

14. David A. Soskis and Frank M. Ochberg, "Concepts of Terrorist Victimization," in Ochberg and Soskis, *Victims of Terrorism*, p. 113.

15. Leo Eitinger, "The Effects of Captivity," in Ochberg and Soskis, *Victims of Terrorism*, p. 86.

16. Edna J. Hunter, "Captivity: The Family in Waiting," in Charles R. Figley and Hamilton I. McCubbin, eds., *Stress and Family II: Coping with Catastrophe* (New York: Brunner-Mazel, 1983), p. 175.

17. A multidisciplinary group of scholars, the Task Force on Families of Catastrophe, studied the Iran hostage crisis and made recommendations. See *ibid.*, p. 167.

18. The government was not allowed to debrief Weir without a representative of the church bureaucracy present, and then only under stringent conditions, even after it was explained that debriefing was standard practice to learn as much as possible from past experience and could possibly aid in the rescue of the remaining hostages. The Rev. Weir himself was glad to cooperate. See Ben and Carol Weir, with Dennis Benson, *Hostage Bound Hostage Free* (Philadelphia: Westminister Press, 1987), p. 176.

19. Hunter, "Captivity."

CHAPTER 7
Meeting the Threat

1. See Parker W. Borg, "International Terrorism: Breaking the Cycle of Violence," Occasional Paper no. 8, Center for the Study of Foreign Affairs, Foreign Service Institute, Department of State, Washington, D.C., June 1987, p. 2.

2. *Ibid.*

3. Geoffrey M. Levitt, *Democracies Against Terror: The Western Response to State-Supported Terrorism* Washington Papers no. 134, Center for Strategic and International Studies, Washington, D.C. (New York: Praeger, 1988), pp. 93–105.

4. *Ibid.*, pp. 25–47.

5. For the text of the Tokyo Economic Summit, see *ibid.*, pp. 115–16.

6. The declarations include the 1978 Bonn Declaration on Hostage Taking and Aircraft Hijacking (Joint Statement on International Terrorism); the 1979 Tokyo Joint Statement on Hijacking; the 1980 Venice Statement on the Taking of Diplomatic Hostages; the 1980 Venice Statement on Hijacking; the 1981 Ottawa Statement on Terrorism; the 1984 London Declaration on International Terrorism; the 1986 Tokyo Statement on International Terrorism; and the 1987 Venice Statement on Terrorism, which supplemented the Bonn Declaration by adding aircraft sabotage. See *ibid.*, "Appendix: Declarations of the Summit Seven on International Terrorism, 1978–1987," pp. 106–18.

7. Mary Mochary, Principle Deputy Legal Advisor, U.S. Department of State, "International Terrorism and Transnational Crime: Diplomatic Issues," presentation before the Third Annual Symposium on International Terrorism and Transnational Crime, Center for International Criminal Justice, University of Illinois at Chicago, August 22, 1988.

8. Jerome W. Klingaman, "The Definition of Low Intensity Conflict and Its Relation to U.S. Defense Capabilities," in *Air Power for Counterinsurgency*, undated, unpublished pamphlet, quoted in Stephen Sloan, *Beating International Terrorism: An Action Strategy for Preemption and Punishment* (Maxwell AFB, Ala.: Air University Press, 1986), p. 9.

9. See Grant Wardlaw's discussion of the roles of the army and the police in counterterrorist operations, ch. 10 in *Political Terrorism: Theory, Tactics and Counter-Measures* (Cambridge: Cambridge University Press, 1982), pp. 87–102. For special operations units, see James Adams, *Secret Armies: Inside the American, Soviet, and European Special Forces* (New York: Atlantic Monthly Press, 1987).

10. Aharon Yariv, "The Role of Intelligence in Combatting Terrorism," presentation before the Third Annual Symposium on International Terrorism and Transnational Crime, Center for International Criminal Justice, University of Illinois at Chicago, August 22, 1988.

Selected Bibliography

ABU IYAD, with ERIC ROULEAU. *My Home, My Land: A Narrative of the Palestinian Struggle.* Trans. Linda Butler Koseoglu. New York: Time Books, 1981.

ADAMS, JAMES. *The Financing of Terror: How the Groups That Are Terrorizing the World Get the Money to Do It.* New York: Simon & Schuster, 1986.

ALNWICK, KENNETH, and THOMAS A. FABYANIC, eds. *Warfare in Lebanon.* Washington, D.C.: National War University, 1988.

ALEXANDER, YONAH, and KENNETH MYERS, eds. *Terrorism in Europe.* London and Canberra: Croom Helm, 1982.

ALEXANDER, YONAH; DAVID CARLTON; and PAUL WILKINSON, eds. *Terrorism: Theory and Practice.* Boulder, Colo.: Westview Press, 1979.

AMOS, JOHN W., III. *Palestinian Resistance: Organization of a Nationalist Movement.* New York: Pergamon Press, 1980.

ANTONIUS, GEORGE. *The Arab Awakening: The Story of the Arab National Movement.* Philadelphia: J. B. Lippincott, 1939.

ARTHUR, PAUL. *Government and Politics of Northern Ireland.* 2d ed. Essex: Longman Group, 1984.

BECKER, JILLIAN. *Hitler's Children: The Story of the Baader Meinhof Gang.* Philadelphia and New York: J. B. Lippincott, 1977.

———. *The Soviet Connection: State Sponsorship of Terrorism.* Kent, England: Alliance Publishers, 1985.

BELL, J. BOWYER. *The Gun in Politics: An Analysis of Irish Political Conflict, 1916–1986.* New Brunswick, N.J., and Oxford, England: TransAction Books, 1987.

———. *The Secret Army: A History of the IRA, 1916–1970.* London: Anthony Blond, 1970.

COOGAN, TIMOTHY PATRICK. *The IRA.* New York: Praeger Publishers, 1970.

CORDES, BONNIE; BRUCE HOFFMAN; BRIAN M. JENKINS; KONRAD KELLEN; SUE MORAN; and WILLIAM SATER. *Trends in International Terrorism, 1982 and 1983*. Prepared for Sandia Laboratories. Santa Monica, Calif.: Rand Corporation, August 1984.

CRELINSTEIN, RONALD D.; DANIELLE LABERGE-ALTMEJD; and DENIS SZABO, eds. *Terrorism and Criminal Justice*. Lexington, Mass.: Lexington Books, 1978.

CRENSHAW, MARTHA. *Terrorism and International Cooperation*. Occasional Papers, no. 11. New York: Institute for East–West Security Studies, 1989.

DARBY, JOHN, ed. *Northern Ireland: The Background to the Conflict*. Syracuse, N.Y.: Appletree Press. 1983.

DAWISHA, ADEED. *The Arab Radicals*. New York: Council on Foreign Relations, 1986.

ERIKSON, RICHARD J. *Legitimate Use of Military Force Against State-Sponsored International Terrorism*. Maxwell AFB, Al.: Air University Press, July 1989.

ESPOSITO, JOHN L., ed. *Voices of Resurgent Islam*. New York: Oxford University Press, 1983.

FARRELL, WILLIAM REGIS. *The U.S. Government Response to Terrorism: In Search of an Effective Strategy*. Boulder, Colo.: Westview Press, 1982.

FIGLEY, CHARLES B., and HAMILTON I. MCCUBBIN, eds. *Stress and Family II: Coping with Catastrophe*. New York: Brunner-Mazel, 1983.

FRANCIS, SAMUEL T. *The Soviet Strategy of Terror*. Rev. ed. Washington, D.C.: Heritage Foundation, 1985.

GALLY, LAURENT. *The Black Agent: Traitor to an Unjust Cause*. Trans. Victoria Reiter. London: Andrea Deutsch, 1988.

HERMAN, MARGARET, ed. *Political Psychology*. San Francisco: Jossey-Bass, 1986.

HUSAINI, ISHAK MUSA. *The Moslem Brethren*. Beirut: Khayats, 1956.

INCIARDI, JAMES A. *The War on Drugs: Heroin, Cocaine, Crime, and Public Policy*. Palo Alto, Calif.: Mayfield Publishing, 1986.

JANKE, PETER, and RICHARD SIM. *Guerrilla Organizations: A World Directory and Bibliography*. New York: Macmillan, 1983.

KAPUR, RAJIV A. *Sikh Separatism: The Politics of Faith*. London: Allen & Unwin, 1986.

KRAMER, MARTIN. *Political Islam*. The Washington Papers, vol. 8, no. 73. Beverly Hills and London: Sage Publications, 1980.

KURZ, ANAT, and ARIEL MERARI. *ASALA: Irrational Terror or Political Tool*. Jerusalem: Jerusalem Post Press, 1985.

LAPIDUS, IRA M. *Contemporary Islamic Movements in Historical Perspective*. Berkeley: University of California, Berkeley, Institute for International Studies, 1983.

LAQUEUR, WALTER, and YONAH ALEXANDER, eds. *The Terrorism Reader: A Historical Anthology.* Rev. ed. New York and Scarbobough, Ontario: Meridian Books, 1987.

LEVENTHAL, PAUL, and YONAH ALEXANDER, eds. *Nuclear Terrorism: Defining the Threat.* Washington: Pergammon-Brassey's. 1986.

_____. *Preventing Nuclear Terrorism.* Lexington, Mass.: Lexington Books, 1987.

LEVITT, GEOFFREY M. *Democracies Against Terror: The Western Response to State-Supported Terrorism.* The Washington Papers. Published with the Center for Strategic and International Studies. New York; Westport, Conn.; and London: Praeger, 1988.

MCLEOD, W. H. *The Evolution of the Sikh Community: Five Essays.* Oxford: Clarendon Press, 1976.

MARTIN, DAVID C., and JOHN WALCOTT. *Best Laid Plans: The Inside Story of America's War Against Terrorism.* New York: Harper & Row, 1988.

MANOGARAN, CHELVADURAI. *Ethnic Conflict and Reconciliation in Sri Lanka.* Honolulu: University of Hawaii Press, 1987.

MELLMAN, YOSSI. *The Master Terrorist: The True Story Behind Abu Nidal.* New York: Adama Books, 1986.

MERARI, ARIEL, and SCHLOMI ELAD. *The International Dimension of Palestinian Terrorism.* JCSS Study no. 6, Jaffee Center for Strategic Studies, Tel Aviv University. Jerusalem: The Jerusalem Post; Boulder, Colo.: Westview Press, 1986.

MIDGLEY, SARAH, and VIRGINIA RICE, eds. *Terrorism and the Media in the 1980s.* Washington, D.C.: The Media Institute, 1984.

MILLER, AARON DAVID. *The PLO and the Politics of Survival.* Washington Papers no. 99. New York: Praeger, 1983.

MITCHEL, RICHARD P. *The Society of Muslim Brothers.* New York: Oxford University Press, 1969.

O'BALLANCE, EDGAR. *Terror in Ireland. The Heritage of Hate.* Novato, Calif.. Presidio Press, 1981.

QUANDT, WILLIAM B.; FUAD JABBER; and ANN MOSELY LESCH. *The Politics of Palestinian Nationalism.* Berkeley: University of California Press, 1973.

RAYYES, RIAD EL-, and DUNIA NAHAS. *Guerrilas for Palestine.* London: Croom Helm, 1976.

SINGH, SATINDER. *Khalistan: An Academic Analysis.* New Delhi: Amar Prakashan, 1982.

SULLIVAN, JOHN L. *ETA and Basque Nationalism: The Fight for Euskadi, 1890–1986.* London and New York: Routledge, 1988.

WALKER, WILLIAM O. III. *Drug Control in the Americas.* Albuquerque: University of New Mexico Press, 1981.

WALLER, MICHAEL. *Peace, Power; and Protest: Eastern Europe in the Gorbachev Era.* Conflict Study no. 209. London: Institute for the Study of Conflict, 1988.

WARDLAW, GRANT. *Political Terrorism: Theory, Tactics, and Counter-Measures.* 2nd ed. Cambridge: Cambridge University Press, 1989.

WEINBERG, LEONARD, and PAUL B. DAVIS. *Introduction to Political Terrorism.* New York: McGraw-Hill, 1989.

WILKINSON, PAUL, and ALASTAIR M. STEWART, eds. *Contemporary Research on Terrorism.* Aberdeen: Aberdeen University Press, 1987.

Index

Guerrillas, 4, 30
  tactics of, 76
  urban, 127
Guerrilla warfare, 155
Guevara, Ernesto "Che," 80
Guilt, 133
"Guilt by association support," 108
Gun running, 118
Gurdwaras, 59
Guru Granth Sahib, 58
Gush Emunim Underground, 43
Guzman, Abimael, 85
Guzmán, Jacobo Arbenz, 79–80

Habbash, George, 22, 40, 41, 115,
    211*nn*.13, 14
Haddad, Wadi, 30–31, 42, 211*n*.13
Hagopian, Hagop, 63
Hague Convention (1970), 153
Hammadi, Muhammad Ali, 22, 155
Hammadi family, 21–22
Handal, Jorge Shafik, 78
Harakat al-Mahrumin (the Movement
    of the Deprived), 100
Harakat al-Tahrir al-Filistini. See Al-
    Fatah
Harakat al-Watiniyin al-Arabiyin. See
    Movement of Arab Nationalists
Hassan, 92, 96
Hawari, Colonel (Abd al-Hamid Labib),
    38, 115
Hawatamah, Nayif, 22, 41–42,
    211*nn*.13, 14
Heros of the Return, 211*n*.14
Herrhausen, Alfred, 69
Hidden Imam, 95
"Higher Council of the Islamic Revolu-
    tion," 97
Higher Shi'a Islamic Council, 100
Hijacking, 125–26, 128, 129; *see also
    specific hijacking incidents*
Hijra, 215*n*.29
Hizballah (Party of God; Islamic Jihad),
    5, 90, 101–4, 110; *see also* Shi'a
    fundamentalism
  doctrinal and ethnic nature of,
    29–30
  Fadlallah's relationship with, 101–2

organization and leadership of,
    101–2
  profile of, 183–84
  rivalry with Amal, 102–4
  social networks in, 21–22
  terrorist activities of, 102–3
Hogefeld, Birgit, 68
Holy Struggle Commandos (Kommando
    Jihad), 94–95, 187
Hostage rescue operations, 156
Hostage-taking, 126
Hunt, Leamon "Ray," 71
Husayn, 92, 96
Hussein, Sharif, 32

Ibn Taymiya, Taqi al-Din Ahmad,
    92–93
Identification with terrorists, 20–21,
    113
Identity
  concept of, 19–20
  group, 20–21
  national. *See* Nationalist-ethnic ter-
    rorism
Ideological groups. *See* Doctrinal ter-
    rorism
Ideologies, 5
  absolutist, 20, 23
  cooperation among groups and, 115
  socialist, 66
Ikhwan al-Muslimin (Muslim Brother-
    hood), 37, 93
Ilom, Gaspar (Rodrigo Asturias Am-
    ado), 81
Imamis ("Twelvers"), 216*n*.32
Imams, Shi'a, 95
Impact of terrorism, 1–2
Imron Zain, Muhammad, 95
India
  Congress-I Party of, 60
  Sri Lanka insurgency and, 56–57
  Tamils and citizenship in, 213*n*.30
Indonesia, Islamic fundamentalism in,
    94–95
Inductive approach to defining terror-
    ism, 208*n*.9
"Innocent victim of society" model of
    terrorism, 16